Handbook for Agricultural Pilots

Handbook for Agricultural Pilots

Fourth Edition

H.R. Quantick

COLLINS
8 Grafton Street, London W1

Collins Professional and Technical Books
William Collins Sons & Co. Ltd
8 Grafton Street, London W1X 3LA

First Edition published in the Hague by
International Agricultural Aviation Centre (I.A.A.C.), 1966
Second Edition, 1968
Third Edition, 1970
Reprinted three times by I.A.A.C. Cranfield
Fourth Edition published in Great Britain by
Collins Professional and Technical Books, 1985

Distributed in the United States of America
by Sheridan House, Inc.

British Library Cataloguing in Publication Data

Handbook for agricultural pilots. – 4th ed.
1. Aeronautics in agriculture
I. Quantick, H.R.
631.3 S494.5.A3

ISBN 0 00 383141 8

Typeset by Cambrian Typesetters, Frimley, Surrey.
Printed and bound in Great Britain by
Mackays of Chatham, Kent

Contents

Foreword

There can be few pilots with Roy Quantick's extensive experience in the R.A.F., as civil airline captain, and in aerial spraying of pesticides, who would be as able as he is to write this improved version of his original *Spray Pilot's Handbook*. It is particularly valuable for this more comprehensive handbook to become available now, and I am grateful to him for asking me to write this foreword.

Now it is becoming more necessary for spray pilots to be competent and responsible, and this handbook will be of considerable help. Pesticides are being criticised, and people are asking if it is essential to spray them from an aeroplane. The critics are worried about powerful and poisonous chemicals being applied by pilots who are not trained in the techniques of application and in the interests of safety without weakening their efficiency. Pilots who study this handbook will be able to show that they are competent responsible people, doing a difficult job well.

Familiarity breeds contempt; we might ourselves be misled into assuming that pesticides can be used without any risk just because we have used them safely for scores of years. Critics of pesticides may also become so familiar with the use of insecticides, herbicides and fungicides that they forget about their benefits and concentrate only upon their disadvantages. It wasn't very many years ago that peas were sold in pods, and when you shelled your own peas, you found that many pods had a maggot in them. Maggots in peas are scarcely important to the well-being of mankind, but many more people died from starvation before pesticides protected their crops. It is human nature also to pay more attention to any drawbacks of aerial spraying, and to forget about the advantages of applying pesticides from the air.

Nevertheless, the aerial spraying industry has a duty to itself and its critics to demonstrate its competence, responsibility and value. Flying at low levels is potentially more hazardous than driving a tractor, both to the pilot and to bystanders when poisonous chemicals are being applied. The airspray industry must continue to show that the risk is small and that the benefits are sufficiently great for the risk to be taken. At the same time, we hope that our critics will also remember that aspirin, for example, is a more toxic chemical than many modern insecticides.

We also have a good record to report. In 1982 in the U.K. there were just twenty-four accidents when spray operators contaminated themselves with pesticides. Ideally, no accidents should occur, but this was a small number and fortunately no deaths resulted.

This handbook is part of the work of making sure no accidents occur in the future. It cannot cover all needs and, indeed, the views expressed in it on the basis of evidence available so far may not be held by everybody, and controversy will continue, but it is a valuable contribution to help develop further the standard and the standing of the airspray industry.

R. J. Courshee
Director
International Centre for the Application of Pesticides
Cranfield Institute of Technology
U.K.

Preface

This handbook was first published by the foundation International Agricultural Aviation Centre (I.A.A.C.) in The Hague in 1966. The second edition was published in 1968 and the third in 1970. The I.A.A.C. moved to the Cranfield Institute of Technology in the U.K. in 1976. It was soon realised that the demand for the handbook was still very keen. The successor I.A.A.C. organisation (under its new constitution) printed three impressions of the third edition as a stopgap while in the process of reorganisation.

Former members of I.A.A.C. will know that as a consequence of international recession, the I.A.A.C. was unable to continue the work that it had done since the days of the European Agricultural Aviation Centre (E.A.A.C.) in 1958, for nearly twenty-two years. However, it is fortunate that it has been possible to complete this new edition.

Since the previous editions, there have been some significant changes in this industry. Aircraft are getting bigger, and turbine power is becoming available for fixed wing aircraft, although turbine powered aircraft are a quantitative jump from the faithful Pawnees. Many more helicopters are being used, probably because they can also be used in other roles to keep up the utilisation. There has not been a great deal of change with chemicals, except the adjuvants, which modify the action of pesticides, and provide their own problems. The techniques of aerial application are becoming refined, as our knowledge of atmosphere physics and droplet behaviour improve. Already, a new generation of atomisers is becoming available giving considerably better droplet spectra than earlier hydraulic energy nozzles. The problems of chemical 'drift' are becoming understood, and techniques are being used to minimise this problem. By definition, an improved efficiency means reducing chemical quantities, and still keeping the pest complex below the economic injury level, and this is our aim in the chemical control of pests.

In the main, this book is directed at pilots. Some of the safety aspects concerning crash survival, aircraft structural integrity, safety helmets, etc., may make heavy reading for some, but it is hoped that this edition will appeal to the training schools who used the earlier editions to supplement the training syllabus. Chemical control of insect pests and vectors of disease will remain the economic method for some time to come, at least until some new method or materials replace them. It is now even more important to use expensive chemicals in the most compatible, acceptable, efficient and economic method.

H. R. Quantick FRAeS

Introduction

Agricultural aviation is a branch of commercial aviation which performs the essential task in production and protection of the world's food and fibre crops. Aerial application is also used in areas such as insect control, particularly those insects that spread disease of animals and man; the application of fertilisers and trace elements; defoliation (to facilitate harvesting); the application of fungicides to suppress plant diseases; seeding; fighting forest fires, and indeed, other important tasks in the protection of biological resources.

The technique of agricultural flying demands from the pilot an area of skill and knowledge quite different from that of other types of aviation. There are too few schools where pilots may be taught, and the average pilot may have had a rather fragmentary introduction into this area. It is interesting to note that as agricultural aircraft are getting bigger and very much more expensive, and this now includes helicopters, it is pressure from the insurance underwriters rather than the licensing authorities that could well provide the incentive for more training schools. Of course, there are notable exceptions, and some countries have recognised agricultural pilots rating as an endorsement on the national licence. These in themselves receive tacit recognition when pilots follow the seasons into another hemisphere pursuing the crop pests.

Some countries where aerial application is a major seasonal industry do not have their own recognised qualification; however, a commercial pilot's licence would probably be the minimum requirement. To fly and operate the new generation of turbo powered fixed wing aircraft and helicopters in the application role requires *training*. Even experienced pilots who have gained all or most of their flying hours on turbo jet aircraft have found themselves on new ground when taking up this role, and have needed intensive conversion.

The agricultural pilot must think of himself as being engaged as much in an agricultural operation as in an aeronautical one. He must know the correct use and handling of agricultural chemicals and fertilisers, and he must know enough about farming to ensure that he can always do an effective job. The agricultural pilot must extend his knowledge about the environment in which he works, and the consequences of his actions within that environment. It would also be a great asset if he can, with experience, be given responsibility for some of the organisation of operations and supervision of ground services. These requirements add to the difficulty of the job; the flying alone calls for a sustained performance of the very highest accuracy, and can be most exacting. Conditions may be uncomfortable, and hours irregular.

This book is intended for pilots who have reached at least the standard of a commercial pilot with regard to normal flying techniques. Even experienced agricultural pilots will find a few useful hints or be reminded of points which they have forgotten. It would not be possible to give full details of all the different types of operation, which differ from country to country and from continent to continent. However, the general principles given are universally applicable, and are a basis for further study of individual types of operation.

This pulication is intended for international use, and must therefore be read in conjunction with local regulations and recommendations. In a few instances there may be some unavoidable conflicts, in which case of course this book does not presume to override local practice.

Acknowledgements

Grateful recognition is due to many people and organisations for advice, criticisms, practical assistance and permissions for the material in this book. In particular: the International Agricultural Aviation Centre (I.A.A.C.) (now incorporated into the Cranfield Institute of Technology) for permission to use material from the historical and technical files; the Department of Aviation, Australia (Flight Standards) for permission to incorporate some parts of the Australian *Agricultural Pilot Manual*; the Australian Bureau of Animal Health, Department of Primary Industry, for permission to incorporate material from the Australian *Aerial Agriculture – Chemical Rating Manual*; the Director General, Environmental Health Directorate, Health and Welfare Canada, for permission to incorporate some parts of the *Aerial Application of Pesticides – Safety Manual*; the Director General, World Health Organization, for permission to reproduce material from the *Guidlines to the use of the WHO recommended classification of pesticides by hazard*; the Director General, Food and Agricultural Organization of the United Nations, for permission to use material from the F.A.O agricultural services bulletins and agricultural development papers; the Secretary General, International Civil Aviation Organisation, for permission to use material from the I.C.A.O. 'Safety in aerial work' circulars; the United Nations Economic Commission for Europe (E.C.E.), for permission to use material presented at the E.C.E. Seminar on Techno-Economic Trends in Airborne Equipment for Agriculture and other Selected Areas of the National Economy, Warsaw, Poland, September 1978; the Cranfield Institute of Technology, for permission to use material from the Short Course on the 'Aerial application of pesticides'; the Editor *The Aeronautical Journal*, Royal Aeronautical Society, for permission to reproduce material from published technical papers; Dr Carrol Voss for the helicopter flying techniques; Jean Haley, for details on flagging, particularly the night operations, from her training manual *Expert Flagging*; Peter Garrison, for his paper on 'Wind shear'; Norman E. Stanley, for his paper on 'Night spraying'.

Aknowledgements are also due to the following people: Mr J. F. Copplestone, Chief, Pesticide Development and Safe Use, Division of Vector Biology and Control, World Health Organization, Geneva, Switzerland; Mr R. S. Trayford, Commonwealth Scientific and Industrial research Organization (C.S.I.R.O.), Australia; Mr Alan Lavers and Mr B. Speight, Shell Research Ltd, U.K.; Mr Darrol Stinton, Airworthiness Division, Civil Aviation Authority, U.K.; Mr John Spillman, Professor of Applied Aerodynamics, Cranfield Institute of Technology, U.K.; Herr Gorzel, Director, Interflug, German Democratic Republic; Mr Ron Amsden, former Head of Applications Department, Fisons Agrochemical Division (now F.B.C.), U.K.; Mr Dick Courshee, Director, International Centre for the Application of Pesticides (I.C.A.P.) at the Cranfield Institute of Technology, U.K.; Dr Steve Parkin (I.C.A.P.); Mr John Parker, Head of Bio-aeronautics, Cranfield Institute of Technology, U.K.; Mr Joe Kosier, Schweizer Aircraft corporation, U.S.A.; Mr Desmond Norman, N.D.N. Aircraft Ltd, U.K.; Mr Bill Bowker, Bowker Air Services Ltd, U.K.; Dr Carrol Voss, Ag Rotors Inc., U.S.A.; Professor Norman B. Akesson, University of California Davis, U.S.A.; Mr Ladi Marmol, A.D.S. (Aerial) Ltd, U.K.; Mr Pat Millar, Millar Aerial Spraying Ltd, U.K.; Mr Tom Bals, Micron Sprayers Ltd, U.K.; Mr Jim McMahon, Micronair (Aerial) Ltd, U.K.; Mr Roy Woodley, Civil Aviation Authority, U.K.; Mr C. J. Freeman, Department of Aviation, Australia; Mr Tom Hamill, Flight International, U.K.; Dr Ian Perry, Consultant in Occupational Aviation Medicine, U.K.; Mr Bill Kessinger, Flight School Manager, Ayres Corporation, U.S.A.; Mr Timothy Sander, Micronair (Aerial) Ltd, U.K.

And to the following organisations: Transavia (N.S.W.) Pty Ltd, Australia; the Commonwealth Scientific and Industrial Research Organization (C.S.I.R.O.), Australia; Shell International Chemical Co., U.K.; the Cranfield Institute of Technology, U.K.; ICI Plant Protection Ltd, U.K.; Fisons Agrochemical Division (now F.B.C. Ltd), U.K.; International Centre for the Application of Pesticides, Cranfield, U.K.; Flight International, U.K.; Ecological Physics Research Group, Cranfield Institute of Technology, U.K.; Her Majesty's Stationery Office, U.K.; the Royal Aeronautical Society, U.K.; Schweizer Aircraft Corporation, U.S.A.; Piper Aircraft Corporation, U.S.A.; Simplex Manufacturing Company, U.S.A.; Spraying Systems Company, U.S.A.; Cessna Aircraft Company, U.S.A.; ADS (Aerial) Ltd, U.K.; AG-Rotors Inc, U.S.A.; Millar Aerial Spraying Ltd, U.K.; Bowker Air Services Ltd, U.K.; Trent Air Services Ltd, U.K.; Ayres Corporation, U.S.A.; Delavan Manufacturing Company, U.S.A.; Longman Group Ltd, U.K.; Associated Book Publishers Ltd, U.K.; the Decca Survey Co. Ltd, (now Racal-Decca Survey Ltd), U.K.; Bell Helicopter Textron Inc, U.S.A.; Transland Inc, U.S.A.; Micronair (Aerial) Ltd, U.K.; Pilatus Britten Norman Ltd, U.K.;

Ciba Geigy, Switzerland; Pilatus Aircraft, Switzerland; Interflug, German Democratic Republic; W.S.K. Swidnik, Poland; Micron Corporation, U.S.A.; Meilec Works, Poland; Pezetel, Agricultural Aviation Services, Poland; Micron Sprayers Ltd, U.K.; U.S. Department of Agriculture, U.S.A.; New Zealand Aerospace Industries Ltd, New Zealand; NDN Aircraft Ltd, U.K.

To the new and especially 'young' pilots

Listen very hard to the 'old' pilots about techniques, incidents and accidents. Physical skills only come after practice, experience comes a lot later. Learn to know where dangers can loom. Learn from the mistakes of others – *you won't live long enough to make them all yourself.*

1
Safety aspects of aircraft used by application pilots

'Agricultural aviation' was first identified as a means of combating crop pests by Alfred Zimmermann, a German forester in Detershagen. His patent letter, dated 29 March 1911, described the use of aircraft in the application of pesticide (in this case lime-water) in the control of the nun moth (black arch moth) in the European forests. Despite this visionary approach, suitable aircraft were only available after the war, as well as trained pilots able to perform this task. Early experiments were conducted in the 1920s in many countries, and practical results were recorded by Neillie and Houser (August 1921) in the U.S.A., and Professor V. F. Boldyrev (July 1922) in the U.S.S.R.

The first specially designed aircraft to distribute agricultural chemicals was the Ag-1 developed in 1949–50 at the Texas A. and M. Aircraft Research Centre. The project was initiated by the National Flying Farmers Association, and was carried out under the sponsorship of the Civil Aeronautics Administration, the U.S. Department of Agriculture and the Texas A. and M. College System. The Ag-1 was followed by other experimental aircraft (Ag-2 and Ag-3) which incorporated pilot safety characteristics with regard to field of view and structural arrangements for protection of the pilot in crashes. These experimental aircraft laid the foundations of design philosophy for nearly all subsequent specialist aircraft. The Piper Aircraft Corporation, who assisted in the experimental Ag-3 aircraft, was the first major aircraft manufacturer to produce a specialist aircraft – the Piper PA-25 Pawnee (plate 1.1).

There are four main groups of aircraft used throughout the world at the present time:

- Group 1: ex-military aircraft, e.g. Boeing Stearman, Grumman Avenger (TBM).
- Group 2: ex-civil aircraft, e.g. Douglas DC-6, Antonov AN-2M, DHC Beaver, Pilatus Turbo Porter, Piper Aztec.

Plate 1.1 Piper PA–25 Pawnee (photo: Piper Aircraft Corporation)

- Group 3: specialist agricultural aircraft, i.e. Piper Pawnee, Ayres Thrush, Schweizer Ag-Cat, Cessna Ag-Truck, Embraer Ipanema, Cmelak Z-37, Transavia Skyfarmer T-300A, etc. (see appendix 1).
- Group 4: helicopters.

Since the experiments with the Ag-1, 2 and 3 and series production of the Piper PA-25 Pawnee and Cessna Agwagon got under way, it is astonishing to find that over the following two decades very little improvement has been seen in the basic design exemplified by the Ag-1. In some cases the agricultural pilot is exposed to considerable potential danger, particularly in the group 2 aircraft. Modifications and adaptations can only go so far before economics and the law of diminishing returns prevent the aircraft coming anywhere near the structural and safe integrity of a specialist aircraft. The following list will give some idea where crash survival could be jeopardised:

(1) Seat anchorages and harness anchorages.
(2) Room to wear a safety helmet.
(3) Incorrect geometry of the upper torso restraint straps.
(4) G switches in the hot leads from alternators and batteries (particularly turbine engines).
(5) Fuel tanks too close to the cockpit area. Some high wing aircraft have fuel located right up to the wing attachment points.
(6) Access doors.
(7) Non-recessed instruments and equipment, cockpit clutter of lethal sharp projections.

(8) Batteries: heavy Ni-cads to have recessed contacts.
(9) Recesses inaccessible for clearing out chemicals and dirt; corrosion protection.
(10) The overload situation.
(11) The rough field operation.
(12) The fatigue life.
(13) Hoses, valves and chemical carrying system inside the cockpit area, non-approved gas pressurisation system.
(14) Post-crash hazard: the threat to the pilot's survival posed by fire, drowning, exposure, including exposure to chemicals, following the impact sequence.

Some of the items in this list are self explanatory, others will be looked at in greater detail. Also the design criteria and the limits that are imposed on airframes, particularly the group 2 aircraft. The re-engine with propeller turbine power units is also studied, and the loading problem on the aircraft structure caused by excessive airspeed. The studies originate from the registration authorities in those countries with the appropriate experience in these areas.

A survey of crop spraying accidents from those countries that publish the appropriate statistics indicates that the main causes of accidents are collisions with obstructions, usually electric wires, trees, and some-

Plate 1.2 Ag-2 Agricultural and Forestry Aircraft (photo: Transland Aircraft)

times fences. Stalling out of the turns and during manoeuvring comes next, and almost the smallest percentage of accidents is due to engine failure – in several cases this was due to running out of fuel. Fortunately for the agricultural pilot, the main cause of accidents results in the aircraft striking the ground at approximately the minimum flying speed of the aeroplane. Because of the low speed at contact, this type of accident is definitely survivable. It follows, and is now generally accepted, that a large proportion of the serious and fatal injuries associated with these crashes could be prevented by suitable aeroplane design coupled with the use of a suitable restraint harness and safety helmet. The following ten recommendations for crash-survival design are made by the Crash Injury Research Unit of Cornell Medical College:

(1) Design forward fuselage and cabin structures to resist nominal crash loads as well as flight and landing loads.
(2) Design aircraft structures to absorb energy by progressive collapse.
(3) Design tubular structure to bend and fail outwardly away from the occupants.
(4) Locate the passengers' and pilots' seats as far aft in the fuselage as possible behind the wing.
(5) Locate fuel tanks in, or on, the wings – not between the firewall and instrument panel.
(6) Provide space between the instrument panel and firewall (or nose section) to permit forward displacement of the panel and instrument cases.
(7) Design the instrument panel to be free of sharp, rigid edges in range of pilot's head.
(8) Fabricate the instrument panel of ductile material and/or use an energy-absorbing shield on the panel face.
(9) Mount instrument cases on shear-pins and/or as low as possible on the panel.
(10) Provide shoulder harness, safety belts, seats and seat anchorages of sufficient strength to resist failure up to the point of cabin collapse.

In plate 1.1, the Piper PA-25 Pawnee (this is an early version) gives an idea of the configuration which embodied the safety criteria as outlined. The pilot sits high up and has a good field of view forward and down. The cockpit allows sufficient room to wear a safety helmet. Roll-over bars strengthen the cockpit area. Access doors are sufficiently large for ease of entry (and rapid exit). The hopper is placed almost over the centre of gravity affording little change in trim, particularly during an emergency dump. Most of the western aircraft follow this general configuration.

The following section on airworthiness codes and risks is an extract from a paper given by Mr Darrol Stinton to the Royal Aeronautical Society Agricultural Aviation Group Symposium at the Cranfield Institute of Technology (1982) and is reproduced with the kind permission of the author and the Royal Aeronautical Society.

Airworthiness codes and risks

Around 40% of the agricultural aircraft outside the U.S.S.R. and Eastern Europe are American. Not surprisingly the airworthiness and technical standards set in the U.S.A. have a profound effect upon standards elsewhere. The aircraft represent variants from the Piper PA-25 Pawnee to the powerful and effective turboprop powered Turbocat and Ayres Thrush, both leading towards 5 tonne gross, with overload. Many such aeroplanes started life with piston engines and the trend is to re-engine with turbo propeller units. While this increases their operational effectiveness and flexbility, it introduces certification problems when it comes to flying qualities, especially handling, where:

$$\text{Flying qualities} = \text{handling (control + stability)} + \text{performance} + \text{functioning of systems}$$

Published airworthiness codes set the standards. Those particularly relevant here affect stability with:

(1) Defined power settings and configurations.
(2) Flying control.
(3) Trimability.
(4) Engine handling.

For example: it must not be possible to pull back the power lever of a turboprop in flight and enter the reverse pitch range inadvertently, yet it is absolutely vital at times for a pilot, when making his approach with 55% of his take-off weight gone, to be able to put his often under-flapped aeroplane down accurately on a short strip and select reverse power almost in one movement. Therefore, one cannot, perhaps, apply the same design approach to an agricultural aeroplane as one can to a third-level mini-airliner with the same engines.

In the U.K., the relevant section of the *British Civil Airworthiness Requirements* (B.C.A.R.) is section K for agricultural aeroplanes. It is

Plate 1.3 Ayres Turbo Thrush 500 U.S. gallons hopper (1893 litres), dual control version (photo: Ayres Corporation)

comparatively straightforward to certificate such aeroplanes imported from abroad when type certificated to the *Federal Aviation Regulations*, FAR part 23, and the earlier *U.S. Civil Aeronautics Manual*, CAM 3, but there are particular difficulties with the next step, i.e. when dealing with a U.S.A. agricultural aeroplane type certificated as shown in table 1.1, for example: CAM 3 is accepted by the U.K. Civil Aviation Authority (C.A.A.) as a code against which the aeroplane can be assessed. CAR 8, on the other hand, is a terse and short document which says, in effect, 'if you can fly it, you can have it certificated (i.e. in the required category)'. This code was designed to fit ex-military aeroplanes

Table 1.1 Codes and categories

Code and category	Weight (lb)	AFT CG (in AOD)	Longitudinal stability
CAM 3 Normal	6000	29.0	Stable
CAR 8 Restricted	6000	30.0	Unstable
CAR 8 Restricted	7400	30.5	Unstable

Table 1.2 The agricultural overload

Authority	Design 'n'	Overload 'n'	Maximum % increase in take-off weight
FAA (U.S.A.)	3.8 (Normal) (4.4 Utility)	2.5	52 (76)
CAA (U.K.)	3.8 (Normal) (4.4 Utility)	3.0	27 (47)

after the War. The U.K. authority cannot certificate an aeroplane to it, because it is not part of the package of reciprocal agreements; it has no equivalent standard in the U.K. Therefore, it is part of the job of the Airworthiness Division to look at and draft a set of flight requirements for such aeroplanes, taking into account the real differences from conventional aeroplanes.

Longitudinal stability and overloads

The normal category certification is applicable to an aeroplane with a structure designed for 3.8 g, while design for utility category works to 4.4 g where

$$3.8 \text{ g} = 1 + 2.8 \text{ applied}$$

$$4.4 \text{ g} = 1 + 3.4 \text{ applied}$$

For practical (utilitarian) work operators want to carry heavier loads, which hoppers usually provide – in the sense that a hopper to carry solids by volume will contain a much heavier liquid load of higher density. Operators therefore tend to pack their aeroplanes to the maximum, working well beyond certificated limits. In recognition of the tendency, while not specifically controlling the reality, the Federal Aviation Administration (F.A.A.) allows overload to a reduced limit (table 1.2).

The C.A.A. apply the following restrictions which reduce the + 27% normal and + 47% utility overloads to whatever value satisfies:

- Climb gradient to 4.5% at the weight, altitude and temperature on take-off.
- Fatigue limit for the structure.
- Design limit of the hopper.

This enables aeroplanes to carry relatively heavy loads, around 50 to 60% of their take-off weights. Turbopropeller engines, which have enormous power in hand and are light weight, enable ag-machines to be fitted with bigger hoppers, thus increasing the trend to higher loads.

Figure 1.1 is to refresh the memory about what is meant by neutral and positive stability (the same principles can be applied to an aeroplane in plan view, for the directional stability case). The natural longitudinal stability of such ag-aeroplanes is degraded by the large mass of liquid swilling backwards and forwards in the hopper and its measurement becomes academic in practice and a worry for the certification pilot and design surveyor. The phenomenon is worsened by the 'P-effect' of the propeller, which is much further forward of the C of G (fig. 1.2). A rotating propeller causes several complicated effects, especially when it is pitched or yawed, and is no longer more or less normal to the airflow; together they add up to the P-factor, or P-effect (Stinton, 1983). Power is destabilising; furthermore, flap deflection causes instability, and a number of ag-aeroplanes either have no flaps, or maximum deflection is limited to around 15°, to achieve at least a token in the direction of stability requirements.

The answer is not to increase static and manoeuvre margins, because that increases the control forces needed to manoeuvre, and increases pilot fatigue – especially in hot and humid conditions. Baffles do not necessarily solve the problem because they lengthen dump times, especially with solids. If specialised baffling is resorted to, then one can foresee specialised metered dump systems being needed as a matter of universal necessity. Metered dumping is inevitable anyway with some of the modern highly toxic, high value loads which can be very expensive and dangerous to discharge completely in an emergency.

The requirement to dump the hopper load rapidly (in the U.K. the present requirement is five seconds for a single-engined aeroplane and ten seconds for twins) without encountering excessive stick forces is fraught with difficulty. When a large liquid load is dumped, an aeroplane pitches nose up. It has been found possible to run out of nose-down elevator against stick push forces of 40 lbf (182 N) or more, in an attempt to check excessive divergence. Two causes contribute to this:

(1) The release of around one half of the total weight makes the aeroplane leap upwards, before the angle of attack can be reduced by pilot action.
(2) The fall of a large mass of liquid induces a downwash in the surrounding air.

Taken together, the relative airflow is caused to have a powerful down-

NEUTRAL STABILITY

In the simplest case of longitudinal stability:

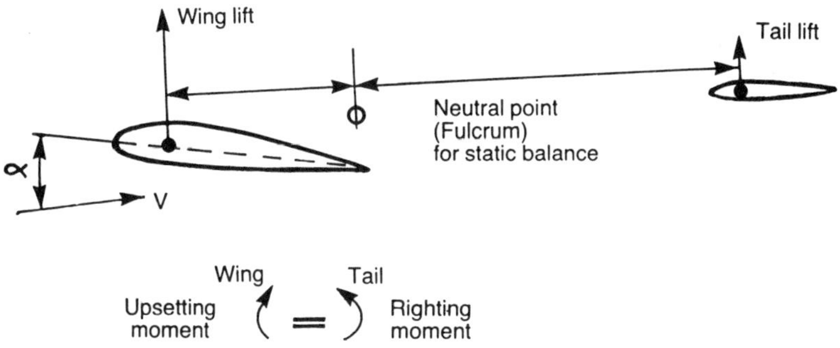

When the centre of gravity of the aircraft is located at the neutral point the machine is neutrally stable.

POSITIVE STABILITY

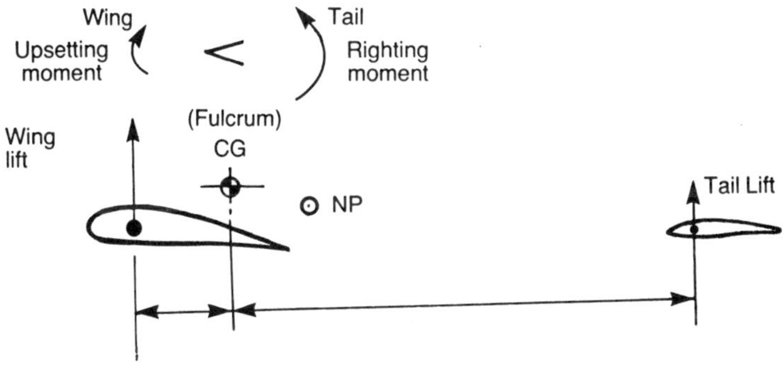

For longitudinal stability the centre of gravity must lie forward of the neutral point so making the righting moment greater than the upsetting moment.

The CG (static) margin is the distance between the centre of gravity and neutral point. The bigger the margin the more stable the aircraft.

Fig 1.1 Aide memoire for longitudinal stability (Stinton, 1982)

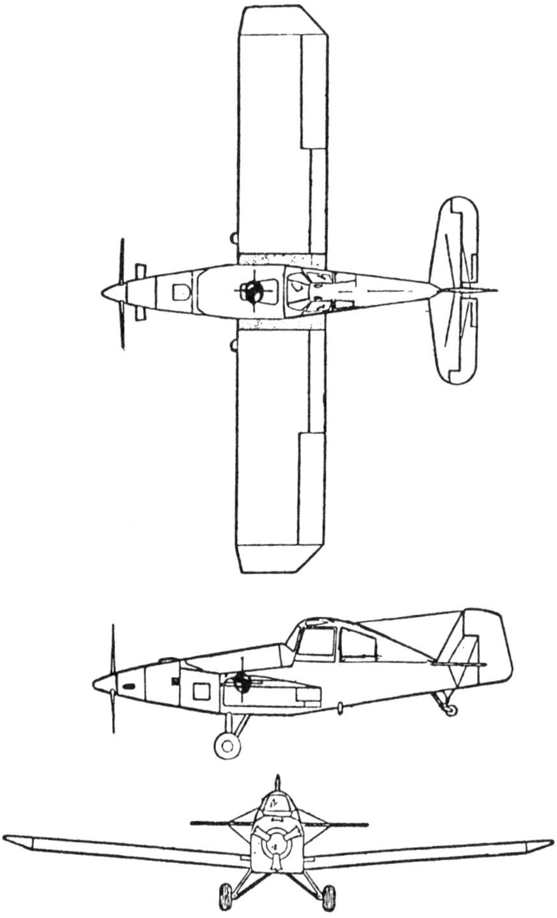

Fig 1.2 Ayres S2R Turbo Thrush

wards component. Longitudinal stability points the aircraft into the relative flow, pitching the nose upwards.

It follows that as structures become more efficient, proportionately heavier agricultural loads will be carried, increasing the problem. Yet, to counter the effect by reducing longitudinal stability, or increasing control authority with quickened rate of response in pitch, could lead to reduced safety. There is a need for a careful assessment and development of control surface characteristics for such aircraft, which has not been done so far. Control forces might be light enough to enable a pilot to work through a hot ten-hour day without excessive fatigue. There is a tendency for pilots to have accidents mid-afternoon and this

Plate 1.4 Emergency dumping (in the U.K. the present requirement is 5 sec for a single engine aircraft and 10 sec for a twin) (photo: Interflug, Berlin, D.D.R.)

might be due to drowsiness, especially in hot countries. Time spent turning, for example, when the pilot is using large control movements, can occupy 40% of the total sortie time (including ferrying) i.e. some four hours in ten. But care is needed, because control forces that are too light can lead to accidents.

It should be added, looking again at fig. 1.1, that directional stability can also be degraded more than a little for similar reasons. Propwash is vigorously destabilising directionally with many turboprop installations, causing aeroplanes to suffer reduced yaw damping in turbulence, causing the nose to swing from side to side.

Plate 1.5 Simplex emergency dump door (photo: Pilatus Aircraft)

Weight and balance

To control the degradation of stability it is becoming increasingly necessary to call for weight and balance information to be provided by operators for their pilots. C of G ranges are often expanded by manufacturers to cater for effects of overloads. The introduction of pilot (and sometimes crewman) weights which can frequently vary between 80 kg and 120 kg, well aft of the C of G, then cause C of Gs to move outside forward limits in some cases, and with the load and/or fuel gone, to move outside aft limits in others.

One answer to the problem, but not with this generation of Western aeroplanes, could be more frequent use of vertical hoppers. These are used in Eastern Europe, e.g. Cmêlak, Belphegor, and the by Australian Transavia for their Skyfarmer. But, in general, Western hoppers tend to be disposed lengthwise, with attendant C of G movement when attitude is changed.

New thinking

To achieve productivity one has to ensure utility, where:

Utility = versatility + (payload capacity × block speed)

= variable geometry + cost/ton mile per hour

Variable geometry (which costs money) may be anything from a variable pitch propeller and retractable gear to variable sweep, by way of slats, flaps and rotary wings. It can also mean the ability to change the internal configuration for different payloads. The question is what degree of variable geometry can be afforded? In addition the designer must also think of the logistics, i.e. the whole problem of supply, repair and maintenance in support of flying operations. Fortuitously, aeroplanes are less limited by ground bearing conditions than trucks. If ground transport can get onto a strip then so can most agricultural aeroplanes.

In the past, there was a tendency to develop existing machines by modification for the agricultural role. Today, special aeroplanes must be designed from the drawing board. Hopper loads are heavy and voluminous. Designers cannot afford to waste such lost volume, and crashworthiness is vital, which is why the NDN Fieldmaster project, in fig. 1.3, incorporates a strong load-bearing stainless steel hopper. There is also room for a second occupant (either an instructor, mechanic or ground crew), which is becoming a necessary feature for such operations and training.

Nosegears are becoming more common, especially for aeroplanes designed with turbopropeller engines. Such power-units can be ten times as expensive as piston engines, which run on costly avgas, while kerosene (avtur) is more available in remote areas. Operators are beginning to argue that they cannot afford to spend almost $250 000 on

Plate 1.6 Pezetel M-15 Belphegor turbo jet agricultural aircraft; note the twin vertical hoppers (photo: Pezetel Warsaw)

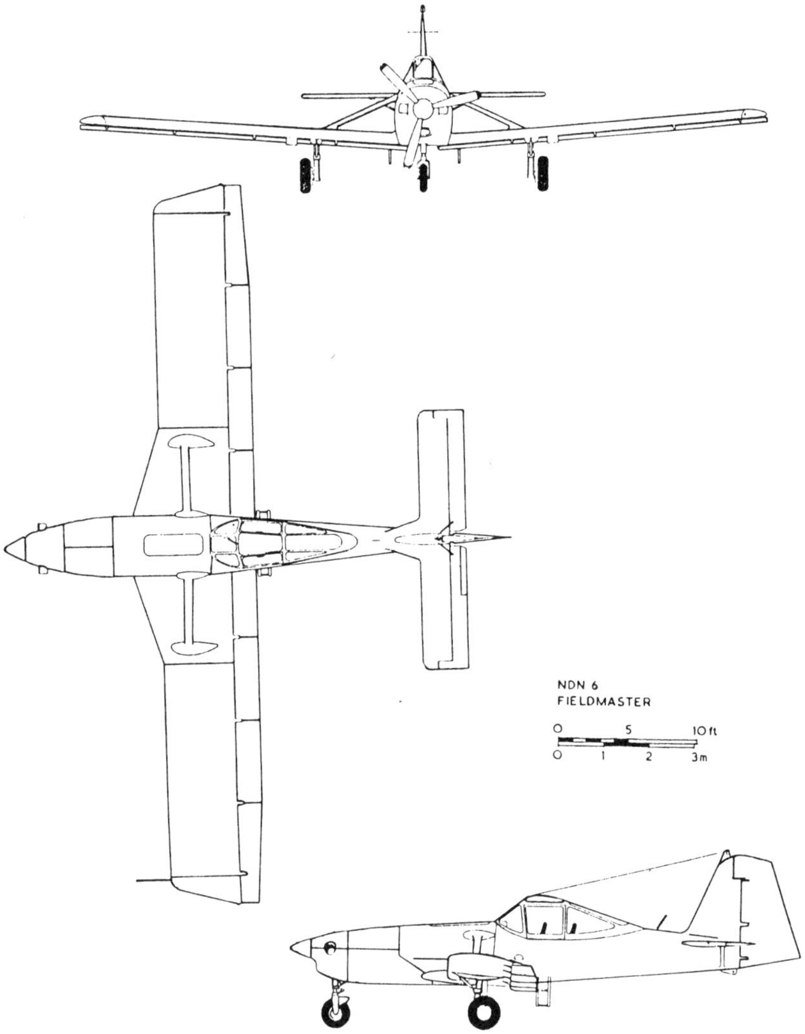

Fig 1.3 NDN Fieldmaster (NDN Aircraft Ltd)

specialist aircraft to have them damaged on take-off or landing, because of the extra skill needed to operate with tailwheel gear. This view implies a need for flaps which, as have been noted, can cause stability problems. Even so, tailwheel gear can often be better than nosegear for economic short-field operations, but it needs more pilot skill. For an example of an agricultural aircraft re-engined with a turbine engine see fig. 1.4.

For return on investment, aircraft of this kind must have long ferry ranges: at least 300 nm (556 km) with hopper empty. With a hopper filled with fuel some agricultural aeroplanes have transatlantic range. A requirement appears to be to spread loads between 0.89 to 1000 lb/acre (1.0 to 1120.8 kg/ha). Large parts of the world are hot, and they can be high, so that the aim should be to operate from 900 ft airstrips to 50 ft screens (274 m to 15 m) at altitudes around 5000 ft amsl (1524 m) in ISA to ISA + 30°C. Minimum spray speed should be sufficient for a steep wing-over to 100 ft (30 m) at the end of each run during which the airspeed should not drop to less than 1.2 V_S. Minimum spray (or swath) speed works out to be not less than about 100 kts; the upper limit is, say 200 kts (185 to 370 km/h).

Structural design loads

This section is after I.C.A.O. 1968. Many pilots appear to be unaware of the serious consequences which can result from their disregard of the various limitations placed on their aircraft. This problem is most acute in the case of those agricutural aircraft for which a substantial increase in take-off weight has been permitted under the provisions of A.N.O.s, or other regulations. This section explains the reason for these limitations and should serve to illustrate the need for great care on the part of the pilot if structural safety is to be maintained.

The fact that an aeroplane can be operated through a wide range of weights and speeds and be subjected to a variety of different flight conditions makes it impossible to specify a single criterion or even several criteria which would completely cover its entire structural strength requirements. The present practice is to consider the widest possible range of operating conditions that the particular aircraft type

Fig 1.4 Schweizer G-164D Turbine Ag-Cat

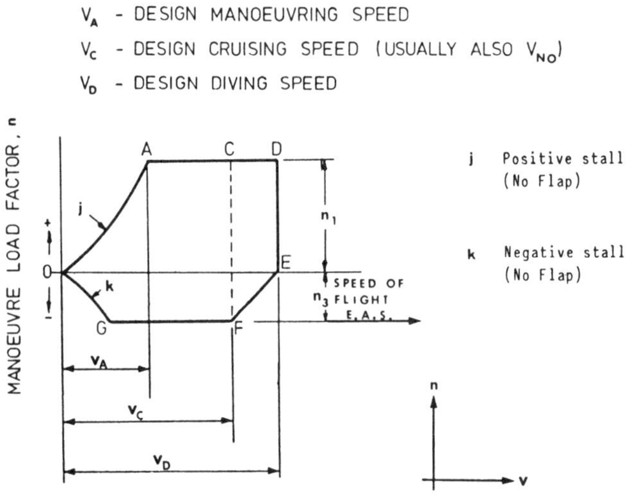

Fig 1.5 Typical manoeuvre envelope (ICAO, 1968)

is likely to encounter and to specify strength–speed 'envelopes' for a given design gross weight.

Loads imposed on the aircraft structure during symmetrical manoeuvres may be presented graphically in the form of a *V–n* diagram, often called a 'manoeuvre envelope'. A typical manoeuvre envelope is shown in fig. 1.5. The vertical axis of the graph is the load factor *n*, which is simply the ratio of the total lift produced by the aircraft structure to the actual weight of the aircraft. To make this relationship clear, we can take the example of an aeroplane in a balanced steep turn maintaining a constant airspeed with a 60° angle of bank. As many of you will recall from student days, this manoeuvre will subject the aircraft to a force of '2**g**', i.e. twice the force of gravity. Because the aircraft is in a stage of equilibrium, the lift it is producing in the turn must equal twice the force of gravity. In other words, the ratio of the lift to the weight of the aircraft is 2:1. The horizontal axis of the graph is the aircraft speed, *V*, and as long as the aircraft is never operated at a combination of *V* and *n* outside the manoeuvre envelope, it remains structurally safe.

Aeroplanes also have to be designed to cope with vertical gust encounters in flight. Here the conditions are similar to the manoeuvre case, except that it is the gust itself which introduces the loads to the structure by effectively changing the angle of attack of the aeroplane. The effects of gust loading can also be presented in the form of a *V-n* diagram, which in this case is called a 'gust' envelope. A typical gust envelope is shown in fig. 1.6. On each of the two V–n diagrams, the points A, B, C, D, E, F and G serve to define the basic flight design cases for the aeroplane and the results obtained by investigating the loads represented by these various points are usually sufficient to specify the speeds and limit load factors which must be used. Limit loads are defined as the greatest which the aircraft is likely to meet in service, and in the U.K. and in Australia (as an example) are specified for normal category aircraft by the following:

$$n1 \text{ (max. `positive } g\text{')} = 2.1 + \left\{\frac{24\,000}{W + 10\,000}\right\}$$

where W is the design maximum weight; but $n1$ need not be greater than 3.5 and shall not be less than 2.5.

$$n3 \text{ (max. `negative } g\text{')} = -1$$

A slightly different formula is used in America to determine limit loads, but as the resulting positive load factors obtained do not vary significantly, the discussion in this article is valid for American as well as for British and Australian designed aircraft.

The strength of agricultural aircraft

The types of light aircraft which are used in aerial agriculture are nearly all designed to a manoeuvre envelope only, because they are not

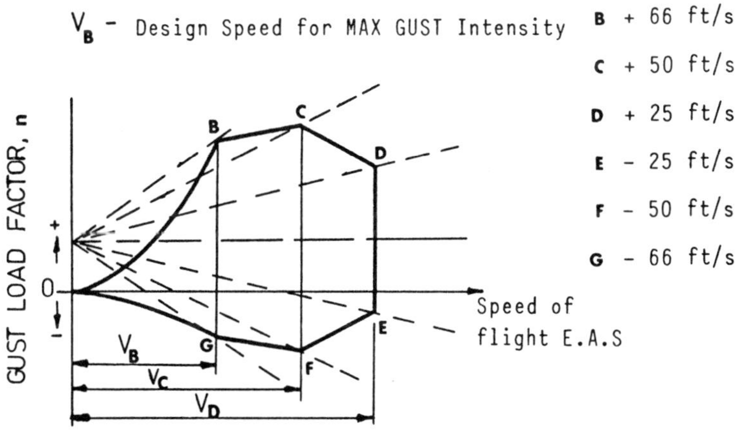

Fig 1.6 Typical gust envelope; note that 1 ft/s = 0.3048 m/s (ICAO, 1968)

'gust critical' at their design gross weights. The discussion which follows will therefore mainly concern the manoeuvre envelope and we will examine a representative envelope for a *non-agricultural aeroplane* and show what is involved structurally when it is adapted to aerial agricultural work.

In Australia, for example, when an aircraft type is cleared for aerial agriculture, an increased maximum take-off weight (TOW) may be allowed after an assessment of its performance, previous service experience, and any other relevant factors. The maximum agricultural TOW which will be permitted in the particular case is based on the aircraft's original design strength and its design gross weight. Virtually all agricultural aircraft are authorised to operate at an increased TOW and the net effect is comparable to a reduction in strength. The extent to which this occurs is clearly set out in fig. 1.7, which shows flight strength envelopes drawn for a typical light aircraft. The outer one is for the aircraft as originally designed and the inner one is as converted to agricultural use with the greater TOW. Operation beyond the positive and negative load factor boundaries will result in structural damage and ultimately in structural failure, so that for the aircraft to retain the same structural safety margin at the higher TOW, it is necessary to impose more critical operational limitations.

Although the difference in load factor may not appear to be large, it represents for a typical aircraft of 3000 lb design weight a reduction in limit load of approximately 15%. This means that the limit load is becoming more easily attainable, particularly when it is remembered that the flight controls were designed to function under the more generous limitations of the original load factor. It will also be noted that not only are the load factors lower, but the stall boundaries have

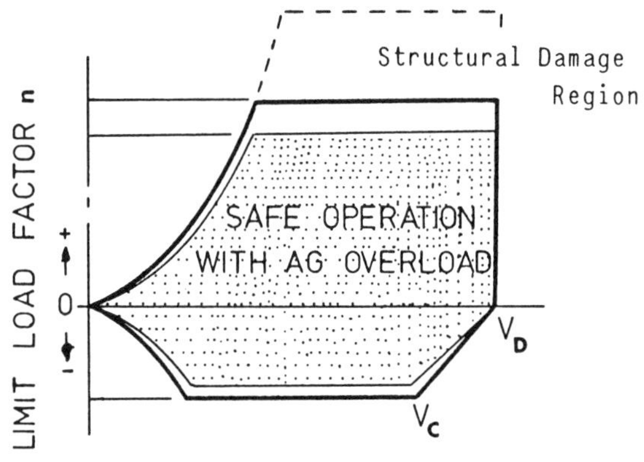

Fig. 1.7 Flight strength envelope (ICAO, 1968).

moved, giving higher stalling speeds. It is also possible that the aircraft will have now become 'gust critical'. Although the higher weight aircraft may react less violently during turbulence, this effect is more than offset by the higher stresses present. As a result of this, the structure could be damaged or even fail in flight due to a gust encounter, quite irrespective of how carefully the aircraft is flown.

It will be realised that operations at an increased weight involve a higher risk of structural failure than other forms of flying, but this has been justified in the past on the basis that agricultural aircraft will normally fly in reasonably good weather, that they will be handled carefully by competent pilots with due regard to their heavier loaded condition and that their *payload is quickly disposable*. The pilots' handbooks published by the manufacturers of some of the different aircraft type used in aerial agriculture contain a statement that the aircraft is '150 per cent stronger than it need be'. Such statements are merely commerical presentations of the very fundamental fact that all aeroplane design requirements call for a safety factor of at least 1.5 between the limit and ultimate loads. These statements can be dangerously misconstrued in some ways.

Pilots have, for instance, interpreted the 1.5 factor as meaning that they can overload the aeroplane by 50% or fly up to 50% above placard speeds without getting into trouble. This is an extremely perilous supposition, particularly in the case of speeds. Aerodynamic loads vary as the square of the speed, so that increasing a speed 1.5 times will increase the aeroplane loads 2.25 times; double the speed and the loads increase by four times, and so on. Figure 1.8 shows the effect of an increase in speed above the design placard value. This is for normal gross weight and shows that even under these conditions a 23% increase in speed over the allowable value may result in structural failure.

Maximum take-off weight

A check has shown that with very few exceptions, agricultural aeroplanes are consistently operated at weights in excess of the maximum agricultural TOW permitted. At the high stress levels associated with such practices, the risk of failure of some part of the aircraft structure is high. The risk of structural failure through fatigue is also dramatically increased. For example, 10% additional weight can account for 30 to 40% reduction in the safe life of the principal structure elements.

Rough handling

Flight tests in connection with fatigue studies have shown that some pilots operate their aircraft up to measured limit load factors of 3.0 **g**.

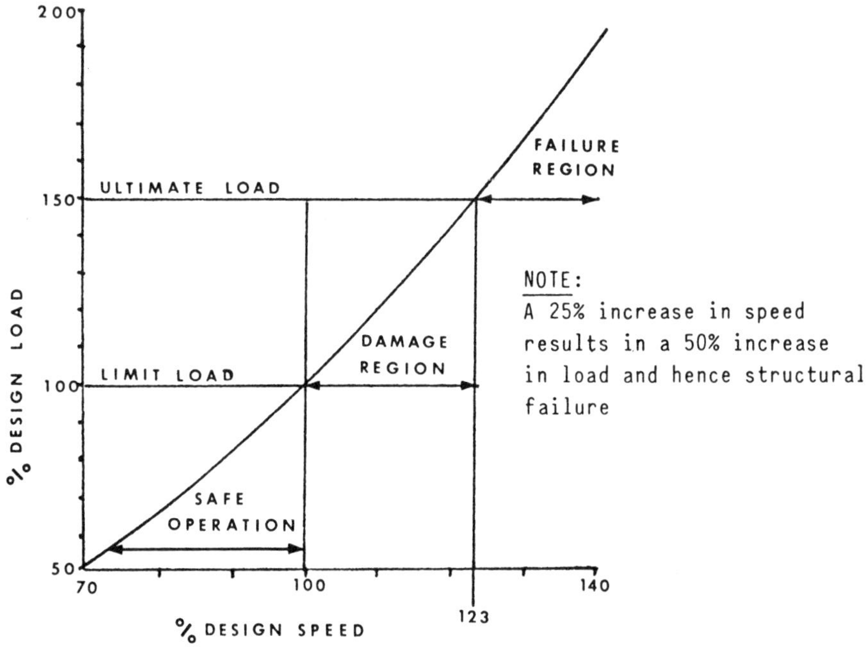

Fig 1.8 Variation in applied loading with speed (after ICAO, 1968)

While this is safe at normal design weights, it is most hazardous at any higher weight and adversely affects fatigue life. The effect of 'bunting' to close hopper doors is another factor which can affect fatigue life, as one bunting operation does fatigue damage equivalent to an additional 'ground–air cycle'. The practice of doing ground pivot turns under engine take-off power also adds to the onset of early fatigue failure of both engine mounts and landing gear components.

Excessive airspeed

The use of flaps to reduce speed in turns invariably means that flap speeds are exceeded. In one classic example of this the pilot was operating his aircraft overloaded with flaps down at 30 knots above the normal placard flap speed. This aircraft subsequently suffered serious wing flutter which could easily have destroyed it. Other cases of exceeding placard flap speed have been noticed during take-off operations.

As a result of investigations into the likely effects of permitted increase in maximum weight of aeroplanes undertaken in some countries, it has been concluded that, while on the ground of structural strength alone some increase would be justified, the effect of the increase on fatigue life could be extremely severe. To illustrate a theoretical case, the Air Registration Board in the U.K. considered an aeroplane of conventional design, having a positive manoeuvring load factor of 3.5, operating continuously on agricultural missions of 15 minutes duration. Assuming the maximum take-off weight for each flight to be at or near the maximum permissible, the safe life of the wings of such an aeroplane was estimated to be in the order of 5000 to 10 000 flights (1250 to 2500 flying hours). It was concluded that:

(a) If the maximum permitted weight of such an aeroplane is increased by 10%, a reduction of 25% in estimated safe fatigue life of the wings would result;
(b) If the maximum permitted weight is increased by 20%, a reduction of 45% in estimated safe fatigue life of the wings would result.

Having regard to these findings, it is considered inadvisable to permit any overloading of aircraft engaged in these operations beyond the point at which the structural requirements for non-aerobatic aeroplanes are met. In fact, due to the frequency of landings and take-offs the conclusions point to a need for a reserve factor on the structural design load factors to ensure a reasonable fatigue life of the main components of such aeroplanes.

The future

The statistics of the U.S.A. Federal Aviation Administration reveal that there were twenty-five in-flight failures per year on average over a period of ten years or so with light aircraft types, as a result of operations outside the design envelopes. These casualties have occurred to aircraft operating on a normal gross weight basis only, and as many of the same types are being used for aerial agriculture at higher weights, it is obvious that the seriousness of exceeding operational limitations cannot be over-emphasised. It may be argued by some that twenty-five in-flight failures per year is a reasonable figure to expect from the operation of about 73 000 light aircraft. However, when some adjustment is made for the relative flight time utilisations of agricultural as compared to normal operations, the expected in-flight failure figure increases at least *six-fold*, even disregarding any considerations of the effect of overloads and structural fatigue.

While it can be said that less than 3% of all aircraft accidents are caused by structural failure, their occurrence has a far greater psychological effect than the 80% or so caused by 'human factors'. The confidence that some pilots have in their ability to 'get away' with a certain amount of abuse of their aircraft has undoubtedly stemmed from their accumulated experience with some of the very robust earlier types, i.e. ex-military, but we now have to realise that modern aeroplanes do not possess the design conservatisms which were built into their predecessors. Today, through refined analysis techniques, structural margins of safety have been reduced to a few per cent and because of this, operational excesses can easily damage or fail modern light aircraft types at their normal design weights. Hence operations at the maximum agricultural loadings require the highest standards of airmanship and the strictest adherence to all appropriate limitations.

It should now be quite clear that flight safety is seriously jeopardised by deliberate or careless neglect of the structural limitations placed on agricultural aeroplanes. In this section however, we are more concerned with emphasising the dire physical consequences which might result from these practices, so that all who are directly concerned with agricultural operations will appreciate the urgency of the problem.

Region of reversed command

The shaded region in fig. 1.9 is one in which a reduction of airspeed requires an increase in power in order to maintain altitude. It can be encountered in any phase of agricultural flying and in itself is not dangerous provided the pilot is aware of the problems associated with low speed, low level flying. For example if a pilot inadvertently allows his airspeed to drop too low on a swath run he will have to add power to maintain level flight. This could lead to his starting a pull up manoeuvre with little or no power left available, and little airspeed to convert to altitude. Agricultural operations do not usually afford the pilot altitude to convert to airspeed. High angle of attack low speed flying even with high application of power should therefore be avoided.

Mismanagement of fuel system

An agricultural aircraft is engaged in repetitive work involving a great number of take-offs and landings, and it is only too easy, especially when he is getting tired, for the pilot to become careless about carrying out take-off checks each time. However unless a habit is made of checking the fuel continually, sooner or later it may be forgotten. Fuel valves must also be checked for the selection of the correct tank; there will be no time at low level to change to another tank after the one in use has run dry.

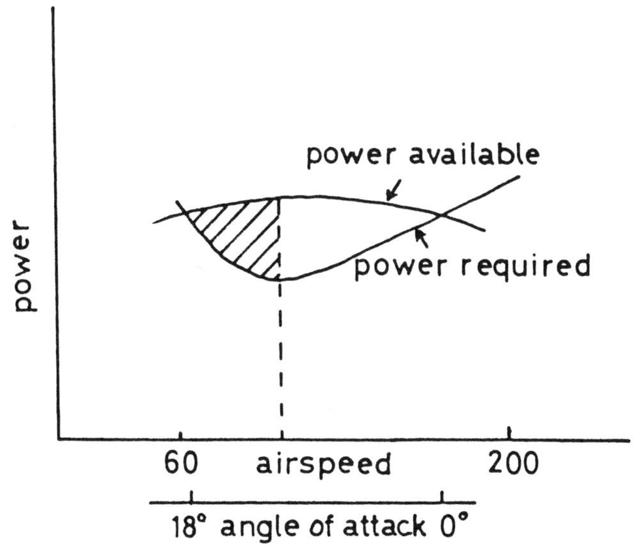

Fig 1.9 Region of reversed command (figures are examples)

Overloading

The loading of the aircraft for the application run is the pilot's responsibility. He must use his training, experience and judgement to determine what the safe load for his aircraft is when working from a given airstrip. This in turn is also dependent upon the type, length and condition of the given airstrip. The paved runway on level ground near sea level provides the best operating conditions, but the use of grass, dirt or gravel strips is frequently necessary and each provides problems of take-off and landing unique to the particular surface involved. Grass may slow the take-off (or increase the run needed) while bare clay or dirt strips provide hazards of mud when wet, and dust and dirt when dry which can clog carburettor air filters and generally make a disagreeable dust cloud around the loading area. Gravel and sand on the strip cause pitting of propellers and damage to wing surfaces, particularly lowered flaps, and to tail assemblies.

The liquid load can be accurately gauged by markers on the tank visible from the pilot's cockpit. The visible marker may be made possible by simply having a clear see-through section on the end of the tank, properly scaled for the tank volume. Or a clear tube may be attached at the bottom and top of the tank, in which the liquid level rises to match the tank level. The visibly marked tank also enables the pilot to check his load when in flight and prevents running out of material during the pass across the field. The density of the liquids used will usually be less than that of water, since the petroleum base solvents and many of the hydrocarbon chemicals are lighter than an equivalent volume of water. However, some solutions, particularly of dissolved solids in water will increase the density and also, when technical concentration materials are used, they may be heavier than water. It is therefore desirable to check on the liquid density and to be careful that an excessive load is not put in the aircraft accidentally through using the same volume but of a higher density material.

In New Zealand there were two fatal accidents in 1979 where overloading appears to have been a contributing factor. In each case the loading vehicle gauge had been previously changed and no subsequent calibration check carried out. It is obvious that a procedure is necessary for load weighing of solids and correct calibration of the loading gauge is most important (Quantick, 1979).

Whole body impact tolerance

Historically, aviation medicine has been primarily concerned with human tolerances to the body as a whole. The development of restraint systems, studies of crash impact protection and survival, have all focussed on the human organism as an entity. Thus, statements have arisen out of context that the body 'can take *x* number of **g**s'. Such assertions have no meaning without also taking into consideration the particular characteristics and the conditions under which the decelerative forces are applied. Physical factors which have been identified as influencing human tolerance to impact forces include: magnitude of the forces, direction of the force (body orientation), distribution of the forces, onset rate (rise time), duration of impact, and the method of restraint or constraint (Snyder, 1971).

Impact (abrupt acceleration; deceleration) is characterised by forces of very abrupt onset, short duration, and high magnitude. It is generally considered that impact involves the occurrence of forces of less than 0.2 s duration (Stapp, 1961). The literature on restraint systems and tolerance tests of subjects is extensive. The most authoritative paper on human voluntary impact tests is by Stapp (1970). Protected only by the lap belt restraint in current civil aircraft, human subjects have been voluntarily tested to 26 **g**. In a series of tests, Lewis and Stapp (1957) concluded that minimum contusions would result when decelerative force exceeded 10 **g**, at 300 **g**/s rate of onset, for 0.002 s duration. By 13 **g**, at the same onset rate and time duration, soreness and muscle strain would be expected. At the highest level studied 26 **g** (at 850 **g**/s for 0.02 s) although the subject complained of severe pain lasting for

30 s post-impact and back strain for two days, no lasting injury was reported. In this case, a 3 in nylon military lap belt was used; impingement pressure was calculated to be 89.5 lb/in^2 and belt loads were measured at 4290 lb. Up to 15 **g**, at these levels of time duration and onset rate, have subsequently been considered safe for human volunteer subjects (for subjective pain threshold and only transient injury).

For the forward-facing position, with lap belt restraint only, Stapp (1970) concluded that 'rates of onset between 250–1600 **g**/s and 11.4–32.0 peak **g** can be sustained against a lap belt restraint up to approximately 90 lb/in^2 average load, with no significant injuries resulting. It has been found that seated human occupants restrained by a 3 in lap belt only and subjected to aircraft crash forces can survive 30 **g** peak at rates of onset below 1500 **g**/s with only minor reversible injurious effects. When this is increased to more than 38 **g** at 1300 **g**/s, the immediate effects of deceleration are greater than at 45 **g** peak at 500 **g**/s.

However, as has been pointed out by Swearingen, *et al.* (1962), the arcing trajectory as the body goes forward to the limits of the belt and then jack-knifes over the lap belt is sufficiently great, so that if the torso is not also restrained, the lap-belted occupant will almost certainly strike the forward structure, instrument panel, and other surfaces, and even though whole body loads of a 30 **g** deceleration are survivable with no more than minor injury, fatal injuries at far lower levels can result from the head striking the sharp forward structure. Thus, upper torso body restraint is necessary for effective crash protection of the seated forward-facing general aviation aircraft occupant. Such protection offers the single most important advance that can be made in present crash survival, since most serious injuries, and fatalities, involve head and chest trauma resulting from upper body contact with the forward structure during deceleration flexion.

Use of upper torso restraint increases whole-body human tolerance limits to approximately 50 **g** peak (at 500 **g**/s rate of onset for 0.25 s duration) (Stapp, 1949). U.S. Air Force design recommendations have been given as 45 **g** for a duration of 0.1 s or 25 **g** for a duration of 0.2 s (Air Force Systems Command, 1969).

An FAA advisory circular specifies acceptable installation methods for shoulder harness attachment, based upon work by Young (Anon., 1967; Young, 1966). Upper torso belts should be fitted at an angle of $-5°$ to $+30°$ from the shoulder (horizontal), and lap belt installations should be between 45° and 55° for best use of the body's pelvic structure (see fig. 1.10 for body restraint systems).

Observations by the U.K. R.A.F. Institute of Pathology direct attention to the need for integrated systems of safety equipment and in the particular case of light aircraft the findings indicate that the

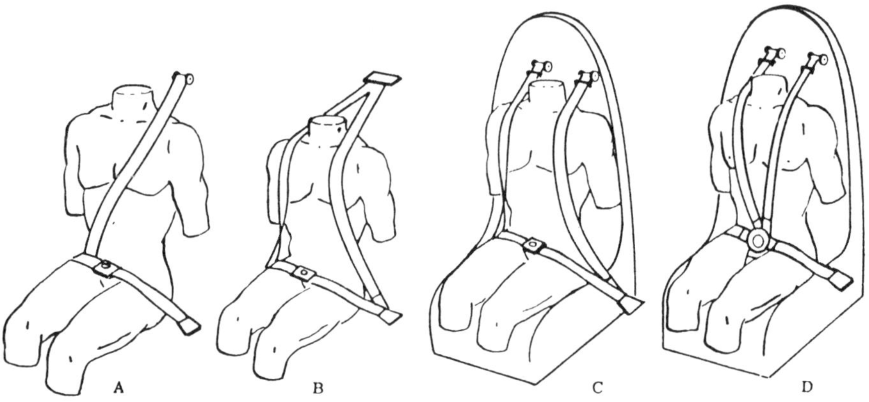

Fig 1.10 Body restraint systems; four examples, all with inertia reel devices: A, a lap belt with a single outboard over the shoulder belt; B, an inverted yoke, coming together behind the head in a single belt to attach to inertia reel mounted in roof structure (Hamill Manufacturing Co.) – the inertia reel could also be mounted on the floor structure at the base of the seat or in the seat back; C, double torso belt, with either a single or double attachment behind the seat; D, five-point restraint system, featuring crotch strap and single-point emergency quick release (Pacific Scientific Co.).

combination of protective helmet and shoulder harness would provide the most significant means of reducing the number of fatalities in accidents (Mason, 1973). The problem of submarining (sliding under and out of the harness) has been considered and has been relegated to an acceptable risk easily preventable by the use of a crotch strap (five point harness).

Safety helmets

Studies on the mechanisms of injury in modern light aircraft crashes show that injuries generally are not attributed to the crash forces themselves but rather to consequential factors like structural collapse of the cockpit area, failure of the safety belt, seat fittings and flailing of the body against protruding objects or the inner structure of the cockpit within the occupant's environment. In particular, injury severity in modern light aircraft crashes is largely determined by the severity of the head injury (Swearingen *et al.*, 1962). It follows, therefore, that all precautions should be taken to protect the head.

A comprehensive survey of literature on single engine light aircraft crash injuries by Pearson (1961) showed that from a group of 236 occupants, 44 received skull fractures of which 28 were fatal, 72 had brain injuries of which 23 were fatal (23% fatalities from head injuries). The data on accidents in agricultural aviation in the Netherlands, to Dutch agricultural aircraft, show that from 1950 to 1963 inclusive twenty-six accidents occurred to aircraft and six to helicopters. In two accidents the pilot was killed and in six accidents the pilot received serious injuries, of which five were cases of serious head injuries. So in 15.6% of these Dutch accidents serious head injuries occurred (Fournier, 1964).

Pearson (1962) states that among 623 occupants during crashes 11% received injuries to the skull, 26% to the brain and 13% to the face. He also shows that skull and facial injuries occur considerably more often when the tie-down attachments are broken or ineffective. Brain injuries were sustained by 45% of those occupants whose seat failed and by 36% of those whose belt failed. Head area injuries were sustained also by occupants using a shoulder harness, but apparently they were less severe than for the occupants not using such a harness. The failure of seatbelt or seat, and consequently the severity of injuries, is influenced by variable factors at principal impact, like the velocity, the angle between the flight path of the aircraft and the terrain, the deceleration at the impact, and the structural collapse of the aircraft. Pearson (1962) goes on to state that with an effective tie down, the increase of the injury severity as a function of impact velocity is small, and furthermore, under impact velocities from 30 to 39 m.p.h., 31% of the sustained injuries were to the skull, brain or face, at 40 to 49 m.p.h. 40%, at 50 to 59 m.p.h. 39%, and at 60 to 69 m.p.h. 34%.

As far as impact angle is concerned, with effective tie down 13% of the injuries were to the skull, brain or face at impact angles up to 22°, 48% at angles from 23° to 37° and 51% at angles from 38° to 52°. So impact angle is an important injury producing factor.

From the foregoing it will be clear that the possibility of head injuries (to skull, brain, face) during a crash is too great to ignore. These injuries are mainly attributed to hitting of the head against the instrument panel or other forward structures, protruding or other injury-producing objects within the occupant's environment. It will be obvious that the contact between the head and the injury-producing objects should be prevented as far as possible by appropriate measures, such as the use of a shoulder harness, removal of protruding objects within the cockpit and, last but not least, the use of a *safety helmet*. In general, one may require that in view of the hazards inherent to agricultural flying (low level flying, operation from unprepared strips) a good agricultural aircraft should provide the maximum protection in the event of a crash. The groundspeeds during crashes usually are not high and therefore good protective measures will offer the occupants a good chance to survive the crash, in most cases even without injuries. Practice has shown that the use of a good safety helmet in addition to these measures can raise the survival potential appreciably (Fournier, 1964).

The argument for wearing protective helmets in aviation rests on the high incidence of serious head injury in crashes, and the extent to which this can be reduced by the use of helmets. The R.A.F. in 1943 showed that head injuries comprised 40% of all crash injuries and 20% of fatal injuries. In 1953 a review of over 2000 U.S.A.F. cases showed that 24% of all major injuries were head injuries and that 14% of fatalities were due to this cause. This survey included cases in which protective helmets were worn, and it was demonstrated that use of a helmet reduced the major and fatal head injury rates from 24% to 14% and from 14% to 7.4% respectively. Since the time of the accidents reviewed, there have been major advances in helmet design. It will be appreciated that brain injury can result from:

- Direct penetration of the skull;
- Deformation of the skull with or without fracture;
- Rotational deceleration;
- Linear deceleration.

In the study of the design of safety helmets, Rawlins (1956) formulated the following requirements:

(a) The helmet should be tough.
(b) It should be rigid but not elastic.
(c) The surface should be free of projections to minimise torque.
(d) The surface should be smooth and have a low coefficient of friction to facilitate sliding over the opposed surface.
(e) By uniform deformation it should smooth out the acceleration curve.
(f) It should convert kinetic energy to energy of compression or extension.
(g) It should spread the blow as widely as possible over the head.

He frankly states that 'some of these properties are mutually incompatible and in practice the helmet will never be ideal. However by regarding the helmet as being composed of two parts (an outer shell and an inner lining) something approaching the ideal can be visualised'.

All present-day crash helmets in use with the air forces are composed of an outer shell and inner lining. Their designers certainly have tried to approach the ideal and are improving their products where it is possible.

The civil aviation authorities in Australia consider that safety helmets used in agricultural work should meet all strength and other requirements of British Standard (BS) 2495, 1960, and in addition should be of the fully-enveloping 'bone dome' type. Chin strap buckles, if used, should be of the 'closed' type, meaning that they should be underlain by a padded tongue or strap; the tearing action under impact of an 'open' buckle on the carotid artery region of the neck can be fatal. Another requirement for agricultural work is that all materials used in the helmet assembly should be able to withstand frequent cleansing, preferably with soap and water. The shells of almost all satisfactory helmets of contemporary design are constructed of resin-bonded laminated fibreglass material. Laminated woven nylon does in fact give a rather stronger shell, weight for weight, but the added cost of this material is out of proportion to the strength gained. Most satisfactory suspensions (i.e. harnesses, cradles) are made of woven nylon or terylene.

In addition to the constructional points discussed, a number of other helmet features are important. Some of these strongly influence comfort and hence user acceptance. Helmet weight and balance, coupled with helmet stability and absence of pressure points in the suspension, are probably the most important of these. Although less important than the other factors from the point of view of comfort, excessive helmet weight should be avoided as it adds unduly to the kinetic energy to be dissipated when the helmeted head strikes an object. No arbitrary upper weight limit is placed on helmets, but if design is satisfactory adequate protection should be obtainable for a helmet weight (without accessories) not exceeding 2 lb (0.908 kg).

Because of the wide ranges of size and shape of human heads, satisfactory helmet fitting presents considerable difficulties. A new problem has, however, been introduced by the necessity to fit earphones to helmets. It is essential for both protection and comfort that the sizing of your helmet shall be correct for your head, and that harness adjustments be made meticulously to obtain the best fit possible. It follows that a protective helmet comprises *personal* flying equipment in the strictest sense. Many helmet types rely entirely or mainly on stretch in a harness or cradle for absorbing energy of impact, rather than on energy-absorbing padding within the helmet. In the former type it is essential that the suspension be adjusted to allow as a minimum a clear ¾ inch (2 cm) of air space between the crown of the wearer's head and the inner surface of the helmet shell, with the chin-strap normally secured.

A protective helmet which is very hot to wear will be unacceptable to users. By its very nature a hard helmet must carry some temperature penalty under more extreme field conditions; it is most important that this be minimised however. Recent safety helmet designs incorporate earphones and visors. In particular, for the agricultural pilot are full face visors with positive pressure air feed, or visor mounted filter cartridges.

Health and fatigue

During agricultural operations there is no opportunity for the pilot to relax, and fatigue is a danger. In various countries there is legislation governing maximum duty for aircrew, but this more often than not is concerned with the number of flying hours that may be performed in a week or in a month, while in agricultural aviation it is the period of a day that is the vital factor. Furthermore, no legislation can allow for differences of stamina between different persons, or different conditions of health in the same person. It is more a question of each pilot knowing his own powers and flying accordingly.

Regular meals are very important but sometimes difficult to obtain under field conditions. Some pilots have the dangerous habit of beginning work on an empty stomach at dawn and eating little before mid-day. Energy is derived from food, and 3000 calories are the average daily requirements, 60% of this in the form of carbohydrates. These are most easily available to the body in the form of simple sugars like barley sugar, cane sugar and glucose. It is the blood sugar level that matters most; a reduced level results in an impairment of mental and physical efficiency, for sugars are a source of energy and are particularly valuable in the prevention and relief of fatigue. Symptoms of low blood sugar level include hunger, fatigue, anxiety and behaviour resembling intoxication. Tremulousness may develop, with difficulty or inability to perform fine movements. It is highly dangerous to fly in agricultural operations (even more so than in other applications) when under even the slightest influence of alcohol or drugs.

References

Air Force Systems Command (April 1960) (revision DN3g2, 20 July 1969) *Handbook of Instructions for Aircraft Designers*. Report ARCDM-80-1. Washington DC: Andrews Air Force Base.

Anon. (1966) *Agricultural Pilot Manual.* Issue 3. Australia: Department of Aviation.

Anon. (October 1967) *Occupant Restraint Harness Design Study*. Report No M67-7. Phoenix, Az: Aviation Safety Engineering and Research Division of Flight Safety Foundation Inc.

Fournier, A. W. (1964) 'Crash helmets in agricultural aviation.' *Agricultural Aviation* **6**, (1), 16-19.

I.C.A.O. (1968) *Safety in Aerial Work Part I – Agricultural Operations.* Circular 85-AN/71.

Lewis, S. T. and Stapp, J. P. (1957) 'Experiments conducted on a swing device for determining human tolerance to lap belt type decelerations.' Report ARMDC TN-57-1. 6571st Aeromedical Research Laboratory, Holloman Air Force Base, NM.

Mason, J. K. (May 1973) 'Protective helmets and harness restraint in fatal light aircraft accidents – UK experience.' *Proceedings, Aerospace Medical Association.*

Pearson, R. G. (1961) 'Impact-injury relationships in lightplane accidents.' *Archives of Environmental Health* **3**, 514–518.

Pearson, R. G. (November 1962) 'Mechanisms of injury in modern lightplane crashes, a statistical summary of causative factors.' TCREC Technical Report 62-83.

Quantick, H. R. (February 1979) 'Safety aspects of the aerial application of pesticides.' *Journal of Royal Aeronautical Society*, 176–182.

Rawlins, J. S. P. (1956) 'Design of crash helmets.' *Aeromedica Acta* special edition, 97–123.

Snyder, R. G. (1971) 'Occupant impact injury tolerances for aircraft crashworthiness design.' SAE Paper 710406.

Stapp, J. P. (1949) 'Human exposure to linear deceleration.' Part 11, December. 'The forward-facing position and the development of a crash harness.' WADC AF Technical Report 5915.

Stapp, J. P. (1961) 'Human tolerance to severe, abrupt deceleration.' *Gravitational Stress in Aerospace Medicine* (O. H. Gauer and G. D. Zuideman *eds*) Boston, U.S.A.. Little, Brown and Co., 165–188.

Stapp, J. P. (1970) 'Voluntary human tolerance levels.' *Impact Injury and Crash Protection* (E. S. Gurduian, W. A. Lange, L. M. Patrick and L. M. Thomas, *eds*) Springfield, Illinois, U.S.A.: Charles C. Thomas, 308–349.

Stinton, D. (1982) Royal Aeronautical Society, Agricultural Aviation Group Symposium, Cranfield, U.K.

Stinton, D. (1983) *The Design of the Aeroplane.* London: Granada Publishing.

Swearingen, J. J. *et al.* (1962) 'Kinematic behaviour of the human body during deceleration.' *Aerospace Medicine* **33**, 188–197.

Young, J. W. (1966) 'Recommendation for restraint installation in general aviation aircraft.' RAM Report 66-33, FAA.

2
Distribution equipment and calibration

Introduction

The chemicals used in agricultural work take the form of liquid sprays, granules and dusts, although dusts are becoming rare as an aerial application preparation because of drift problems. The aircraft is fitted with equipment for distributing these chemicals. The equipment must also be calibrated in order that the rate of dispensing the chemicals achieves the correct application onto the crop or other target surface. The equipment and the calibration procedure for liquids and solids are now described.

Spraygear – description

Spraygear is the name given to equipment used for distributing liquids. The following are the main components of an aircraft spraying system (see diagrammatic layout in fig. 2.1).

(1) *Chemical tank* (or hopper). This is either situated internally in the fuselage (in the case of a converted aircraft it usually replaces one or more seats), or is a 'belly tank' attached to the underside of the fuselage. It should be constructed of stainless steel or fibreglass. A contents gauge or sight glass is provided. There is a tightly-fitting lid or filler cap. The tank should be equipped with a device for jettisoning the load in an emergency.

(2) *Filters* are provided to remove matter likely to cause blockages. A basket filter is located at the filling point (recommended screen size: 10–20 openings/cm or 25–50 U.S.A. mesh). A coarser filter is usually situated at the entrance of the pump, for its protection. Another filter, or filters, is situated between the pump and the boom (or in the booms) (see fig. 2.2). The fourth point of filtering is at the nozzle

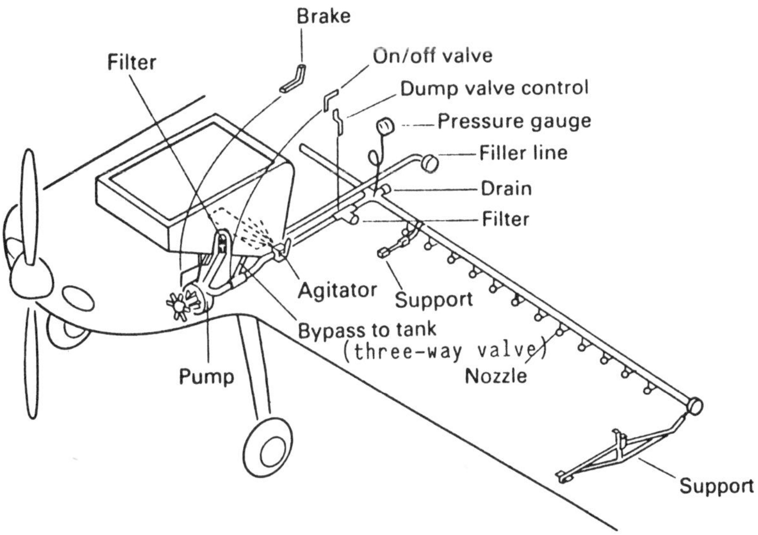

Fig 2.1 Diagram of a typical aircraft spray system. The use of a three-way operating valve ensures that, even with the pressure regulator fully closed, re-circulation continues whenever the spray is off (after F.A.O., 1972)

where the screen size should be just under the orifice size (see plate 2.1 on p. 36).

(3) A *pump* is incorporated in the spray system to supply the liquid under pressure to the atomising equipment. Normal operating pressures are 20-80 lb/in^2 (1.5-5.6 kg/cm^2). Pumps are either centrifugal or, less usually, gear pumps (figs. 2.3 and 2.4). A centrifugal pump can be operated without a pressure relief valve and should be installed at the lowest point in the spray system, to ensure that it remains primed.

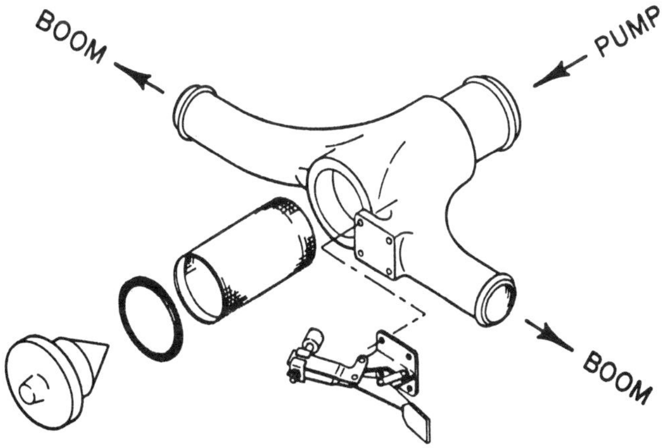

Fig 2.2 Liquid screen filter used between pump and boom (after F.A.O., 1972)

Fig 2.3 Section through a centrifugal pump; these pumps are not self priming and must be located below the liquid level in the hopper

Fig 2.4 Section through a gear pump; these pumps are considered positive displacement pumps and require use of a pressure relief valve (after F.A.O., 1972)

(4) *Pump drive.* Fixed wing aircraft are either fitted with a pump hydraulically or mechancially driven by the engine, or with a pump driven by a windmill mounted in the propellor slipstream. The latter system is relatively cheap and simple though rather inefficient and sensitive to changes in airspeed and power. In the case of helicopters it is impractical to use windmill drive owing to low velocities in the slipstream. Electrical, hydraulic or mechanically driven pumps are used. Where a windmill drive is used, it is important that a brake be provided with which the pilot can stop the pump during flight; this is to guard against undue wear and possible over-speeding if the pump is starved of liquid. There have been cases in which pumps have disintegrated through over-speeding. On positioning flights it is a wise precaution to lock the pump windmill blades with wire to prevent rotation.
(5) *Pressure regulator.* This is usually a gate valve, accessible in flight, and placed in the return-to-tank pipe. Closing the valve causes the system pressure to rise, although even when the valve is fully closed, a by-pass should be provided to allow the liquid to return to the tank.

This guards against burst pipes, and provides agitation of the spray liquid in the tank by continuous re-circulation.

(6) *Pressure gauge.* The pilot must have a spray pressure gauge visible from the cockpit. The pressure at which a spray is emitted has an important effect on spray deposit, as will be seen later. No pressure plumbing should be located in the pilot's area because any leakage, or plumbing failure would be an immediate hazard to the pilot.

(7) *Operating valve.* This controls the flow of chemical from the aircraft, and is operated by a level in the cockpit. It is often a three-way valve, allowing the liquid either to pass to the booms (or atomisers) or to return to the tank (fig. 2.5).

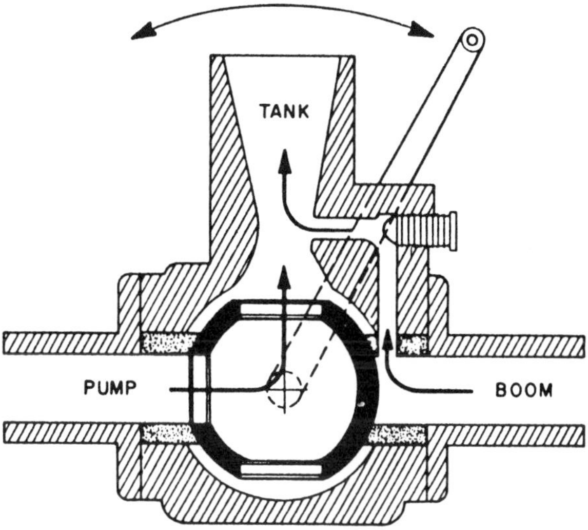

Fig 2.5 Three-way ball valve for aircraft sprayer sharing boom-vacuum position for positive spray shut-off; check valves are needed at each nozzle with this system (after F.A.O., 1972)

(8) *Plumbing.* The system incorporates a return-to-tank. This should be arranged so as to ensure that the chemical is continuously recirculated whenever the pump is running (some chemicals require continuous agitation to prevent sedimentation or separation).

(9) *Atomising equipment.* There are, in the main, two devices by which the liquid may be finally emitted from the system: boom-and-nozzle-gear or rotating atomisers. Both are designed to break the liquid up into droplets of a more or less predetermined size.

Atomising equipment

Boom-and-nozzle gear

The liquid enters spray-booms mounted along each wing. The *boom* is a hollow tube, often of streamlined cross-section, with plugs at the outer ends to facilitate cleaning. The *nozzles* are placed along the boom, and may number between twenty and fifty. The most common type is Spraying Systems' Diaphragm Teejet nozzle. As it is important that no chemical escapes from the system unintentionally, a spring-operated diaphragm is incorporated which shuts off the inlet to the nozzle immediately the pressure in the boom falls below operating level (plate 2.1). Thus at the end of a spray run a positive cut-off is obtained. The liquid entering the nozzle is set in a rotary motion by passing through spiral passages in a small plate known as the *core*. It is then ejected through a small hole in another plate known as the *orifice disc* through which the liquid finally emerges broken up into droplets. Both core and orifice disc can be removed and replaced with others, to control droplet size. A small filter basket is incorporated in the nozzle. Nozzles are also used which produce a hollow cone, a flat fan or solid shaped jet.

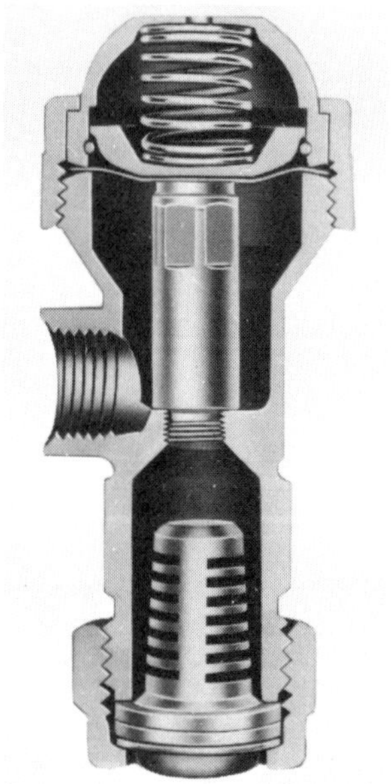

Plate 2.1 Diaphragm check valve and filter incorporated into the nozzle body (photo: Spraying Systems Co.)

Nozzle size

The initial choice of nozzle and adjustments to the spray equipment should be based on the manufacturers' specifications; but remember that their figures will have been obtained using water as the calibration fluid and can therefore only be used as a guide. The formulation flow rate and the ambient conditions may lead to variations in output, so it is therefore essential that an aircraft's calibration is frequently checked.

Fan nozzles can be classified according to their included angle of spray fan produced and their liquid throughput measured with water at a known temperature and operating pressure. For example:

(1) Spraying Systems (U.S.A.) fan jet 8003
= 80° — included angle of operation
and 03 = 0.3 U.S. gallons min (1.14 l/min)

(2) Spraying Systems (U.S.A.) cone jets: cone jets are designated by the diameter of the nozzle orifice and the size of the core used. The orifice is classified in 1/64ths of an inch, so D2 is equal to 2/64 in (0.8 mm) and D4 equals 4/64 in (1.6 mm).

Operating pressure

The throughput of a nozzle is proportional to the square root of the operating pressure; so doubling the spray pressure increases output by 40%. Altering pressure therefore has only a limited effect on spray output. When increased it may overstress the pipework, or when reduced, result in very coarse drops, and so should only be resorted to for fine adjustment. Basic adjustment is best achieved by altering the number or the size of the nozzles.

Spraying Systems' nozzles have been the classic reference for many years. Equivalent nozzles are available from other manufacturers, e.g. Delavan Corporation, U.S.A.; Delavan Ltd, U.K.; Lurmark Ltd, U.K. (Manufacturer's addresses are given in the references at the end of the chapter.) For many applications, nozzles are available which are made of nylon or Kematal ® (acetal copolymer – POM). Kematal ® is the registered trade mark of Celanese Corporation. These nozzles have extremely good resistance to chemical abrasion and corrosion. For aircraft use, a significant weight saving is possible compared to stainless steel and brass. See manufacturers product catalogues for full specifications. Table 2.1 illustrates the nozzle capacity for Spraying Systems diaphragm teejet nozzles.

Table 2.1 Nozzle capacity for Spraying Systems diaphragm teejet nozzles (with water)

Orifice no.	Core no.	Spray pressure lb/in^2	kg/cm^2	Total capacity each nozzle U.S. gal/min	litres/min
D4	25	20	1.4	0.21	0.79
		40	2.8	0.29	1.10
		60	4.2	0.35	1.32
D4	45	20	1.4	0.25	0.94
		40	2.8	0.36	1.36
		60	4.2	0.43	1.62
D6	25	20	1.4	0.32	1.21
		40	2.8	0.44	1.67
		60	4.2	0.54	2.04
D6	45	20	1.4	0.41	1.55
		40	2.8	0.58	2.19
		60	4.2	0.72	2.73
D8	25	20	1.4	0.43	1.62
		40	2.8	0.61	2.31
		60	4.2	0.75	2.83
D8	45	20	1.4	0.59	2.23
		40	2.8	0.84	3.18
		60	4.2	1.04	3.93
D8	56	10	0.7	0.96	3.63
		20	1.4	1.91	7.22

Nozzle orientation

Droplets emitted from the various spray nozzles used in aircraft are affected by the high speed slipstream (fig. 2.6). The angle at which liquid is discharged from the nozzle relative to the slipstream can change the droplet spectra. Hydraulic energy nozzles angled forward and down into the slipstream will produce the smallest droplets. Nozzles pointing directly to the rear of the aircraft will produce the largest droplets, and there is a range of intermediary size droplets for the angles between these two extremes.

Microfoil® nozzle

This is another form of hydraulic energy nozzle consisting of multiple needles for use on aircraft, particularly helicopters (designed by Amchem Products, Ambler, Pa., U.S.A.). The microfoil has been developed for

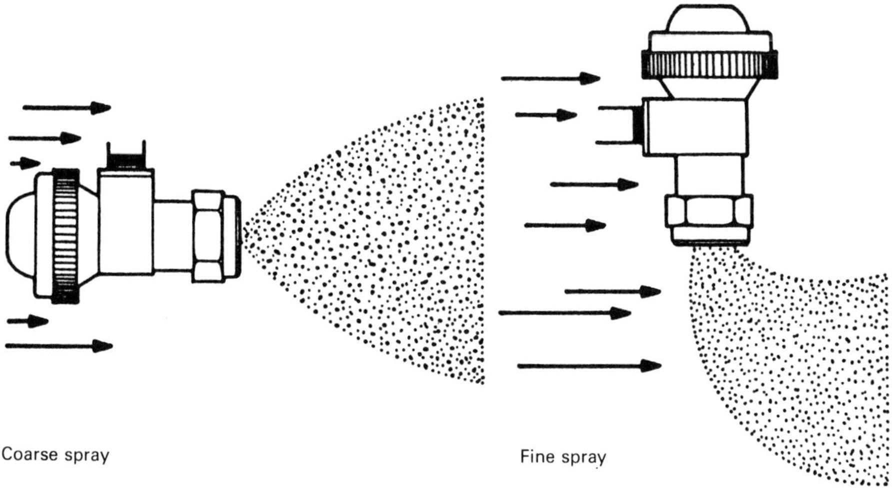

Fig 2.6 Droplet sizes can be varied by changing the orientation of the nozzles in relation to the slipstream (F.A.O., 1972)

producing uniform large droplets in the application of herbicides (low drift application). The nozzle is available with two sizes of needle 0.33 and 0.7 mm diameter. Practically uniform droplets are produced in the size range 800–1000 μm, provided the airstream does not exceed 95 km/h and there is low pressure (0.14 bar) on the needle-like orifices along the trailing edge of the nozzles. Smaller needles cannot be used as they would be difficult to keep open (F.A.O., 1972; Wilce *et al.*, 1974). See fig. 2.7.

Rotating atomisers

The rotating atomisers used on aircraft are usually rotating cage, rotating porous cylinder or rotating grooved and toothed discs. They are either driven my windmills using the slipstream, or by electric motors.

Micronair atomiser

This is an example of a rotating cage atomiser, manufactured by Micronair (Aerial) Ltd., U.K. This is a commonly used rotating atomiser. It consists of a cylindrical gauze rotating around a fixed spindle which is attached to a mounting bracket on the wing of an aircraft, in the case of the AU 3000 compact atomiser, or directly onto a spray boom in the case of the AU 5000 mini atomiser. The AU 7000 is used successfully on Microlight aircraft.

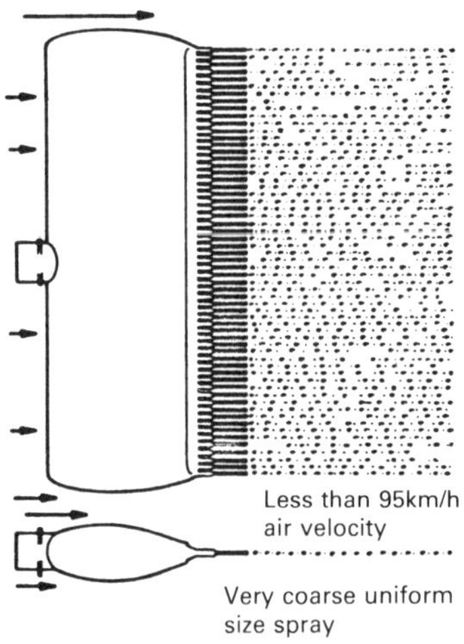

Fig 2.7 Microfoil nozzle; many of these sections make up the complete boom (F.A.O., 1972)

Plate 2.2 Microfoil boom fitted to Bell 47 (photo: Ag Rotors Inc.)

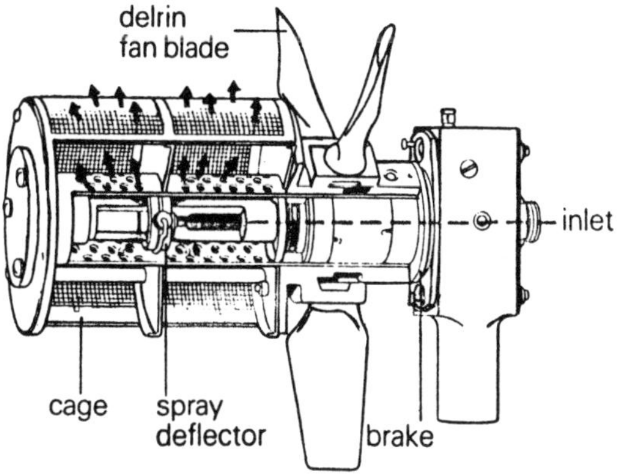

Fig 2.8 Section through a Micronair rotating cage atomiser, type AU 3000

Power is supplied from the slipstream through a five-bladed windmill (AU 3000) or a three-bladed windmill (AU 5000) clamped in a hub which carries the bearing assembly. The pitch of the blades is adjustable and this is used to set the r.p.m. Liquid from the spray boom flows through the hollow spindle and is discharged from a deflector plate which distributes it to the front and rear of the cage. The liquid is then coarsely atomised by being passed through a diffuser tube, and then fully atomised by centrifugal force as it strikes the rotating gauze cylinder (fig. 2.8).

Flow control Flow rate is controlled by means of restrictor plates placed in the path of the spray liquid. Changes in flow rate are achieved by changing the effective hole size in the restrictor plate by means of the variable restrictor unit (VRU). The VRU consists of a fixed plate which has a series of seven differently sized holes around its circumference. A second disc shaped plate with a single large hole moves over this first plate. It is controlled by a graduated cap; rotating the cap locates the single hole in the moving plate over the appropriate hole in the fixed plate.

The standard VRU plate (odd numbers) gives flow rates from 0.154 to 24.43 l/min (AU 3000) and so covers the majority of dose rates. Alternative plates are available to cover other flow rates. Make sure the VRU spring is in good condition to ensure that the plates are kept close together so preventing excessive doses from being applied.

Spray deflector To ensure the spray is distributed evenly along the full length of the cage, a deflector is fitted to the centre shaft. Always consult the manufacturer's instructions when re-fitting the deflector

Plate 2.3 Micronair atomisers (long blades) fitted to a Bell Jet Ranger 11; also Simplex belly-mounted spraying system (photo: A R W Crosse-Upcott)

to make sure it is correctly positioned. Alternative deflector plates and spring housings are available for use when different application rates are required.

Shut-off control Some aircraft are still fitted with hydraulic shut-off valves to give instant control of the spray; however, the diaphragm check-valve offers a less expensive alternative. AU 5000 atomisers are now fitted with secondary shut-off valves internal to the unit as standard.

Hydraulic braking system To stop the atomiser rotating when the plane is not spraying, a hydraulic brake mounted on the hub assembly is locked. The brake disc must not be contaminated with oil or grease. An optional electric brake is available as an alternative to the hydraulic system.

Flow meter Normal methods of spray calibration used with conventional systems are not suitable for ULV calibration, unless employed over large areas. Because of the very slow emission of chemical, the installation of a flow meter is essential for accurate control. A small, stainless steel turbine is fitted to the flowline and its speed monitored by a transducer which relays a signal to a display unit in the cockpit. This unit should include a totaliser. If such a flow meter is to be reliable, it needs to be protected by an efficient filtration system, as the speed of the turbine and its record of the flow will be affected by any foreign bodies in the spray liquid. Flow meters are available for rates between 4 and 410 l/min.

Tachometer unit The tachometer sensor unit is usually fitted to one of the atomisers. The rotation of a ferrous object attached to one of the blade clamping bolts is monitored by a magnetic transducer and the speed then relayed to the cockpit. The rotational speed of an atomiser can drop by 100 r.p.m. when the formulation is being sprayed from it.

Mounting Four Micronair AU 3000 Compact atomisers are usually fitted to an aircraft like the Piper Pawnee. Some of the largest aircraft may be fitted with six units. The Micronair AU 5000 Mini atomisers are light enough to be fitted directly onto spray booms. The number fitted depends upon the required application rate, but a minimum of six units is recommended to ensure an even swath in conventional spraying.

Micronair atomisers can be used on helicopters with the appropriate blades, and have been used most successfully in locust control. Micronair (Aerial) Ltd are producing a new unit for the larger drops that are required for herbicide application and oil-slick control.

Micron aerial atomisers

Experiments have shown that when a spinning disc designed with 'zero issuing' points (teeth) was fed at a suitable rate, droplets of a uniform size could be produced by the breakup of 'ligaments' which issue from the teeth (fig. 2.9). Furthermore, the rate could be increased when comparing the drops formed on the edge of a smooth disc, which is critical to over-feeding. Grooves leading to the teeth also improve the performance.

The Micron X series of atomisers are available in a number of variants. They are either air driven or powered by electric motors. With the exception of the X-15, the X-1, X-4 and X-7 were designed as replacements for hydraulic nozzles on orchard sprayers, and have found response from aerial applicators in the U.S.A. In particular, the X-1 has been developed by Micron Corporation in the U.S.A. as the Micron

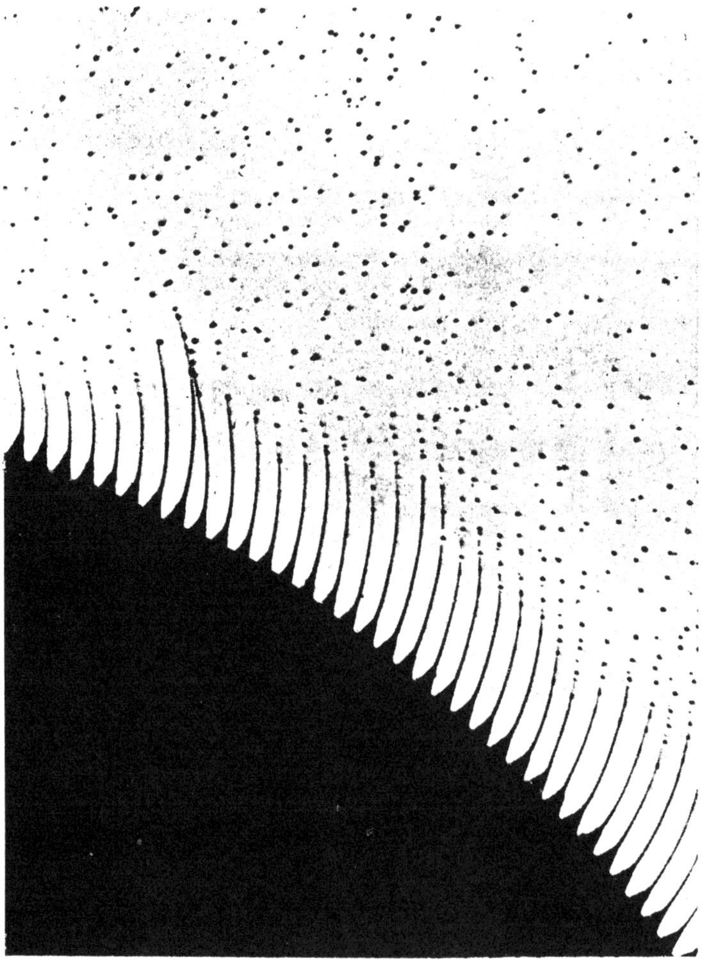

Fig 2.9 Ligaments forming at zero issuing points at the edge of a single rotating disc, breaking into uniform sized droplets (Micron atomiser)

X-1 CDA (Controlled Droplet Application). The Micron X-1 CDA atomising nozzle consists of a single grooved and toothed disc rotating on two ball races and driven by interchangeable airturbines of different pitch angles so that the X-1 can be matched to various airspeeds. Liquid is fed through a fixed central feed tube into the hollow rotating shaft and then through a feed distributor and feed cap which results in the formation of a uniform thickness liquid sheet. This sheet is transferred to the grooves of the atomising disc preforming ligaments, which are then separated by the disc teeth into uniform sized droplets.

The Micron X-1 CDA nozzles are designed as direct replacements on the spray boom with conventional hydraulic nozzles. Micron recommend the following installation for the appropriate aircraft speed range:

80–100 m.p.h. (130–160 km/h 19 nozzles
(red airturbine supplied as standard)
100–120 m.p.h. (160–190 km/h 23 nozzles
(gold airturbine supplied as standard)
Over 120 m.p.h. (190 km/h) 29 nozzles
(blue airturbine supplied as standard)

The Micron Sprayers Ltd X-15 atomiser is available in three forms, arising from the needs of different forms of aerial application (plate 2.4). All are based around a stack of fifteen Ulva discs:

(1) The single air driven units for fixed wing aeroplanes;
(2) The twin-headed motor driven unit for helicopters;
(3) The single-headed motor driven unit for Microlights, etc.

Plate 2.4 Micron Sprayers (U.K.) X-15 atomiser consists of a stack of fifteen Ulva discs (photo: Micron Sprayers Ltd)

Beecomist spray head

The Beeco Products Company, U.S.A. manufactures the Beecomist spray head, which is a rotating porous cylinder powered electrically (model 360) or hydraulically (model 361) (fig. 2.10). The pesticide liquid is fed to the disperser body, where the concentrate is dispered to the inside of the rotary spray head. The concentrate is then expelled by centrifugal force through the sleeve and into the atmosphere in controlled droplets from 20 to 100 microns, depending on the sleeve used. The drive motor provides high speed rotation (10 000 r.p.m. or above) producing controlled droplet size permitting low volume or ultra low volume (ULV) applications.

Porous and perforated sleeve assemblies are available for a variety of pesticides ranging from very low viscosity solutions to wettable powders and heavy flowables.

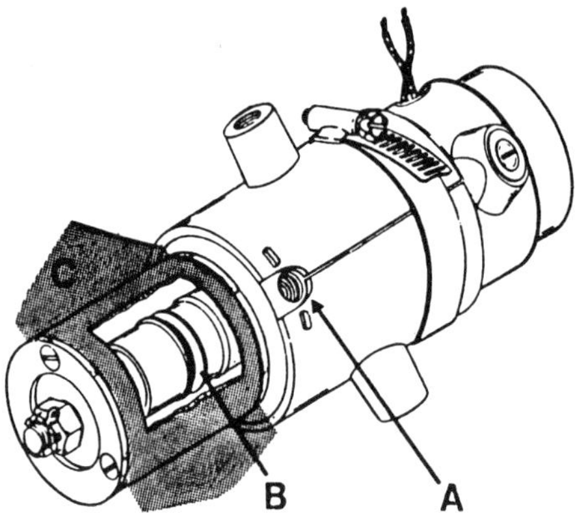

Fig 2.10 Layout of a Beecomist spray head (model 360, electric motor); (A) input to the spray head; (B) disperser body; (C) distribution through the porus or perforated sleeve. Three different sleeve assemblies are available for different volumes and drop sizes

Other types of atomisers

There are other types of hydraulic energy and centrifugal energy nozzles and also special applications, e.g., piezo-electric atomisers, electro-static atomisers, venturi effect atomisers, etc. However, the foregoing descriptions are of equipment most commonly used with aircraft, and principals of operation found virtually world-wide. There will probably be more CDA nozzles utilizing centrifugal energy coming onto the market in due course, as they produce very narrow droplet spectrums, are very light weight and can be fitted as direct replacements on standard aircraft booms.

Electrically driven atomisers

Electrically driven atomisers do not depend on air power, so they are ideal for helicopters where the slipstream may not be sufficient to provide adequate airflow. Other advantages are the ability to set the r.p.m. from the cockpit, and reduced drag. The main disadvantage is the amount of power required, and four or more units may be the limit for most aircraft electrical systems. Agricultural aircraft with turbine engines and alternators in the region of 200 amps or so would not be so restricted.

Droplet spectra categories

Droplet size is expressed as the diameter of the droplet in flight measured in micrometres. One micrometre (1 μm) is 1/1000 mm or 1/1 000 000 m. A 200 μm drop is therefore 1/5 of a millimetre in diameter. Remember that, when a drop hits its target, it will spread and cease to be a sphere and so give a false impression of the size of the original drop. The extent of spread will depend on the formulation and the nature of the surface.

None of the many spraying devices in use produces droplets of just one size. Within any particular spray, there will always be a range of drop sizes referred to as the droplet spectrum, and an understanding of droplet size and its influence on spray recovery is important.

Droplet spectra are therefore categorised according to the average size of their droplets. The two common ways of determining this are the volume median diameter (VMD) and the number median diameter (NMD).

Average droplet size

To obtain the VMD, the drops are ranged in order of size and the volume of all the drops in each size category calculated and the mean evaluated. The diameter of the drop representing this mean is the VMD; half the volume of the spray is composed of droplets smaller than the VMD, and half of it of drops larger than the VMD.

To obtain the NMD, the drops are counted and arranged in order of magnitude. The mean of the total number of drops is then found and the diameter of that mean drop size is the NMD. Half of the total number of drops therefore have diameters below this value and half have diameters above it. On its own the NMD can be misleading in that it is influenced by large numbers of small drops which in fact comprise only a small proportion of the volume of spray liquid.

Occasionally the term mass median diameter (MMD) is seen but, except where spray has been subject to rapid evaporation and consequently varies in specific gravity, it can be taken as the same as VMD for all practical purposes. Both calculations are time-consuming to carry out, for they require the collection and sizing of a large number of drops. However, for most commercial operations, the following equation is usually accurate enough:

$$\mathrm{VMD} = 0.45 \times D_{max}$$

where D_{max} is the diameter of the largest drop.

VMD and NMD are a useful means of characterising sprays, but they give no indication of the range of drop sizes present and, unfortunately, there is no simple means of quantifying this. As a small number of large drops contain more liquid than a large number of small drops, the VMD is always greater than NMD. The ratio of VMD to the NMD has been used as a simple index expressing the dispersion of the spray. Examples of ratio values are:

Spinning cages	3.0 to 5.0
Hydraulic nozzles	
fine sprays	≃ 3.0 to 7.0
coarse sprays	≃ 8.0 to 11.0

The most significant factors affecting drop size are the type of equipment being used and the conditions under which that equipment is operated.

The other factor that will have some effect is the formulation. All water-based sprays (dilutions and emulsifiable concentrates, suspension concentrates, wettable powders, etc.) will behave in roughly the same way, but there will be considerable difference between these and oil-based formulations (such as the solutions used for ULV application). It is impossible to define these differences precisely but always remember that the data given by the equipment manufacturer is likely to refer to water and therefore needs to be checked for all formulations, but particularly oil-based ones.

Flow rate calibration

Accurate calibration of the aircraft is vital for effective spraying: as explained below, unless the precise flow rate of the spray system is known, it is impossible to apply the required dose rate. Calibration of flow rate for conventional application is relatively simple. Because the emulsifiable concentrates (EC) used are diluted with water, the spray's characteristics are very similar to water; and so water can be used as the initial calibration fluid. Any final adjustment will only be minor and can be checked during normal operations.

However, ULV formulations contain much higher concentrations of active materials which are dissolved or sometimes suspended in oil; therefore, if an aircraft has to be flown for ULV calibration, it is advisable to make up a blank formulation with similar physical or flow characteristics to that being sprayed. Remember that only aircraft with hydraulic or electrically driven pumps can be calibrated on the ground; those with wind-driven pumps must be flown.

Calculating flow rate

The flow rate is related to the required volume rate, the aircraft ground speed and the effective swath width – a relationship which can be expressed as the equation:

$$\text{Metric} \qquad FR = \frac{V \times W \times S}{600}$$

$$\text{Imperial} \qquad FR = \frac{V \times W \times S}{495}$$

where FR is the flow rate required in l/min (gal/min); V is the total applied volume in l/ha (gal/acre); W is the measured swath width in m (ft); S is the convenient flying speed in km/h (m.p.h.). The following calculations are in metric units.

Example Calculating the flow rate required from an aircraft fitted with fifty-two nozzles having determined the swath width, been given the volume rate and a convenient flying speed.

Volume rate	= 20 l/ha
Swath width	= 22 m
Flying speed	= 161 km/h
Flow rate	$= \frac{20 \times 22 \times 161}{600}$ l/min
	= 118.06 l/min

Flow rate per nozzle $= \dfrac{118.06}{52\ \text{(nozzles)}}$ l/min

The flow rate required from each nozzle = 2.270 l/min

The calculated flow rate can initially be selected against the manufacturer's specification, but it should always be subsequently rechecked while actually spraying.

Dose rate and target area

The chemical dose rate is usually expressed as an amount per unit area (l/ha or kg/ha) but is occasionally used as a percentage strength of the spray solution.

The total applied volume may vary according to the pesticides' mode of action and the target type. Although the dose rate is given for an area, the foliage surface (leaf index) of the target crop within that area may be much larger. Contact insecticides demand good coverage, and therefore drop size must be reduced. This increases the number of drops from the same volume, and hence provides improved coverage of the area of foliage to be treated. (See appendix 4 for the theoretical plant coverage from 10 l applied volume per hectare.)

Calibration for conventional application

The spraying system's pipework can itself hold up to 30 l of liquid, so first make sure that the pump is primed. Fill the tank with 40–50 l water and then fly the plane at spraying speed. The three-way valve should be set to reach and maintain the required operating pressure. The pilot's control lever can be correctly repositioned using the adjustable stop on the lever quadrant. When the pressure begins to fall, indicating the tank is empty, close the valve. The system is now fully primed and the pilot can return to the landing strip. Assuming a total flow rate of 118.06 l (as calculated in the example), 118.06 l are added to the tank.

The aircraft is then flown again at application speed and the time taken to discharge 118.06 l is recorded, the three-way valve being closed the moment the pressure falls. If the flow rate is correctly set this will be exactly 60 s. For conventional application, a small error in flow rates does not matter; but if the error is greater than 10%, the calibration should be rechecked. If the time is longer, then the three-way valve should be opened further (if it is already fully opened, larger nozzles may have to be selected).

Note that to calculate the quantity of active ingredient (A) required to mix with a known quantity of dilutent (D) to obtain a given concentration of spray:

$$A = \frac{\%\ \text{concentration required}}{\%\ \text{concentration of active ingredient}} \times D$$

Example:
(a) Mix 100 l of 0.5% ai, using a 50% wettable powder.

$$100 \times \frac{0.5}{50} = 1\ \text{kg of wettable powder}$$

(b) Mix 2 l of 5% ai using a 75% wettable powder

$$2000 \times \frac{5}{75} = 133\ \text{g of wettable powder.}$$

Calibration for ULV application

ULV applications use a formulation with a high concentration of active ingredient which is sprayed at a very low dose rate (less than 5 l/ha). ULV spraying therefore requires a very precise knowledge of the actual flow rate which is being emitted. Hydraulic nozzles are not very suitable for ULV application: low flow rates and small droplet size demand the use of nozzles with very small holes and these are easily blocked. It is essential to recalibrate for each formulation as each will have a slightly different viscosity and this will affect the flow rate (remember than an aircraft used for ULV spraying should be fitted with a flow meter).

In the following example, it will be assumed that the aircraft is fitted with six Micronair AU 5000 mini atomisers. The calibration procedure is in two stages: adjusting the flow-rate and setting the droplet size. Unlike conventional hydraulic energy nozzles, these two variables are largely independent and one can be changed without significantly affecting the other. The following details are given:

Volume rate (V) = 2.5 l/ha

Swath width (W) = 25 m

Flying speed (S) = 161 km/h

Flow rate (FR) $= \dfrac{V \times W \times S}{600}$ l/min

$= \dfrac{2.5 \times 25 \times 161}{600}$ l/min

$$= 16.77 \text{ l/min total output}$$

Flow rate per Micronair $= \dfrac{16.77}{6}$ l/min

$$= 2.79 \text{ l/min.}$$

The formula for the flow rate can of course be transposed to give any other value.

Example To find the dose rate per hectare, given the flow rate, flying speed and swath width and using the figures obtained above:

Flow rate = 2.79 l/min per Micronair

Swath width = 25 m

Flying speed = 161 km/h

Dose rate $= \dfrac{FR \times 600}{S \times W}$ l/ha

$= \dfrac{2.79 \times 600 \times 6}{161 \times 25}$ l/ha (six Micronairs)

Dose rate (applied volume) = 2.5 l/ha

Micronair atomiser adjustment

The output from each atomiser is controlled by its variable restrictor unit (VRU). Each VRU has a restrictor plate which has a series of holes of different sizes. A selector plate attached to the adjustment knob exposes any of these holes, thus providing a flow to the atomiser which can be varied. The holes in the restrictor plate are numbered 1–13, odd numbers only. The higher the number, the higher the flow rate, with 13 being the highest and 0 a shut-off position. The standard restrictor plate (odd numbers) gives flow rates from 0.27 to 22.8 l/min (AU 5000).

From the above calculation, it is necessary to select the appropriate VRU setting and system pressure from tabulations (see table 2.2). For a flow rate of 2.79 l/min the nearest setting number (VRU number) is 7. With a system pressure of 20 lb/in^2 the flow would be 2.65 l/min. Set the adjustment knob of the VRU so that number 7 aligns with the datum on the restrictor body. Having established the VRU settings, fine adjustment of the total output from the aircraft is made by varying the system pressure. The VRU setting must always be selected so as to allow a reasonable opening of the control valve (and hence system pressure). This will ensure easy regulation of the application rate.

Table 2.2 Flow through variable restrictor unit (VRU) (Micronair AU 5000). These figures are based on tests with water. Actual flow rates will vary according to the installation and chemical used. Operators should always check flow rates under field conditions.

Setting number	Pressure (p.s.i.)	Flow per minute per atomiser		
		Imp. pints	U.S. pints	Litres
1	20	0.48	0.57	0.27
	30	0.58	0.70	0.33
	40	0.70	0.85	0.40
3	20	1.32	1.58	0.75
	30	1.67	2.01	0.95
	40	1.94	2.32	1.10
5	20	2.55	3.06	1.45
	30	3.20	3.85	1.82
	40	3.78	4.54	2.15
7	20	4.66	5.60	2.65
	30	5.98	7.18	3.40
	40	7.21	8.66	4.10
9	20	7.92	9.51	4.50
	30	10.38	12.47	5.90
	40	11.97	14.37	6.80
11	20	14.96	17.96	8.50
	30	20.24	24.30	11.50
	40	24.64	29.58	14.00
13	20	26.22	31.48	14.90
	30	34.32	41.20	19.50
	40	40.13	48.18	22.80

In this example, the tabled flow rate at 20 lb/in^2 is less than that which is required. A slight increase in the system pressure will bring the flow rate up to the calculated requirement; the tabulations are based on water flow. Actual flow rates will depend on the installation, the chemical used and temperature. Operators should always check flow rates under field conditions.

Final calibration should be done by stop watch either in flight, or with a ground pump connected into the supply line. As it is always advisable to use a flow meter in all ULV applications, the total flow rate would also be a means of final calibration. Flow meters are also a means of early warning of system malfunction. Mistakes in ULV application can be disastrous. Always remember that calibration tabulations or graphs for all atomisers and nozzles are (most probably) based on water flow at a given temperature. They provide the *starting* point in all calibration procedures.

Determining droplet size

The mean size of the spray droplets produced by an atomiser is determined by the rotational speed of the gauze. As the gauze is turned by the fan blades in the slipstream, the speed of rotation is controlled by both airspeed and blade angle. The airspeed is determined by the type of aircraft and spraying operation, hence the droplet size is controlled by the setting of the fan blades. Figure 2.11 gives the approximate relationship between droplet size and rotational speed (r.p.m.), for example, 9000 r.p.m. will produce a droplet size of 100 μm. Having

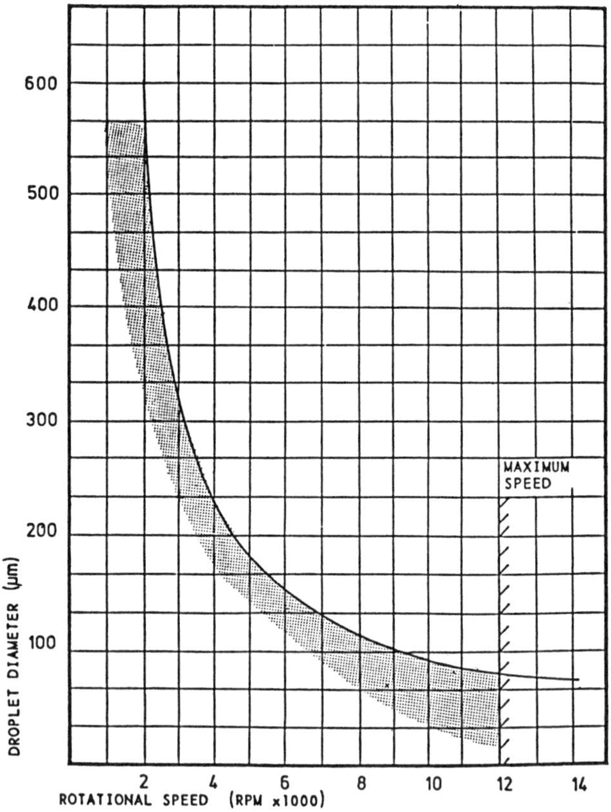

Fig 2.11 Droplet size versus rotational speed (Micronair AU 5000); the graph is based on tests with water; actual droplet sizes will be influenced by the chemical used; operators must check the actual size under field conditions

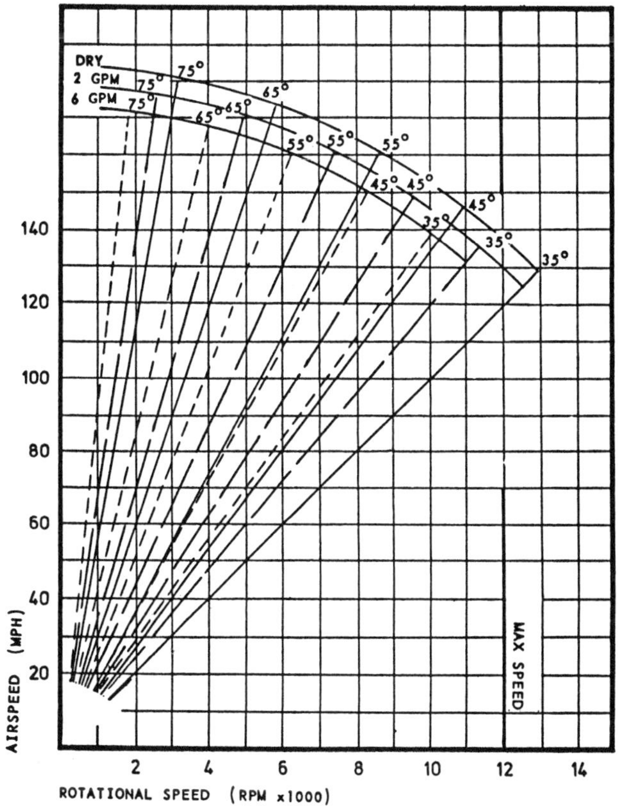

Fig 2.12 Rotational speed versus airspeed (EX 1772 blades, Micronair AU 5000); these figures are approximate only. Actual speeds will depend upon airflow over the atomisers; conversion: 1 gal (Imp.) = 4.546 l, 2 gal (Imp.) = 9.092 l, 6 gal (Imp.) = 27.276 l.

established the r.p.m. it is necessary to find the appropriate blade angle setting to produce this r.p.m. From fig. 2.12 identify the intersection of the rotational speed and the aircraft speed. Extend this point through the flow rate per atomiser and read off the blade angle.

Example Using the figures in the section on calibration for ULV application, with a flow rate of 2.79 l/min per Micronair (or ≃ ½ Imp. gal/min), with the atomiser r.p.m. 9000 (for a droplet size of 100 μm), aircraft speed 161 km/h (100 m.p.h.): from fig. 2.12 the blade angle is ≏ 36°. Set the fan blades on all atomisers to this angle (refer to the manufacturer's instructions).

Note: Pilots will always find in this industry measures expressed in

Imperial, metric and American units. Square measure can offer some unusual units, i.e., Feddans, Manzanas, Fanegadas, etc. In general in this book, units are expressed in metric. However, reproduction of some figures will show Imperial or American units. Pilots must be able to convert speeds, volumes, application rates, linear measure, etc., from one standard to another. Conversion factors are listed in appendix 4.

Spraygear – handling

It is vital to prevent the unintentionial escape of chemical from the system. Chemical leaking inside the fuselage can cause corrosion and, if poisonous, release dangerous fumes in the cockpit. Chemical leaking outside in flight can cause damage to crops and livestock. The system must therefore be checked regularly for leaks; all pipes and hoses must be in good condition and clips and joints secure. Pressure can on occasion reach 90 lb/in^2 (6.3 kg/cm^2) and there must be no chance of a pipe burst. A common source of leakage is from dripping nozzles. They drip either because of weak diaphragm springs or because of dirt lodged in the diaphragm. Strainers must be kept clean. The most common cause of spray gear failure in flight is a clogged strainer. Chemicals should be filtered before or during loading to keep the aircraft system as clean as possible.

A windmill pump must be braked when the spray system is empty. A pump running dry will very quickly overspeed, with consequent damage and even disintegration. The brake is adjustable to compensate for wear in the brake linings. On positioning flights with an empty hopper, a windmill pump should be locked with wire to prevent any chance of it rotating. For pump maintenance refer to the maker's instructions. Many pumps have grease points for lubrication. Seals may occasionally need to be replaced; some chemicals have an abrasive effect. The jettison system, or dump valve, must be checked every day to ensure that it is correctly rigged and ready for use, but does not leak.

Many fungicides and some other chemicals consist of a dispersible powder in suspension in water or oil. Such chemicals must be agitated to prevent the powder from settling out at the bottom of the tank. If allowed to do this, it often sets hard, and will certainly block the pipes and passages of the spray gear. The recirculation system will prevent this while the pump is operating, but a load of such chemicals must not be left unagitated in the aircraft for more than an hour; it should be pumped out of the aircraft back into a storage tank. Cleanliness of the system is vital from the point of view of corrosion. It should be emptied and flushed through with detergent and clean water after work. Chemicals containing copper are particularly corrosive. (Wire brushes should not be used to clean nozzle orifices, for there is a risk of enlarging or distorting the shape of the orifice in course of time; this will affect the droplet size produced.) Use compressed air whenever possible to remove dirt, *never* blow through contaminated nozzles. Some chemicals, particularly the hormone-type weedkillers are dangerous to crops other than those for which they were intended. The damage that is possible with even a minute residue of weedkiller in the aircraft hopper could be enormous. See chapter 4 for the details on aircraft equipment decontamination.

Pilots must always check regularly for any signs of unusual or even excessive vibration, particularly with rotating atomisers. This will be due to either damage, or a build-up of chemical in one or more of the atomiser gauzes, or a bearing failure, or attachments coming loose, or damage to a blade. Vibration will either be felt through the airframe or will be visible at the atomiser or the adjoining boom. If excessive vibration is experienced, the pilot should immediately reduce airspeed as much as possible and land at the nearest suitable airstrip. If it is necessary to fly to another base for rectification, the faulty atomiser must be prevented from rotating by tying it to its bracket. It may not be obvious which atomiser is at fault, and if this is the case tie all the atomisers before flying.

Spreading equipment – description

The use of the term 'spreading' denotes the application of solid material such as fertilisers, granules, micro-capsules, seeds and dusts. The items of equipment are as follows.

Hopper This will be fitted internally in the fuselage, and will usually be the same tank as that used for spraying. A large door is fitted at the top for loading. At the bottom, a gate is fitted for controlling the flow of material. This gate, which slides across the opening of the hopper, is operated by a lever in the cockpit; the rate of flow of material is controlled by regulating the size of the gate opening, for which purpose an adjustable stop is fitted to the operating lever.

Agitator In order to maintain the smooth flow of materials which tend to bridge over the gate opening, and to break up any small lumps, a mechanical agitator is fitted in the lower part of the hopper. A common type takes the form of a rotating squirrel cage, driven via a reduction gear by a windmill placed in the propeller slipstream. The windmill can be braked from the cockpit.

Spreader – venturi type This is the most common form of spreader. It is a tunnel shaped like a venturi tube, mounted below the hopper on the underside of the fuselage so that air from the propeller slipstream enters the front of it. (It is unsuitable for use with helicopters.) Material falling from the gate of the hopper into the spreader is blown out at the rear; the shape of the spreader, together with internal guide vanes or channels, adds a sideways velocity to the motion of the particles, and thus spreads them out behind the aircraft to a width of 20 to 40 ft (7 to 12 m). The channels within such spreaders are irregularly shaped to compensate for the tendency of the propeller vortex to displace particles from one side to the other while they are falling to the ground.

The swath width varies with the speed of the air through the spreader. This speed in turn varies not only with the airspeed in the slipstream (i.e. with aircraft speed and engine power) but also with the rate of flow of fertiliser; the reason for the latter is that the more particles that enter the airstream the more energy is required to accelerate them, and the absorption of this energy results in the slowing down of the air. If too much material enters the spreader, i.e. if the hopper gate is opened too wide, the airstream will no longer be powerful enough to move the material, and the spreader will choke. The symptoms of choking are material falling from the front of the spreader and, after the gate has been closed again, from the rear of the spreader. Choking results in distribution errors and waste. It is prevented by reducing the gate opening, or by flying faster. Some pilots fly with $\frac{2}{3}$ flap, as this increases the drag and, therefore, the power required and the speed of the slipstream.

Spreader – aerofoil type A well-known example of this is the Transland Swathmaster. It is unsuitable for helicopters. The venturi is replaced

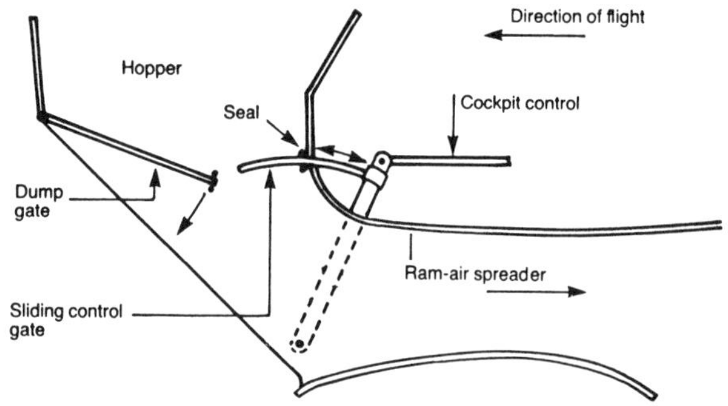

Fig 2.13 Granule application from fixed wing aircraft: simple diagram to show sliding metering gate (after F.A.O., 1972)

by a spreader shaped like a pair of small wings mounted beneath the fuselage. The surfaces of the wings are pierced by a large number of small holes. Material falling from the gate of the hopper meets a flow of air from the propeller slipstream entering a large opening at the front of the spreader, and is carried by this airflow into the 'wings', from where it is blown out through the surface holes. Guide vanes are placed inside the wings to improve distribution and flow. The Transland Swathmaster may also be used for spraying liquids, but only at higher application rates.

Spreader – centrifugal type The increasing use of helicopters for applying solids has given added impetus to the development of centrifugal spreaders. Equipment of this type can also be used on fixed wing aircraft. The particles are allowed to fall from the hopper gate on to one or two horizontal discs, which spin at high speed. The material is flung from the disc or discs by centrifugal force, and distributed laterally behind the aircraft. With granular materials, swath widths of as much as 50 ft (15 m) can be obtained – rather more than is possible with a venturi spreader. The discs are usually driven by electric motors or hydraulically actuated, from a hydraulic pump on the engine power take-off. The centrifugal spreader has the important advantage that it produces little aerodynamic drag compared with the venturi spreader; the latter can cause a marked deterioration in the performance of an aeroplane.

Spreader – Tetrahedron (C.S.I.R.O., Australia) The roughly tetrahedral device is mounted on a flat plate. The load drops from the hopper gate directly in front of the spreader, which intercepts the flow and diverts particles sideways. The spreader does not inferfere with emergency dumping – full loads fall mainly in front of the spreader without passing over it. The Tetrahedron spreader has demonstrated a lower drag penalty than is encountered with ducted spreaders. At application rates of about 100 lb/acre (115 kg/ha) a Piper Pawnee aircraft fitted with a Tetrahedron spreader gives swath widths about 50% greater than those with no spreader fitted. Dispersion rates are improved with flow rates up to about 150 lb/acre (170 kg/ha) but the benefit is most marked at rates of 100 lb/acre (115 kg/ha). Since the spreader has no ducts, blockage is not a problem, and with fewer wearing surfaces than a ducted spreader, it lasts considerably longer.

Helicopter spreaders These can be of the centrifugal type fitted to, or remote from, the helicopter. The latter employs a hopper suspended from the helicopter, under which is the centrifugal spreader (driven by an auxiliary electric motor). The hopper gate is controllable from the

Plate 2.5 The Tetraspreader (Tetrahedron Spreader) as fitted to a Piper Pawnee (photo: C.S.I.R.O., Australia)

cockpit. The advantage of such an underslung system is the quick turn-round time possible. The helicopter need not land to pick up a fresh load.

Helicopters may also employ a separate blower unit driven by the engine which forces air through twin ducts positioned at the base of the side hoppers and out on short booms. Each tank has its own slide gate. An alternative to the ram-air system used on helicopters is the spinning disc. Two such units are mounted either side below each of the side hoppers. The discs are driven hydraulically or electrically, and in opposite directions. Granules are thrown outwards from the front of the spinners and swaths in the order of 15 m are obtained.

Spreading equipment – handling

If the aircraft is a dual sprayer/spreader using the same hopper for both operations, disconnect all spray pipes from the hopper when installing the spreading gear, to prevent them being blocked by dust. Grease the slide of the hopper gate to ensure free movement and prevent unnecessary wear to the operating linkage. Keep the hopper and spreader free of caked fertiliser or dust which tends to build up and block passages, especially during damp weather. Lubricate the agitator according to maker's instructions.

All fertiliser should be passed through a screen of half-inch (1.25 cm) mesh before being loaded into the aircraft, because, if badly stored, it often forms lumps which the agitator will not break up, and by which it may be damaged. (Agitators are sometimes removed when working with free-flowing materials.) Stoppages caused by lumps unable to pass through the gate cause uneven distribution and waste a great deal of time, since the aircraft must be landed to clear the stoppage. Adjust the gate so that material cannot escape unintentionally in flight – dusts may be equally as dangerous as sprays, while fertilisers are expensive and should not be wasted.

Many forms of solid material are hygroscopic and must not be left in the aircraft for long periods in humid weather. Damp material will not flow, and it tends to form lumps. Corrosion is a great danger to

Plate 2.6 Simplex spreader suspended below a helicopter; the helicopter can remain in the hover while changing the unit for a full one (photo: Ag Rotors Inc.)

the airframe and it is accelerated by moist conditions; the spreader, hopper and airframe must be kept clean by brushing, if dry, or by washing with water and detergent, if damp.

Spreading of solid materials

Aerial spreading of solid materials includes seeding and the application of fertiliser or lime on grassland which is too rough, too steep or too marshy for wheeled vehicles or on cereal crops and forests. Dusting is becoming an out-dated technique and does not require discussion.

Fertilisers

Most modern artificial fertilisers are in free-flowing granular form, and run easily from the hopper without any need for agitation, provided they are dry. (In humid climates for this reason they should not be removed from proper storage too soon before use, and, when stacked in the open air in bulk or in bags, should be covered with a canvas sheet.) Some fertilisers such as basic slag, ground rock phosphate, and some forms of potash and lime, do not flow freely and bridge over the gate

Plate 2.7 AN-2 aircraft applying fertiliser; this example of the group 2 aircraft (and its successor the AN-2M) is used extensively by East European countries for all aspects of agricultural work (photo: Interflug, Berlin, D.D.R.)

Plate 2.8 PZL M-18 Dromader; built in Poland, has a 1000 hp piston engine, and a 2500 l or 1500 kg hopper; this version is fitted with a spreader (photo: Pezetel Warsaw)

of the hopper, or even over the agitator itself, and are not really suitable for aerial application except in cases where accuracy is not of primary importance. The flow may be irregular and the coverage on the ground rather patchy. Fertilisers contain one or more of the three elements vital to plant growth, nitrogen, phosphate and potash. The quantity of each is expressed as a percentage of the total material, and is to be found labelled on the packing. The total quantity to be applied per acre depends not only on the degree of concentration of the material but also on factors connected with soil deficiencies and the requirements of the crop.

Fertiliser application rate

This generally varies in practice from about 50 to 300 lb/acre (56 to 340 kg/ha). To calibrate, there is an initial quandary:

(1) It is not known how wide the swath would be.
(2) Until the swath width is known, it is not possible to calculate flow rate required in kg/min.
(3) Until the output required is known, it is not possible to find the swath width that can be obtained at the particular output!

In the case of sprays, it is possible to obtain a starting point using water. With solids it is not possible to use a substitute that would have the same behaviour characteristics. With fertilisers and seeds, the same problem exists. With some types of spreaders, the swath width is considerable affected by the mass flow.

Initial calibration can be done on the ground by timing the flow of a measured quantity of product through the hopper gate. (Jack the aircraft into the flying attitude first, and use a low gate setting.) With the approximate settings established, it is necessary to fly the aircraft and dispense a quantity of product across a line of collectors. If it can be arranged that the collectors have a measured funnel of say 357 mm, this will give an area of 1000 cm^2. The collectors would be spaced at about 1 m intervals across the swath. One gram of the collected product on this area would represent 100 kg/ha. If the products deposited in the collectors at each location are weighed, the deposit rate may be determined in kg/ha as follows:

$$\text{Deposit rate} = \frac{K \times W}{A}$$

where the deposit rate is in kg/ha; K (constant) = 10^5; W (weight collected is in g; A (area of collector opening) is in cm^2. This procedure offers an economical method of calibration of flow and deposit rate, before further flying tests are made for swath width (Amsden, 1984).

The relationship between flow rate (kg/min) and application rate (kg/ha) is given by:

$$\text{kg/min} = \frac{\text{kg/ha} \times \text{km/h} \times \text{m}}{600}$$

where the ground speed is km/h and the swath width is m.

Table 2.3 gives the fertiliser flow rates required for every metre of flight spacing for four aircraft speeds. From this table we can see that if it is proposed flying at, say, 150 km/h to apply 200 kg/ha it will require 50 kg/min for each metre of swath spacing. It can be expected that the swath spacing would be around 9 to 12 m, so start the flying trials at a gate setting intended to give around:

$$9 \times 50 = 450 \text{ kg/min to } 12 \times 50 = 600 \text{ kg/min.}$$

If the first flight is made at a gate setting which, on the ground gave 450 kg/min, and this resulted in an actual flow of 500 kg/min then the 'ground' curve could be corrected accordingly (Britten and Rose, 1959). If the effective swath appeared to be say, 11 m, then the second flight would be made with a gate setting judged to give about 550 kg/min. The result of this flight would give another correction for the 'ground' curve, and another figure for the swath width. If the latter proved to be 10 m, then a third flight should result in an adequately accurate gate setting for a known swath width.

Table 2.3 Flow rate calibration (for fertiliser)

Fertiliser application rate (kg/ha)	Flow rate (in kg/min) required for each 1 m between flight lines, at a ground speed (in km/h) of			
	100	125	150	175
100	16.66	20.83	25.00	29.17
200	33.33	41.67	50.00	58.34
300	50.00	62.50	75.00	87.50

These trial and error tactics may seem laborious at first sight, but as long as they are systematically planned, a rapid build-up of information on the equipment performance and fertiliser flow characteristics results in easier attainment of the correct settings.

When applying herbicidal or insecticidal granules, the application quantities are of the order of 5–15 kg/ha. Table 2.4 gives the granule flow rates required for every metre of flight spacing for the same four aircraft speeds.

Table 2.4 Flow rate calibration (for granules)

Granule application rate (kg/ha)	Flow rate (in kg/min) required for each 1 m between flight lines, at a ground speed (in km/h) in			
	100	125	150	175
5	0.833	1.04	1.25	1.46
10	1.66	2.08	2.50	2.92
15	2.50	3.125	3.75	4.375

This table can be used in exactly the same manner as table 2.3. To calculate the quantity of a formulation (X) required to apply the recommended amount of active ingredient per hectare (A) with a formulation containing $B\%$ active ingredient:

$$\frac{A \times 100}{B} = X$$

For example, applying 0.25 kg ai/ha of 5% granules:

$$\frac{0.25 \times 100}{5} = 5 \text{ kg granules/ha}$$

References

Amsden, R. C. (1984) 'The aerial application of solid materials.' Short course on the aerial application of pesticides. Cranfield Institute of Technology, U.K.

Beecomist Spray Head. Beeco Products Company, Industrial Park, Fort Washington, Pa. 19034, U.S.A.

Britten, F. R. J. and Rose, G. J. (1959) 'The distribution of granular fertilizer from light aircraft.' *Proc. 1st Int. Agric. Aviat. Congr.* 210-220.

C.S.I.R.O. (September 1981) *Rural Research*. Quarterly journal of C.S.I.R.O. Australia, 22–25.

Delavan Nozzles. Delavan Corp., P.O. Box 100, West Des Moines, Ia. 50265, U.S.A. Delavan Ltd, Gorsey Lane, Widnes, Cheshire, WA8 0RJ, England.

F.A.O. (1972) 'The use of aircraft in agriculture.' Agricultural Services Bulletin 16.

F.A.O. (1974) 'The use of aircraft in agriculture.' Agricultural Development Paper 94.

Micron Atomisers. Micron Sprayers Ltd, Three Mills, Bromyard, Herefordshire, HR7 4HU, England. Micron Corporation, 1424 West Belt Drive North, Houston, Texas 77043, U.S.A.

Micronair Atomisers. Micronair (Aerial) Ltd, Bembridge Fort Sandown, Isle of Wight, PO36 8QS, England.

Spraying Systems Nozzles. Spraying Systems Co., North Avenue @ Schmale Road, Wheaton, Illinois 60187, U.S.A.

Transland Spreader. Transland Systems and Equipment, 24511 Frampton Avenue, Harbor City, Ca 90710, U.S.A.

Wilce, S. E. *et al.* (1974) 'Drop size control and aircraft spray equipment.' *Agricultural Aviation* **16** (1), 7-16.

3
Application – spraying and spreading

Introduction

The chemicals dispensed by aircraft onto crops fall into four general categories: insecticides, fungicides, herbicides and defoliants or desiccants. This chapter describes the general characteristics of these groups and certain of the additives (adjuvants) which, in general, enhance the effects of the active ingredient (ai). The pilot must be aware of the effects on deposition by varying the flying height and speed, and the all important aspect of unwanted *drift*. The aeroplane itself can influence deposition as aerodynamic effects from propeller traction and wing tip vortices modify the dynamics of the air in the proximity of the crops. Atmospheric effects are also described.

Types of chemical used in spraying

Spraying operations require the application of the following general categories of chemical.

Insecticides Insecticides work in three different ways to achieve their object. Contact poisons kill by direct contact with the insect. Stomach poisons are deposited on the plant for the insect to eat. Systemic poisons are absorbed by the plant into its system, and kill insects which suck the plant juices. The first two require a moderately fine spray with good cover in order to reach the insect itself; with the third, a coarser spray is used, the object being merely to place some of the chemical on each plant.

Fungicides These are chemicals designed to control fungus diseases in plants. They are generally compounds of copper, zinc, manganese, sulphur or tin, which can kill germinating fungus spores on the plant.

To do this, they are deposited on the leaves and stems; in order to cover the surfaces as well as possible, a fine spray is used, and an underleaf coverage is in most cases advisable.

Herbicides Selective herbicides are those which are applied to a crop to kill weeds without damaging the crop. They include DNOC, a contact chemical which soon kills the green parts of the weed on which it lands, and the hormone-type weedkillers, MCPA, MCPB, 2,4-D and 2, 4, 5-T. The latter are chemicals which are absorbed by the weed via its leaves, reaction of the plant and dying off being slower than with DNOC, and they can be applied with a coarse spray.

Defoliants and desiccants Chemicals of a herbicidal action used to defoliate a crop (e.g. cotton, soya beans) in order to facilitate mechanical harvesting; or to desiccate, which means to hasten the dry-ripening of the crop (e.g. rice) in order to reduce time or cost of drying after harvest. Some chemicals in use for these purposes are: pentachlorophenol, salts of endothall, tributyl phosphorotrithiate. Sodium chlorate should, if possible, be avoided for its fire hazard.

Preparation of the spray liquid

Chemicals are formulated as follows:

Dispersible powders These are finely-ground powders which are mixed with water or oil for use. They must be thoroughly mixed and repeatedly agitated to prevent sedimentation. Once a sediment has formed it may set hard and be almost impossible to re-mix.

Emulsifiable liquids Emulsions are mixtures of immiscible liquids, for example oil and water. As the liquids are usually of differing density, they may have to be agitated to prevent them settling into layers.

Solutions in either oil or water.

Chemicals, which are generally supplied in concentrated form, are mixed either with water or oil for spraying. The manufacturer's directions for mixing must be followed carefully. In preparing a spray liquid 'adjuvants' may be used, but only if the chemical product would not be adversely affected. In every case the manufacturer or his agent should be consulted.

Thickeners for water-based herbicidal sprays could reduce the drift.

Hydroxy-ethyl cellulose thickeners (e.g. Hercules Vistik) should be used at concentrations of 1% or less in water. The thickening property is influenced by the temperature.

Sticking agents improve the adhesion of a spray residue and make it rain-proof, which is not always advantageous.

Spreaders improve the wetting properties of a spray. Both stickers and spreaders are seldom needed as extra adjuvants with modern chemical formulations.

Foaming agents are used in a rather new technique of foam spraying which appears to reduce drift. Special foam creating nozzles are required when using these adjuvants.

ULV products These chemical products are ready for use and do not require any preparation. They might be the straight undiluted chemical, or a factory-made formulation consisting of the active ingredient and a non-volatile carrying liquid.

Application rate

The *application rate* is the total quantity of material applied per acre or per hectare. It must be distinguished from the *dosage rate* which is the amount of *active ingredient* per acre or per hectare. For example, ½ kg of active ingredient (ai) may be applied in 5 l or 100 l of water per hectare; the dosage rate is the same, but the application rate is varied. It is normal to refer to application rate as 'high volume' (HV), 'medium volume' (MV), 'low volume' (LV), 'very low volume' (VLV), and 'ultra low volume' (ULV). The actual values of these definitions have now been tabulated by the European and Mediterranean Plant Protection Organization (E.P.P.O.). It should be noted that other definitions of the same terms are in use, but E.P.P.O. strongly recommends the general use of the definitions. For the values of these spray volumes, refer to the tabulation in appendix 2.

Location and number of nozzles or atomisers

Generally speaking, spraying at heights below 50 ft, it is incorrect to space nozzles at even distances along a sprayboom from wingtip to wingtip. This is because of the airflow characteristics; the motion of the aircraft produces a number of vortices, of which the three biggest are the one caused by the propeller and ones situated at either wingtip. The propeller vortex is in effect a spiral flow round the fuselage, in the direction of propeller rotation. Thus with aircraft where the propeller is righthanded tractor (i.e. clockwise seen from the cockpit), some of the spray emitted from the boom near the starboard wing root tends to be displaced underneath the fuselage and across to the port side. (Most marked with the higher powered aircraft.) To compensate for this, extra nozzles should be installed on the starboard side. The wingtip vortices, of which the port rotates in a clockwise direction seen from the rear and the starboard in an anti-clockwise direction have the useful effect of spreading the spray out sideways beyond the wingtip and thus allowing a swath width greater than the wingspan. However, they also have the effect of raising the finer droplets away from the ground to a position from which they can drift away altogether.

To prevent such losses the spray booms can be shortened, or the outboard nozzle locations blanked off with plugs. These airflow effects on the distributed swath are not noticed with the majority of spray aircraft operating at heights above 50 ft, so the nozzle spacing can be even along the boom.

Flying height

Amsden (1972) listed the factors which determine the height from which pesticide should be applied. These are as follows.

(1) The velocity of the cross-wind component relative to the flight path;
(2) The aircraft design characteristics;
(3) The composition of the spray spectrum being used;
(4) The specific gravity of the spray liquid (or particles);
(5) The rate of evaporation from the spray droplets.

All these factors may vary from one operation to the next, and even within a single flight. The relationship between spraying height and the cross-wind component can be expressed as

$$H \times U = C \quad \text{(the } HU \text{ products equation)}$$

where H is the height of the wing (or rotor) above the crop in metres (m) and U is the cross-wind component in km/h. C is a constant.

The difficulty is the determination of the constant. It is estimated, however, by observation of the biological effectiveness of sprays applied under a number of known conditions with a swath width determined at a particular height. If the aircraft is too low, distribution of the spray will become less even owing to the effect of vortices. This is particularly true with the larger rotating atomisers. Excessive drift is liable if the aircraft is flown too high. The maximum wind speed is usually determined as a safety criterion. With wind speeds above about 15 m.p.h. (25 km/h) for the average single engine crop spraying aircraft, the orographic turbulence is very uncomfortable to experience, and it is difficult to maintain the correct flying height. It is natural under these conditions to creep up in height.

At the other extreme – modern aircraft with good visibility from the cockpit – it is quite possible to fly with the wheels virtually touching the crop. Impressive as this may appear to the uninformed, it results in less even distribution; also the swath width is narrowed. The distance between the aircraft and the crop should be about half the wing span if full use is to be made of the downwash in distribution.

There is therefore a *minimum* wind speed for a given *HU* factor. In table 3.1 these limits are 14–25 km/h for an aircraft with an 11 m wing span; in this example, the constant *C* is set at 80.

Table 3.1 Variation in flying height with wind speed where *HU* = 80 (after Amsden, 1972)

Height (*H*) (m)	Wind speed (*U*) (km/h)	
2.0	40	
2.67	30	
3.2	25	↑
4.0	20	Operating
5.0	16	limits
5.7	14	↓
8.0	10	

Table 3.2 shows terminal volocities of water droplets. The evaporation of water droplets is illustrated in table 3.3. In this case the rate of fall in still air of a 200 μm drop is a little over 2 ft/s (0.61 m/s). Such a drop will evaporate comparatively little in falling 20ft (6.1m) to the ground. A drop initially 100 μm in diameter will start to fall at rather less than 1 ft/s (30.5 cm/s). Evaporation during fall will now be important in slowing its fall still further and it could not in fact fall to the ground from 20ft; it will have evaporated completely by about half way. The drop initially 50 μm in diameter will only survive about 1 ft (30.5 cm) of free fall at this humidity.

Table 3.2 Terminal velocities of water droplets

Droplet diameter (μm)	500	100	50
Terminal Velocity (ft/s)	6.93	0.89	0.24
(cm/s)	210	27	7.3

Table 3.3 Approximate lifetimes of drops of pure water in air at 15°C and 40% relative humidity

Initial diameter (μm)	Lifetime (s)
50	4
100	16
200	63

Swath width

Figure 3.1 shows an idealised situation. In practice, the ground patterns will be more irregular, but the principle is shown that there is only one swath spacing that will produce uniform overall distribution. For practical examples, see figs 3.2–3.4.

Speed

The vortices produced by the wing of an aircraft in level flight increase in size and intensity as the speed decreases. (Wingtip vortices are described in greater detail at the end of this chapter.) Thus at low speeds the swath width will be greater than at higher speeds. The downwash from the wing also increases as the speed decreases, and is greater if flaps are lowered. Therefore if underleaf cover or penetration of the crop with the spray is desired, it helps to fly as slow as possible, (bearing in mind the safety aspect and the need for a speed margin to clear obstacles at the end of the run). (Helicopters flying at the lower speeds display greater downward air velocities than a fixed-wing aircraft of similar weight.)

Determination of distribution

The accurate determination of spray distribution, droplet size, and swath is too difficult a process for everyday use in the field. However, the

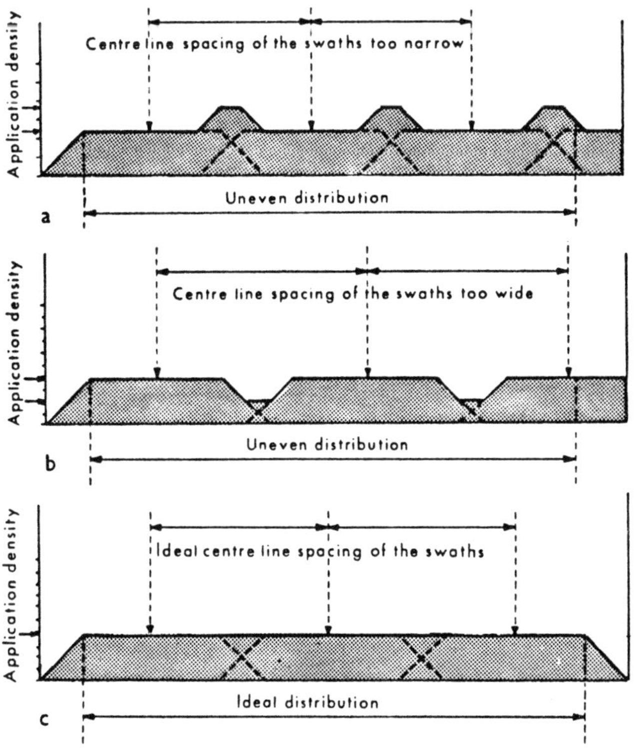

Fig 3.1 The relationship between application density and swath spacing

following test serves to give a good general idea. On a field (or airstrip) mark out a run of about 100 yards (90 m) lying parallel to the wind. Fill the aircraft tank with water and a colouring substance (e.g. nigrosine, a black substance soluble in water, at 4 oz to 10 gal or 250 g to 100 l) and make a run into wind with speed, height, and spray pressure held constant at values corresponding to typical operational conditions.

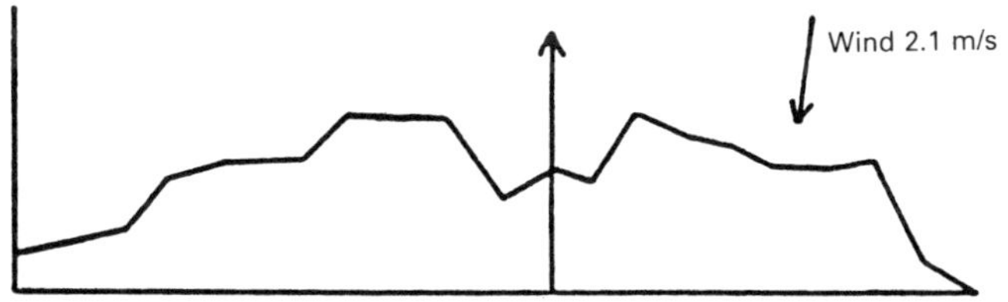

Fig 3.2 This shows the distribution pattern (by volume) of an Ag-Cat with nozzles under the wings but not under the fuselage with a consequent gap in the centre of the swath

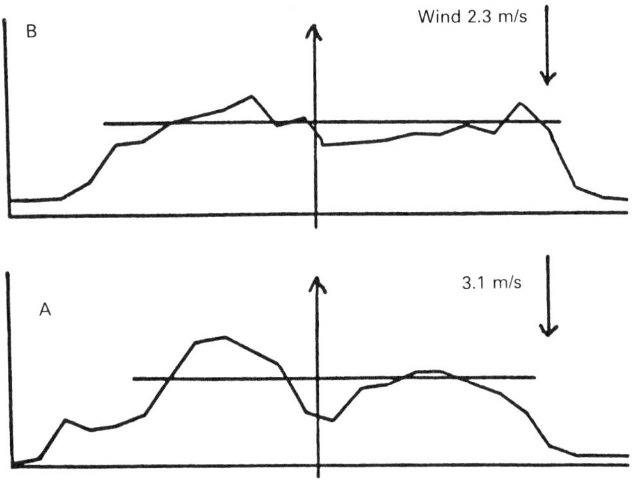

Fig 3.3 This shows the influence of flying height and speed on the distribution from a Piper Pawnee PA-25. In A the height is around 1.5m and the speed 95 m.p.h.; in B the height is 2 m with a flying speed of 85 m.p.h. Flying too low and too fast reduces the swath width (in this case from 18 m to 16 m) and creates an uneven distribution

A strip of adding machine paper (or similar) about 25 m long is placed on the ground at right angles to the spray run and half way along it. The aircraft should be flown once along the run into wind spraying all the way. The pattern will then be visible on the paper. The trial may be repreated crosswind for comparison.

Practical examples

The preceding section dealt with distribution on a theoretical level and figs 3.2–3.4 illustrate distribution patterns which occur in practice. For each type of aircraft there exists a certain maximum spraying speed above which it is almost impossible to obtain an even distribution, even if nozzle placement were changed.

Meteorological considerations

Wind

Spraying is normally carried out only when the surface wind is less than 15 m.p.h. (7 m/s) and for certain operations only when considerably less than this. Thus, from the point of view of aircraft handling, wind is not likely to present a very great problem provided that the area is not one of exceptional turbulence. Spray runs are normally carried out cross-wind, ensuring that the ground speed and therefore the application rate are the same in both directions of flight. The wind will displace the spray sideways from the track of the aircraft, by a distance varying according to aircraft height and wind strength. To cover the field completely, it will be necessary to make one or more additional runs beyond the upwind boundary to allow the spray to fall at the very edges of the field.

When flying cross-wind, fly on the downwind side of the markers (flagmen), so that the spray drifts clear of them, and in light winds make each succeeding run upwind of the last so as to avoid flying into the spray cloud of the previous run. (Even if the chemical is not dangerous, the droplets may cloud the windscreen.) It is sometimes necessary to fly parallel to the wind. It may be possible to compensate to a certain extent for variations in ground speed by flying faster into wind and slower downwind, but when the wind is stronger than about 10 m.p.h. (5 m/sec) it will become advisable to fly in one direction only, to preserve even distribution.

A gusty wind causes irregular spray distribution and in such cases work may have to stop even though the mean wind strength is within the limits for the job.

Rain

Most chemicals must dry on the plant before rain, or the rain will wash

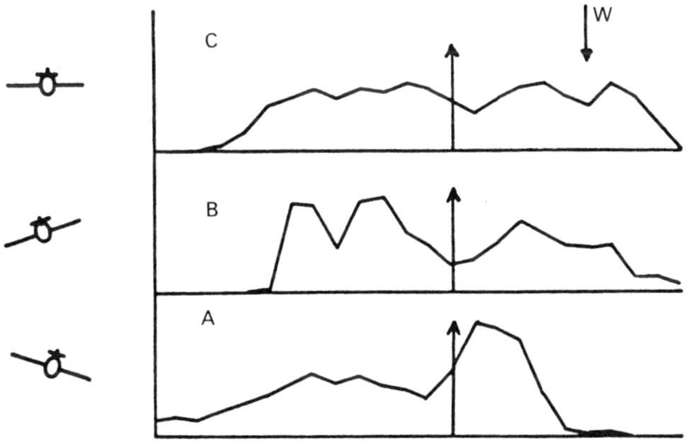

Fig 3.4 This depicts the distribution from an aircraft which started spraying when incorrectly lined-up. At first the right wing was too low (A); the pilot then over-corrected and the left wing was too low (B); C shows horizontal flight

them off and they will have no effect. Therefore, do not spray if there is a likelihood of rain before the spray has dried, and do not spray a wet crop unless it is in the process of drying out rapidly. Other chemicals need to dry for several hours before rain; the manufacturer's directions for use should be consulted.

Temperature and humidity

Some chemicals do not act effectively if applied under the wrong conditions of temperature and humidity (refer to manufacturer's instructions).

Drift (liquids)

'Drift' as a hazard means the movement of chemical to a place other than that for which it was intended, and arises from the fact that droplets and particles float in the air for a certain time after being emitted from the aircraft. The smaller the droplet, the greater its surface area in proportion to its weight, and the slower it falls through the air. Table 3.4 indicates the distance drifted for different size droplets.

Table 3.4 The distance drifted by water droplets while settling 10 ft (3.05 m) in an air flow averaging 3 m.p.h. (1.34 m/s) (assuming no evaporation)

Droplet diameter (μm)	Classification	Distance drifted
500	Light rain	7 ft (2.1 m)
200	Drizzle	16 ft (4.9 m)
100	Mist	50 ft (15.25 m)
30	Cloud	500 ft (152.5 m)
15	Coarse aerosol	2000 ft (610 m)

(1 micron = 0.001 mm)

The danger of drift lies in the fact that the chemical may reach a crop other than that for which it was intended, and may damage that crop. For instance, all selective weedkillers can also kill a wide range of agricultural and horticultural crops, and in some cases damage is caused by minute quantities of chemical. Chemicals can also kill bees and fish, and contaminate crops intended for human or animal consumption. The extent of the danger depends on the chemical used. Some are scarcely dangerous at all, but with a few others even the vapour could be dangerous.

It must also be remembered that drift causes chemical to be lost from the crop being treated, and may reduce the efficiency of the treatment. (Drift may on occasions be intentionally utilised to penetrate deep crops and forests, or to cover large areas quickly where precision is of secondary importance. This is often done with a fine aerosol spray or mist, which may remain airborne for a considerable time.)

Factors affecting drift

Droplet size From table 3.4 it can be seen that the smaller droplets can drift further. A compromise must be found between the size of droplet required for an effective treatment, and a size which will keep the drift value within acceptable limits.

Nozzle or atomiser location Droplets entering the wingtip vortices may be thrown upwards to heights of several metres above the aircraft. From there they will drift further. Nozzles or atomisers should be located to keep as much spray as possible away from these vortices. Spray booms will normally end a metre or so inboard of the wingtips.

Flying height Again, the higher a droplet is released into the air, the further it is liable to drift. For the majority of droplets (generally those of 120 μm and larger) the stronger the surface wind, the lower the aircraft should be flown. (See the *HU* products equation and table 3.1 earlier in this chapter.)

Wind speed and direction The wind speed and direction must be monitored closely to ensure that they are within safe limits for the job in hand. A change in either may occur during the day and require work to cease.

Orographic turbulence and thermal currents Both these factors can cause droplets to be carried upwards to heights from which they can drift long distances.

Humidity and temperature Under certain conditions droplets can diminish in size quite rapidly by evaporation. Smaller ones evaporate more quickly, having more surface area in proportion to mass. There is therefore less risk of drift in humid conditions. It may be an advantage in dry conditions to use an oil-based spray rather than a water-based one.

Atmospheric stability Under conditions of strong stability, vertical air movements can almost be completely suppressed. This cuts off the horizontal airflow near the ground from the general airflow above, with the result that the ground level flow can be poorly defined and highly variable in direction. In these situations, spray drift cannot be predicted either in terms of the quantity remaining airborne or the direction.

Atmospheric instability It is possible to keep drift within acceptable limits under conditions of atmospheric instability. One of the reasons is that because of turbulence, there is an exchange of air between the crop canopy and the airflow above and droplets are filtered out of the airflow more efficiently. However, to assess this aspect it is necessary to know some of the parameters of the crop canopy (roughness lengths) and turbulence intensity, which need special equipment, as there is no way of direct measurement of turbulence intensity (not yet at least). It is also beyond the scope of this handbook to explore these mechanisms further.

Methods of reducing drift

Invert emulsions The invert emulsions (see chapter 4, section on classification by formulation) are where the oil phase is continuous and the water broken up as small droplets. These are widely used with phenoxyacid herbicides for controlling trees and brushy species along power lines, rights of way, ditches and roadsides. The average VMD has to be made very large in order to reduce the number of 'small' droplets. This means a reduction in coverage and so the application rate must be increased.

Viscosity additives These are materials like Decagin, Vistik, Norbak and others which make the liquids very viscous and thus produce large drop sizes in a manner similar to the invert emulsions. The uses are also similar.

Special nozzles Some nozzles are designed to produce large droplets, e.g. Delavan 'raindrop' nozzles, *ca* 1500 μm. Micronair produces a special cage for the rotary atomiser for herbicide application. The microfoil boom is another version, but these cannot be used over 95 km/h. However, they are ideal for helicopters at the flow rates required.

Foam spray applicators These are another version of viscosity additive materials. The various foaming agents were developed for fire fighting equipment. Foaming bubbles are formed which cling together in clusters and have a very adhesive quality as well as attaching to plants and other surfaces.

Note that there are some new 'drift retardant additives' appearing on the market which do not act or behave strictly as the first two items, but do modify the droplet spectrum. Drifgon (TM) is one such additive (Drifgon (TM) is the trademark of Sanitek Products, Inc. U.S.A.).

Points for pilots to remember in minimising drift

(1) Do not fly higher than is required for an even distribution across the swath. Maintain this height.
(2) Always monitor the wind. Keep an eye on the windspeed and direction versus line of flight.
(3) Never open the spray valve before the correct spraying height is reached. Close the spray valve before climbing out.
(4) Stop work if the temperature becomes too high and/or the relative humidity too low.
(5) Be aware of the possibility of inversion layers early in the morning and in the evening after a hot day. For still air, particularly for inversion conditons, aerial spraying should not take place (unless the job calls for very large drops and narrow swaths, i.e. herbicide application).
(6) No wind does *not* mean no drift.
(7) Be aware of the characteristics of the spray liquid you are working with. Evaporation reduces the droplet size making them drift prone.
(8) Never fly with leaking equipment.

Distribution of fertilisers

Most jobs, including all those on cereal crops, require distribution of a very high accuracy. With some fertilisers, mainly those containing nitrogen, inaccuracies become apparent very soon by causing uneven growth or colour in the crop, in the form of stripes across the field, or patchiness. Uneven growth of cereals causes the deeper parts of the crop to lodge (i.e. be flattened by the wind) more easily than when all the stalks are of the same length. As fertilisers become available with higher concentrations of nitrogen, accurate distribution becomes more difficult and errors become more apparent.

A gusty wind also gives rise to patchy and uneven distribution, particularly where the fertiliser particles are small and light. It may help in such a case to fly as low as about 10 ft (3m) so that the fertiliser

Plate 3.1 NDN 6 Fieldmaster agricultural aircraft powered by a Pratt and Whitney PT6A-34AG 750 h.p. (560 kW) engine; this version is fitted with a spreader applying fertiliser (photo: NDN Aircraft Ltd)

falls to the ground quickly and is less likely to be displaced by gusts. Great attention must be paid to accurate calibration and correct application rates. The amount of material applied must be constantly checked against the acreage treated. (See chapter 2 for details about calibration.)

Flying

Under many conditions, as when treating forests or hill-country grazing, it becomes difficult and even unnecessary to obtain exactly even distribution, and marking may be impossible. On hillsides, it is necessary to follow approximately the contours, while in forests markers are often hard to see. However, with field crops at least two markers (flagmen) must be provided and followed accurately. The flow of fertiliser must begin and end exactly at the beginning and end of the runs, so that none falls outside the field at all. There is no reason why, with practice, a pilot should not be able to drop the fertiliser right up to the edges of the field without any more wastage than with a ground machine of the spinner type. The exact moment for opening or closing the gate can be judged by the position of the field boundary in relation to some part of the aircraft such as the edge of the instrument panel, and a ground observer can then report the accuracy of the drop.

Drift (granules)

Drift is a less important factor with granular materials than with sprays or dusts; granules are not displaced more than a few yards by the wind under normal weather conditions, and allowance can be made for this by the markers. With basic slag, lime and other materials composed of fine particles, it is necessary to fly as low as possible when there is any wind, if drift is to be avoided. In rough country, however, the dangers of very low flying may be too great, and the drift is in any case not dangerous; it merely results in loss of material.

Low flying would, however, often accentuate the high and the low deposit rates across the treated swath (fig. 3.3 A).

Wingtip vortices

The efficiency of aerial spraying has improved considerably in certain areas; for example, formulations and adjuvants, and a new generation of rotary atomisers with better control of the droplet spectrum (better VMD/NMD ratios). There has been little improvement in the aircraft as an application platform, apart from the pilot protection aspects and general reliability. Current aircraft look very similar to the first generation of specially designed aircraft. Apart from vintage sport clubs, agricultural aviation is the only area where biplanes are in regular use.

The aerodynamics of the lifting surfaces produce effects which the agricultural pilot has had to live with for many years. Wider swath widths would greatly improve the productivity of the regular type of low and high volume spraying. However, the present generation of aircraft have a number of aerodynamic shortcomings, notably the drag imposed by the general shape and the equipment attached. The wingtip vortex has probably been the most significant barrier to improving the evenness of deposition across the effective swath. If it were possible to reduce the wingtip vortex, or better still eliminate it altogether, an immediate improvement in deposition and application efficiency would be possible.

There have been a number of attempts to do this with devices like end-plates, and other modifications to the wingtip. As, by and large, agricultural aircraft are still flying with regular style wingtips, it is doubtful whether these modifications justified the expense. As this is a very important item, we will look a bit closer at the mechanism.

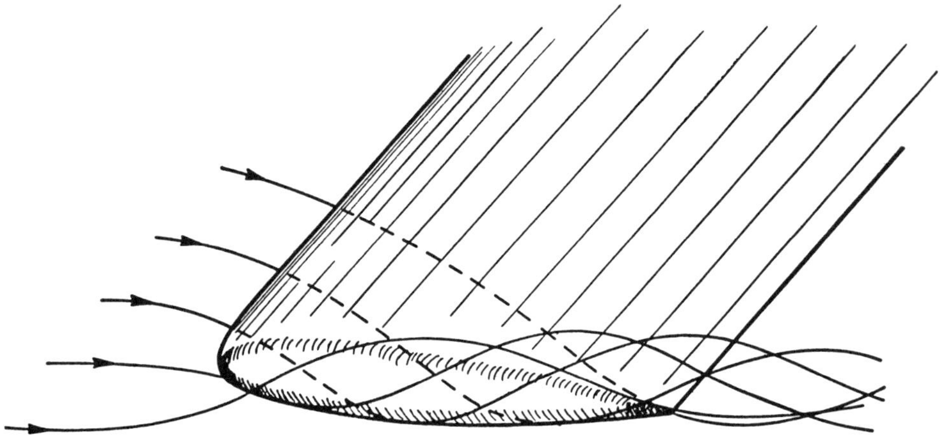

Fig 3.5 Streamline flow close to the tip of a lifting wing (Parkin and Spillman, 1980)

In generating lift, the wing of an aircraft causes the airflow near each wingtip to swirl round the tip from lower to upper surface, as in fig 3.5. This swirling motion increases directly with increase in wing lift and varies inversely with aircraft speed at a given lift and flying height. Thus a crop spraying aircraft, which is generally heavily loaded and has to fly relatively slowly, generates a strong swirling motion near each wingtip. If the aircraft has nozzles near these tips the spray from them will be swept into these swirling flows and some of it will be thrown into the air above and behind the tips, to be blown away from the target area if there is a slight crosswind. Even if the span of the spray boom is significantly smaller than the wing span, the smaller droplets from the outer nozzles can be entrained and thrown upwards.

With volatile sprays such as those with a large water content, evaporation can occur so quickly that quite a large number of the smaller sized droplets generated can be affected. If the aircraft flies close to the crop the effect of ground proximity is to materially increase the swirl velocities. Research at the College of Aeronautics at the Cranfield Institute of Technology (U.K.) (Parkin and Spillman, 1980) has resulted in a modification to a Piper Pawnee wingtip in an effort to reduce the effects of the wingtip vortex on spray deposition. The geometry used is shown in fig. 3.6. The varying camber and twist across the spans of the sails is essential to allow for the changes in local airflow direction which occur as the distance from the actual wingtip surface increases.

Although the three sail geometry wingtips were used in the trials, the results were very promising. In the results of two series of tests using the different wingtip configurations, the amount of spray above the height of the aircraft was reduced to 40% of the squared tip values by fitting the sails, irrespective of the wind condition. It is this part of the spray which is likely to be blown completely off-target and constitute a hazard or pollution.

It is beyond the scope of this section to explore the aerodynamics of the prototype sails, but as work is still going on in this field, a five-sail tip version is expected to be tested soon. If this proves as good as expected, commercial exploitation is likely to follow. Future agricultural aircraft could look quite different to the present generation of aircraft as efforts by the designers produce drag reducing devices; wingtip sails may be one answer. For the time being, the agricultural pilot will still have to live with wingtip vortices as even the very latest agricultural aircraft are still using conventional wingtips.

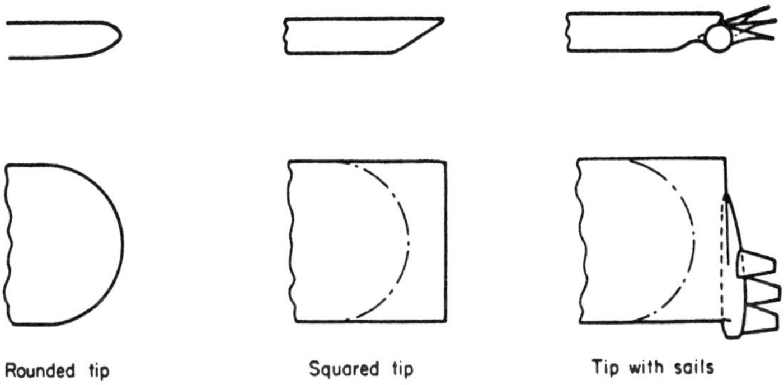

Fig 3.6 Geometry of wingtip sails tested (Parkin and Spillman, 1980)

References

Amsden, R. C. (1972) 'Wind velocity in relation to aerial spraying of crops.' *Agricultural Aviation* **14** (4) 103–107.

Anon. (1978) *Handbook for Agricultural Pilots* 3rd edn. Bedford, U.K.: I.A.A.C. Cranfield Institute of Technology.

F.A.O. (1972) 'The use of aircraft in agriculture.' Agricultural Services Bulletin 16.

Parkin, C. S. and Spillman, J. J. (1980) 'The use of wingtip sails on spraying aircraft to reduce the amount of material carried off target by crosswind.' *J. Ag. Eng. Res.* **25** (1).

Wilce, S. E. *et al.* (1974) 'Drop size control and aircraft spray equipment.' *Agricultural Aviation* **16** (1), 7–16.

4

Safety aspects of chemicals used by application pilots

This chapter uses material from the Aerial Application of Pesticides Safety Manual *(Health and Welfare Canada) and is incorporated with the kind permission of the Director General. Also, extracts are taken from the* Aerial Agriculture – Chemical Rating Manual *(Australian Bureau of Animal Health) and are incorporated with the kind permission of the Pesticides Co. ordinator.*

Introduction

Pesticides used in crop protection vary in toxicity from harmless to potentially hazardous. This chapter describes the classification of pesticides and the significance of the LD_{50} values. Pilots and ground staff should not come into contact with any pesticides, and the operations are organised in such a manner as to avoid accidental contamination. However, pilots will know that their training assumes the possibility of engine failure, or other equipment malfunction whilst in flight, and will practise the appropriate actions. The same assumption applies to accidental exposure to chemicals. This chapter outlines the action to be taken in the event of contamination, and also decontamination of personnel and equipment.

Classification of pesticides

Information pertaining to pesticides and pesticide use is rather complex and extensive. In the following pages this information has been divided into three classifications, namely:

(1) By purpose (which may also be descriptive of the mode of action);
(2) By formulation;

(3) By chemical composition (i.e. the active ingredient which may be described by a chemical name or trade name).

While this breakdown is needed for an understanding of the subject matter, it must be borne in mind that information from all the three subdivisions comes into play in the solution of any pest control problem.

Classification by purpose

The broad division of 'pests' into insects, weeds and fungi, naturally evolves the terms (a) insecticides, (b) herbicides, and (c) fungicides. In this classification the terms 'insect' and 'insecticide' include such pests as spiders and mites.

Insecticides

The chemical compounds used to control insects are subdivided in accordance with their mode of action:

A *Contact insecticides* kill primarily through direct contact with the insect. The chemical is absorbed through the external body surfaces of the insect in sufficient quantity to be lethal.
B *Residual insecticides* are taken up by the insect from a leaf or other treated surface.
C *Stomach poisons* must be eaten by the insect to be effective; external contact is not sufficient.
D *Systemic insecticides* are absorbed by, and flow through, the system of a plant or animal in sufficient quantity to protect it against the insect at points remote from the point of application.
E *Fumigants* vaporise and effect control by contacting the insect in the vapour form.

Since insect development progresses through several distinct stages during the life cycle, different stages may require control by different insecticides. Thus insecticides may be classified on the basis of the stage of development which they control most effectively:

(1) *Adulticides* are most effective against the adult form of the insect.
(2) *Larvicides* are more effective against the grub, worm, or larva of the insect.
(3) *Ovicides* are most effective against the egg stage of the insect.

In addition, some insecticides may be specifically referred to in accordance with the particular type of pest they are capable of controlling, such as *aphicides* for the control of aphids, and *acaricides* for the control of mites.

Herbicides

Chemical compounds used to kill or inhibit undesirable plant growth may be subdivided in accordance with their selectivity and mode of action:

A *Contact herbicides* are those that kill primarily by contact with plant tissue, rather than as a result of translocation. Only that portion of the plant contacted is directly affected, and the effect is usually rapid. Complete coverage is necessary for complete control.
B *Systemic or translocated herbicides* act more slowly, taking perhaps several weeks for maximum effect, and are capable of movement within the plant away from the site of application.
C *Growth regulators* alter the growth characteristics of plants. Careful timing and application are necessary.

Herbicide treatments are either:
Non-selective to kill or suppress all vegetation in the treatment area.
Selective to kill or suppress some plants without affecting others.

Selective herbicides may also be classified according to the time of application, as follows:

(1) *Pre-plant herbicides* are applied to the soil before seeding of the crop. (Some types must be incorporated into the soil after application.)
(2) *Pre-emergent herbicides* may be applied following seeding of the crop, pre-emergent to the crop only or pre-emergent to both crop and weeds.
(3) *Post-emergent herbicides* are applied following emergence of the crop, or weeds, or both.

Fungicides

Fungicides are chemicals which control the causes of many plant diseases. There are two main types, as follows:

A *Protective fungicides* are applied before the invasion of the disease begins, and will destroy any spores as they germinate.
B *Eradicant fungicides* will control fungi already established in the host plant.

Most fungicides are contact materials, or have very limited systemic action. Thus, as is the case with contact herbicides, the objective must be complete coverage.

Classification by formulation

Biologically active chemicals need to be put into a form in which they may be dispersed evenly at the required rate; in other words, they need to be formulated. The common formulations are solutions, emulsions, suspensions, dusts, and granules. Although some chemical compounds may be adapted to all formulations, others may be limited by their physical properties to only one or two.

The type of formulation will to a great extent govern the total volume of material which has to be distributed to disperse evenly the active chemical ingredient at the required rate per unit area. Thus the choice of high-, medium- or low-volume application is dependent upon the formulation.

The least volume of material would obviously be distributed if the active ingredient (also referred to as the 'technical material') were not formulated (i.e. diluted) at all. Such a method is now available and is known as the ultra low volume technique (ULV).

Ultra low volume (ULV)

This method requires equipment which will evenly distribute very small quantities, 2–16 oz (60–500 ml) of liquid per acre (0.4 hectare). With this equipment, any insecticide which is itself a liquid may be applied undiluted or as a very highly concentrated solution. Owing partly to limited information on effectiveness, toxicity, and drift hazards, only a few insecticides are currently registered for ULV application.

Unless the chemical is registered for ULV application, and the appropriate equipment is employed, a formulation of the technical material (and therefore a greater volume) is used. The available formulations are as follows:

A *Solutions* When a chemical compound (dry or liquid) is dissolved in a liquid, the result is a solution. Such a solution may be in water, or in an organic solvent. Most pesticides are relatively insoluble in water (phosphamidon being a notable exception), and must be dissolved in an organic solvent before being added to the water.

B *Emulsions (from emulsifiable concentrates)* Oil solutions to be diluted with water are formulated as a concentrate, with emulsifying agents added to permit the oily product to disperse in water to form an emulsion. This gives the thin, milky liquid which is characteristic of an emulsion, by which the oil-carried pesticide is dispersed through the water diluent.

C *Invert emulsions (from emulsifiable concentrates)* In this case a water solution is formulated as a concentrate and dispersed in oil to form an emulsion; that is, the water-carried pesticide is dispersed through an oil diluent. This results in a thick mayonnaise-like mixture, which is used when drift control is of prime importance.

D *Visco-elastic emulsions* Special chemicals can be added to an emulsifiable concentrate so that it is less easily broken up into droplets. With any given nozzle, emulsions of this type tend to give larger droplets.

E *Particulate sprays* Special materials are available which will swell greatly in water without dissolving, when mixed with a water-based spray. When such chemicals are prepared as sized particles, and sufficient water is made available, the result is a 'particulate spray' which may be pumped and sprayed, but yet contains particles which are all of approximately the same selected size.

F *Suspensions (from wettable powders)* Wettable powders are formulated by mixing the active ingredient, together with special wetting agents, into a clay-like powder. When mixed with water, the result is a suspension, which usually requires constant agitation to maintain a uniform mixture.

G *Colloidal formulations* These are sometimes referred to as 'flowable paste' or 'suspensible solids', and are in a finely divided state. Because of smallness of particle size, specific gravity of the suspending medium, and the presence of suspending and dispersing agents, the formulation remains almost indefinitely in a suspended state and also highly fluid.

H *Dusts* consist of clay-like materials carrying appropriate amounts of active ingredient. Dusts are intended to be used exactly as supplied, without further dilution or mixing.

I *Granules* are formulated by mixing the active ingredient with a clay-like material, in a process which yields relatively large particles or granules carrying the required level of pesticide. Granules are used to facilitate placement of the active ingredient, and can be specially prepared to suit particular circumstances.

J *Additives* or adjuvants of various kinds are available to modify or improve the properties of the spray liquid according to need, particularly in the case of solutions. Spreader-stickers are additives which will help the spreading and adhesive properties of the spray solution. Thickening or foaming agents may be added to a spray solution to produce a viscosity that is useful in reducing the number of fine particles in the spray cloud. Several varieties of these adjuvants are available.

Classification by chemical composition

Biologically active chemicals for pest control are mainly organic compounds. Organic compounds are those which contain carbon atoms in their chemical structure. Most organic compounds are synthesised or manufactured from basic chemical components, but some are extracted from plants and are therefore called 'botanicals'. Organic compounds used for pest control are members of various group or 'families' of chemicals. Each group contains chemical compounds which have some common characteristics, and any one group may contain insecticides, herbicides, and fungicides.

Probably 90% of all the compounds that possess useful pesticidal or herbicidal actions can be classified, on the basis of chemical composition and structure, into no more than a dozen major classes. Four of these contain compounds responsible for almost all of the aerial applicator's toxicological problems: the dinitrophenols, the carbamates, the chlorinated hydrocarbons, and the organophosphates.

Dinitrophenol compounds

Dinitrophenols derive their name from a phenol ring to which are attached nitrogen-oxygen radicals. Belonging to a family of dye chemicals, they are a strong yellow in colour, and stain any organic material with which they come in contact. This group is considered to be quite toxic, and may be employed as herbicides, insecticides, and crop desiccants. The most common member of the group is dinoseb.

Carbamate compounds

This family of compounds is typified by a particular arrangement of nitrogen, carbon, and oxygen in the chemical structure. Members of the group are insecticides: carbaryl, aminocarb, methomyl; herbicides: propham, triallate, barban; fungicides: maneb, metiram, zineb. The chemicals of this group are, in general, less persistent in the environment. The toxic hazard to humans and animals is mild with the above herbicides and fungicides, but some of the insecticides have a high acute toxicity.

Organochlorine compounds (chlorinated hydrocarbons)

All pesticides in this group contain chlorine, carbon, and hydrogen; some also contain oxygen and sulphur. Most chlorinated hydrocarbons are insecticides. Many of these compounds have relatively high persistence in soil, food, and feed, and tend to accumulate in the fatty tissues of man and animals. The best known members of this family are DDT, aldrin, dieldrin, chlordane, endrin, lindane, BHC, heptachlor, methoxychlor, toxaphene and endosulfan. Others, such as dicofol, contain oxygen and are acaricides. There are other chlorinated compounds which are placed in different groups because of special features of their chemical structure.

Organophosphorus compounds ('organophosphates')

Most organophosphorus compounds are derivatives of phosphoric acid. They contain phosphorus, carbon, and hydrogen; some also contain hydrogen, oxygen, and frequently sulphur. Many members of the group have a high acute toxicity, and all act as cholinesterase depressants. Most of the group are insecticides, and some of them are acaricides also. This group is less persistent in soil, food, and feed for animals; many are combustible. Common members of the family are parathion, phorate, azinphosmethyl, dimethoate, fenitrothion, fenthion, malathion, diazinon, temephos, phosphamidon, TEPP, methidathion, leptophos.

Safety in the use of chemicals

An evaluation of the 'safety' of pesticides used in agriculture involves an understanding of the terms toxicity and hazard. *Toxicity* can be defined as the potential of a pesticide to cause injury when administered to or absorbed by the body of a treated organism through various routes. *Hazard* (or risk) on the other hand, is the likelihood that injury will result from the normal or expected use of the pesticide. A formulation of parathion, kept tightly sealed in a container in a locked pesticide store presents little hazard, although it is a highly toxic pesticide. However, the mixing and subsequent application of this parathion by a person not wearing adequate protective clothing nor adhering to prescribed safety directions, exposes that operator to extreme hazard. This section outlines the chemical factors used in evaluating the hazards associated with pesticides and advises on how these can be minimised.

Application of pesticides is a serious business. Their great usefulness rests in their ability to interrupt the life processes of insects, fungi, weeds and other pests. Many of these biologically active chemicals, if used carelessly, can also have adverse effects on humans, animals and wildlife. All should be handled with great respect. Knowledge is the key. The aim of this book is to provide some of this knowledge so that all who apply pesticides from the air clearly understand associated hazards and thus have the incentive to run a clean operation.

Each person involved in the manufacture, handling, distribution and use of pesticides must be conscious of the need to avoid, as far as possible, breathing, swallowing or absorbing through the skin, significant quantities of the materials they handle. Adequate knowledge and sensible application of safe and accepted practices are fundamental to the protection of operating personnel, the public and the environment. In every instance of pesticide application *someone* has to assume responsibility for the conduct of the operation. This management function should ensure:

- The least toxic effective pesticide is used.
- Application is at the minimum dosage effective for the current stage of development of the particular pest.
- Application equipment is regularly maintained and calibrated.
- Every effort is made to get the maximum amount of spray on target.
- All personnel involved are fully briefed on safety procedures, are properly supervised and protected.
- Liaison is arranged in advance with local medical facilities.
- Personnel receive regular physical examination, including blood cholinesterase determinations.
- Persons never work alone with pesticides, as prompt help may be required in case of accident.

Experience has shown that if proper precautionary measures are observed even the most toxic compounds can be used safely. It is fundamental that personnel at all levels of responsibility be thoroughly briefed in good practice associated with pesticide usage.

Toxicity of chemicals

Pesticides are two-edged swords because they are not selectively toxic only to the intended target organisms. Most are poisonous to humans and animals as well as pests. Thus everyone working with pesticides should have some knowledge of their toxicity and potential hazard. With the exception of mercury compounds, most common fungicides have low mammalian toxicity. The majority of herbicides have a relatively low toxicity to animals including man. Some pose a major risk to sensitive crops in adjacent areas through drift. Insecticides constitute the main hazard to men and animals. In general, the organophosphorus compounds are more toxic than the carbamates or organochlorines. The effects of carbamate exposure tend to be more rapid but less severe and not as long-lasting as those which follow intoxication from organophosphorus compounds. The hazard with organochlorines is usually lower at the time of application but, because of their stability, they can pose a hazard through contamination of the food chain. Thus, consideration must be given to the possible accumulation of harmful residues, and care must be taken to prevent contamination of bodies of water.

Some of the organophosphorus insecticides (e.g. parathion) are highly toxic and, in addition to special protection for all personnel handling or applying such materials, care should be taken that spray does not reach animals, birds, or men on the ground at time of application. Sprayed fields should not be entered until the spray deposit has dried. Work which brings personnel into contact with treated crops should be delayed for 3–7 days.

Not only do pesticides vary widely in their toxicity, but it is also important to note that some present only an acute hazard, some produce a hazard only after repeated exposure, and some have both acute and chronic effects. Toxicity may vary with the type of formulation used, with the route of absorption into the body, and with body weight. The susceptability of humans to poisoning by a pesticide may also differ somewhat with age, sex and nutritional state and ambient conditions.

Lethal dose (LD_{50})

The accepted method of recording the relative toxicity of a pesticide is the LD_{50}. This is the statistical estimate of a dosage which, when administered, will kill 50% of the test animals under stated conditions. This is the accepted yardstick for denoting acute toxicity but care must be exercised in its interpretation. The figures designating LD_{50} values express the lethal dose in milligrams per kilogram body weight of the test animal. The dose required to kill a 200 g rat will be about twice the amount that would kill a 100 g rat.

Rats, mice, rabbits, birds, dogs and fish are commonly used in laboratory tests, but because the various animals generally react differently to the same treatment, the LD_{50} value may vary considerably from one animal species to the next. Test conditions and the history and status of the animal colony have a profound effect on the result. Thus the LD_{50} values are very useful in classifying pesticides according to their toxicity, so long as it is recognised that the values are not absolute and should be expressed as a range.

Toxicity also varies with the route of absorption into the body. LD_{50} values are thus determined for different routes of administration; oral, dermal or inhalation routes being of most practical significance. It must be remembered that a pesticide of high oral toxicity may be much less toxic by dermal administration. When using LD_{50} values to compare toxicities of pesticides it is imperative that data from the same animal species and the same route of administration should be used every time.

Another way of expressing relative toxicity as employed in the case of fish (and other organisms of low body weight) is the LC_{50}, the lethal concentration value normally expressed in milligrams of the active constituent per litre of water (mg/l) for a certain period. This is the concentration which produces 50% mortality within the specified time. In all cases, the *higher* the value given for LD_{50} or LC_{50}, the *less* toxic is the pesticide.

W.H.O. criteria for classification of pesticides

The World Health Organization (W.H.O.) recommended classification of pesticides by hazard is listed in table 4.1 (World Health Organization, 1975). These toxicity values are based on the amount of active material (technical material), not the formulated product. The acute oral LD_{50} values corresponding to the probable *lethal* doses of technical material if taken orally by a human adult of average size are given in table 4.2.

Table 4.1 Criteria for classification of pesticides (World Health Organization, 1975); the terms 'solids' and 'liquids' refer to the physical state of the product or formulation being classified

	LD_{50} for the rat (mg/kg body weight)			
Class	Oral		Dermal	
	Solids	Liquids	Solids	Liquids
1a Extremely hazardous	5 or less	20 or less	10 or less	40 or less
1b Highly hazardous	5–50	20–200	10–100	40–400
11 Moderately hazardous	50–500	200–2000	100–1000	400–4000
111 Slightly hazardous	Over 500	Over 2000	Over 1000	Over 4000

Table 4.2 The relationship between LD_{50} and probable lethal dose of technical material taken orally by a human adult

LD_{50} value	Lethal amount
5	few drops
50	one teaspoon (5 ml)
500	one ounce or 2 tablespoons (30 ml)
5000	500 ml
15000	1000 ml

Toxicity to mammals

Table 4.3 give the acute toxicity ratings by LD_{50} values for oral and dermal absorption; that is, milligrams of toxicant per kilogram of body mass.

Chemical compound	Oral LD_{50}	Dermal LD_{50}
Insecticides		
Aldrin	35–70	100–200
Amidophos	13–21	118
Aminocarb	21	280
Azinphos-methyl	7–25	200–280
Carbaryl	400–900	>4000
Carbofuran	5	–
Chlorpyrifos	135	200–2000
DDT	112–800	2510–3000
Diazinon	76–600	200–1200
Dieldrin	40	60
Dimethoate	200–300	400–1150
Endosulfan	18–110	74–130
Endrin	3–18	10–120
Fenitrothion	130–673	300–3000
Fenthion	190–310	330–1300
Leptophos	43	>800
Malathion	500–1900	4000–5000
Methidathion	25	155
Methomyl	17–24	250–5000
Methoxychlor	5000–7000	>3000
Mexacarbate	15–63	–
Naled	250–550	800–1100
Parathion	3–30	7–200
Phosmet	230–300	>3000
Phosphamidon	9–30	107–143
Propoxur	80	>2400
Rotenone	25	–
Temephos	1000–1500	1400–4000
Tetrachlorvinphos	1100	>4000
Trichlorfon	450–650	>2000
Herbicides		
Alachlor	1200	3500
Amitrole	1100–25000	>10000
Asulam	4000	1200
Atrazine	2000–3000	–

Table 4.3 – *continued*

Chemical compound	Oral LD_{50}	Dermal LD_{50}
Avenge	320–450	770
Barban	600–1350	>1600
Benazolin	>3000	–
Bentazon	500–1100	>2500
Benzoprop	716	>1000
Bromoxynil	250	–
Chloramben (salts)	3500	>3160
Chlorbromuron	2150	>1000
Chlorfenac	1780	>3160
Chloroxuron	3700	–
Chlorpropham	3800	–
Cyanazine	149	1200
Cyprazine	1200±200	–
2,4-D	300–700	800–1500
Dalapon	1000–9000	>2000
2, 4-DB	700	–
Demeton-methyl	60	–
Dicamba	566	–
Dichlone	3–12	–
Dichlorprop (esters)	400	1400
Dinoseb	15–50	135–200
Diquat	30–440	>750
Disulfoton	3–12	20
Dodine	1000–2000	2500
Endothall	35–80	100–750
Fenoprop	650	–
Linuron	1000	–
MCPA	700–1000	>1000
MCPB	700	–
Mecoprop	650	–
Metobromuron	2000	>10200
Metribzin	698–2345	>1000
Monolinuron	2100	–
Naptalam	1770	–
Niclofen	2630	–
Paraquat	25–250	50–500
Phemedipham	>4000	4000
Picloram	8200	>4000
Prometryne	2500	–
Pronamide	5360–8350	>3160
Propanil	560	>1000
Propham	1000–9000	–
Simazine	5000	–

Table 4.3 – *continued*

Chemical compound	Oral LD_{50}	Dermal LD_{50}
2,4,5-T	300–800	>1000
TBA	750	–
TCA	3370	–
Triallate	675	–
Fungicides		
Anilazine	2700	–
Captafol	2500	–
Captan	8400–15000	–
Chlorthalonil	>3750	>10000
Coppers (fixed)	3000–6000	–
Fentin hydroxide	108	5000
Folpet	>10000	–
Mancozeb	>8000	–
Maneb	1000–8000	>1000
Metiram	6400	–
Nabam	395–400	–
Thiabendazole	3100	–
Zineb	1000–8000	>1000

Toxicity of solvents

Some solvents and adjuvants are themselves toxic and can be hazardous. Skin irritation, or crop phytotoxicity of a pesticide formulation may be due to the solvent used and not the active constituent of the pesticide. Some adjuvants are highly toxic and require the same handling and storage precautions as do pesticides. Absorption of a pesticide through the skin is often increased by the presence of a solvent in the formulation.

Hazards to pilots and ground crews

The preceding section of this chapter deals with chemical considerations in evaluating the toxicity of pesticides to humans. Operators using pesticides must be aware of the possible danger of exposure:

- From absorption through the skin (and/or cuts and abrasions);
- From skin irritation;
- From ingestion;
- From inhalation.

A thorough understanding of the possibility of exposure to pesticides, an appreciation of the consequences and adherence to safe practices will keep exposure to a minimum. Should accidents occur, decontamination procedures should be carried out quickly and medical advice should be sought. Recommended medical treatments are outlined in the following chapter.

Markers working in fields during pesticide application must take special precautions against pesticide contamination. Markers *must* wear white overalls, boots or shoes and a washable broad brimmed hat. They should:

- Always work into the wind when marking,
- Never stand where they can be sprayed or subjected to drift,
- Stand at least 50 m from the edge of a crop so aircraft is not spraying when it passes,
- Not touch or walk through freshly sprayed crop,
- Move away from mark when aircraft is approaching and 300 m away on spray run. If unable to get clear of aircraft lie face down on ground with hands beneath body until aircraft passes,
- Shower and change into uncontaminated clothing if accidently contaminated, and at the end of a spray job,
- Wash face and hands with soap and water before smoking, eating or drinking.

Cholinesterase levels

The poisoning action of both organophosphorous and carbamate pesticides occurs when the pesticide inhibits the activity of an enzyme in the central nervous system. This inhibition reduces or even blocks the transmission of nervous impulses, resulting in impairment of action, or in extreme cases, total paralysis of heart or lung action. The enzyme involved is *acetylcholinesterase* (AChE), and is found also in the red cells of the blood. Another enzyme, *cholinesterase* (ChE) which occurs in blood plasma, is also inhibited by these pesticides. Although the quantitive effect depends on the individual pesticide, it may be said in general that the plasma ChE is inhibited more readily, and its activity recovers more quickly than is the case with the red cell AChE, when one of these pesticides is absorbed into the system.

Both blood enzymes have a potential diagnostic value. The activity of plasma ChE may begin to decrease within a few minutes of accidental absorption of pesticide. Typically it may reach its lowest value within an hour or so, after which it may begin to recover rather quickly in the case of carbamate absorption, and be nearly normal within a few hours, while with organophosphorous compounds recovery is usually a matter of a few days. The AChE of the red cells usually responds less rapidly and less markedly to accidental pesticide absorption, and recovery of activity is slower, typically requiring three or four weeks. Both enzyme measurements provide useful and complimentary information relative to pesticide absorption and are frequently used on occupationally exposed workers to determine, before outward signs of poisoning occur, whether certain operations involve an exposure hazard. When these blood enzyme measurements are to be made for this purpose, it is essential that pre-exposure values for each individual be determined, since there is a wide variation in normal values among individuals. Also, analytical procedures and interpretation of results are related to the pesticide(s) involved.

Action in the event of accidental poisoning

It must first be emphasised that a properly organised aerial application operation would include advance preparation for medical service. This must include the location of doctors, hospitals or other medical centres. It must also be established that the doctors or staff are equipped for pesticidal poisoning, particularly if any of the previously mentioned chemical groups are to be used. Ensure that adequate supplies of atropine (tablets or ampoules) and pralidoxime chloride vials (2-PAM) are available. Ensure that the medical service *is available* during the spraying programme and that the staff are briefed as to the details of the work to be done, the area of operations and the pesticide chemical group being used.

It is beyond the scope of this book to detail the full range of treatment for pesticide poisoning as it is extensive; however, knowledge and propt action could *save a life*. It is essential to recognise symptoms as early as possible. Some persons may not show symptoms of poisoning until up to eight hours after exposure. Never disregard headaches, dizziness, nausea, or diarrhoea within twenty-four hours after working with an organophosphate pesticide: *always* consult a doctor. The exact nature and severity of the symptoms depend upon the particular chemical and the duration and intensity of the exposure. *Even in mild cases, never omit medical attention.*

Acute symptoms of poisoning usually appear within:

30 minutes after inhalation
15–60 minutes after swallowing
2–3 hours after skin contact.

In cases of moderate severity, the symptoms usually reach their peak within 4–8 hours, and may persist for several days.

General symptoms

In general, the symptoms which indicate that pesticides poisoning has occurred are as follows:

Mild poisoning

(Note that mild symptoms may be the beginning of a progression to severe symptoms.) Symptoms include headache, fatigue, skin irritation, loss of appetite, dizziness, weakness, nervousness, nausea, perspiration, diarrhoea, eye irritation, insomnia, thirst, restlessness, irritation of nose and throat, loss of weight, soreness of joints and changes of mood.

Moderate poisoning

(Note that moderate symptoms may be the beginning of severe symptoms.) These symptoms include nausea, trembling, muscular incoordination, excessive saliva, blurring of vision, feeling of constriction in the throat and chest, difficulty in breathing, flushed or yellow skin, abdominal cramps, vomiting, diarrhoea, mental confusion, twitching of muscles, weeping, excessive perspiration, profound weakness, rapid pulse and cough.

Severe Poisoning

Vomiting, loss of reflexes, inability to breathe, uncontrollable muscular twitching, constriction of pupils (to pin-point pupils), convulsions, unconsciousness, severe secretion from respiratory tract, fever, intense thirst and increased rate of breathing.

First aid treatment

- *Move well away from any pesticide.* Quickly move the patient to a safe uncontaminated location, and remove any contaminated clothing.
- *If breathing is very weak or has ceased*:
  (1) Give artificial respiration;
  (2) Oxygen can be beneficial.
- *If pesticide has been swallowed*:
  (1) If the patient has not vomited, induce vomiting *immediately*. Do this by introducing a finger into the throat, or by giving warm salt water (30 ml of salt in a glass of warm water);
  (2) Give milk or cold water freely;

(3) Again induce vomiting if vomit fluid is not clear, *but do not* induce vomiting if the pesticide solvent is a petroleum distillate, such as fuel or kerosene.

Do not give anything by mouth to a person who is unconscious, or having convulsions.

- *If pesticide is splashed in the eye*:
  (1) Wash the eye with clean water *immediately*; speed is essential to prevent injury to the eye;
  (2) Use large amounts of clean water to gently irrigate the eye;
  (3) Continue for at least fifteen minutes;
  (4) Boracic acid solution may be beneficial.
- *If pesticide is spilled on the skin*:
  (1) Remove all contaminated clothing; cover the patient with clean clothing or a clean blanket;
  (2) Wash the skin thoroughly with plenty of soap and water *immediately, and repeat again*;
  (3) Clean under finger nails and toe nails.
- *If respiration becomes weak or irregular*:
  (1) Give artificial respiration, maintain breathing and prevent worsening of condition;
  (2) Oxygen can be beneficial;

  Artificial respiration takes precedence over all other first aid procedures.
- *If convulsions occur*:
  (1) Keep the patient warm and dry;
  (2) Prevent injury, use gentle restraint.
- *If unconsciousness occurs*:
  (1) Ensure patient can breathe adequately (may need to pull tongue forward to prevent blocking the throat);
  (2) Keep patient warm and dry;
  (3) *Do not give anything by mouth to an unconscious person.*
- *If the pesticide is an organophosphate or carbamate and symptoms are severe*:
  (1) Administer 2 atropine tablets of 1/100 grain or 0.6 mg each, *but do not* given atropine if the patient is already turning blue because of inadequate respiration, or is unconscious.
  (2) *Obtain medical attention as quickly as possible* (i.e. implement the emergency procedure as previously planned for the particular operation).
  (3) *Advise the attending doctor if atropine has been administered.*
  (4) Although 2-PAM is listed as a requirement in first aid kits, *it must not be used without medical supervision.*

(5) *Atropine* is antidotal in cases of *organophosphorus* and *carbamate* poisoning; 2-PAM is antidotal in cases of *organophosphorus* poisoning *but not carbamate* poisoning as its use is *contra-indicated.* 2-PAM may be used in conjunction with atropine (*but not for malathion poisoning*).

It must also be strongly emphasised that self-diagnosis and self-treatment are dangerous. It must be prevented by arranging for continuing medical supervision. An example of the risks involved is that with some operators it has been the practice to take atropine tablets to 'prevent' orhanophosphate poisoning. *This is dangerous.* Atropine has its proper place in treating proven clinical cases of such poisoning, but it can be dangerous if taken otherwise. Atropine is a potent drug in its own right, and if taken in the absence of organophosphate or carbamate poisoning, may lead to serious illness. The same applies to 2-PAM. Furthermore, the indiscriminate use of atropine or 2-PAM can mask early symptoms, so that further exposure is permitted, and can make clinical diagnosis extremely difficult. The consequences can be very serious.

An examination of recommended lowest levels of depression of cholinesterase from a number of chemical manufacturers are: 50% of the individual's 'normal' in whole blood; 60% of the individual's 'normal' in erythrocytes, 40% of the individual's 'normal' in plasma. Below these levels, remove the person from the pesticidal area until the chlolinesterase has recovered again.

It does not necessarily follow that the above levels mean that the individual is showing any of the signs of illness, as previously described, but that a small further exposure could cause dramatic deterioration. It must be remembered that these levels could be above that which is already providing behavioural changes which could, of course, go unnoticed. It is not possible to postulate the lowest levels for pilots (Quantick and Perry, 1981).

This is a rather discouraging picture of the hazards involved in handling pest control chemicals. It is not intended to frighten pilots and other personnel but to warn them that constant vigilance is the price of safety. It has been proved that safety is possible by the generally good record of many who have handled the organophosphates and chlorinated compounds in large quantities for many years. Better equipment, such as botttom-loading systems for spray planes, closed-circuit loading systems, newly designed helmets with integral visors, and masks for pilots, can help. For ground personnel, the fundamental principal of safety is more basic and simple. It consists of thinking in advance about each move and making it deliberately. All members of an aerial application team should observe each other for signs of toxicity as these are sometimes more obvious to others than to the victim himself. It should always be remembered that repeated small exposures may constitute a greater danger than the large, single dose.

For *emergency action* in case of a *major crash or spill* remember:

- If your clothing is contaminated with pesticide get it off quickly, then wash the skin.
- If your clothing is soaked with pesticide rip it off and jump into the nearest water as fast as possible.
- DO NOT HESITATE.

Decontamination

The great majority of pesticides can be removed by washing aircraft, vehicles, and equipment with soap and water, and then flushing with clean water. Mild detergents can be applied. Stiff bristle brushes will remove compacted chemical desposits after wetting. Some materials may corrode aircraft parts and fittings rapidly. Dry materials should be removed from inside the aircraft fuselage structure, or the vehicle cabin, by means of an air hose or an industrial vacuum cleaner. Tyres should not be forgotten in the decontamination process.

Decontamination requires large volumes of water, so it is absolutely essential to use an uncontaminated water source. Every effort must be

Plate 4.1 The cleaning and decontamination of aircraft is greatly assisted if access is possible into all the recesses of the airframe: Piper Pawnee Brave PA-36-300 (photo: Piper Aircraft Corp.)

made to channel the washings from the decontamination into a sump or other safe disposal area where no hazard to humans, animals, or wildlife can occur. Some pesticides require special treatment for proper decontamination. This applies particularly to spray mixtures containing 2,4-D, 2,4,5-T, MCPA, dicamba, picloram, etc.

Do not eat, smoke or drink during decontamination operations. The following procedures should be followed in decontamination procedures with different chemicals.

(1) *Water based spraying mixtures* The amine, potassium, and sodium salts of the phenoxy acid herbicides are water-based for mulations. The residues are water-miscible or may be made soluble by treatment with alkali. The recommended decontamination procedure for such spraying mixtures is:

- Flush sprays, hoses, tanks, etc. with clean water.
- Discharge the washing soda mixture through the nozzles and rinse system twice with clean water.
- Fill tank with water and add household ammonia at a rate of 1 part/100 parts of water.
- Pump this ammonia solution through the system.
- After ensuring that all parts have been contacted, allow the ammonia solution to stand in the closed spray system for 2–3 days.
- If washing soda is not available, the use of ammonia alone at the rate of 2 parts/100 is effective.
- The entire spray assembly should be finally washed out with cold water.
- Treat mixing and loading equipment similarly.

(2) *Oil-based spraying mixtures* The active material in oil-based spraying mixtures – such as oil concentrates, emulsifiable concentrates and invert emulsions – is insoluble in water but soluble in oil. Examples of these are ester formulations of 2,4-D and 2,4,5-T. The decontamination procedure following aerial spraying of these formulations is:

- Add 3 l of kerosene, 500 g of washing soda and a little detergent to every 100 l of water and use this solution to fill the spray tank or mixing vessel.
- Allow solution to contact all component parts and stand for 2 h.
- Discharge solution through nozzles and hoses and rinse twice with clean water.

For close inspection, individual application equipment parts and components after decontamination and drying should be stored in plastic bags or sheeting using silica gel to absorb any moisture.

(3) *Cleaning of aircraft and spray equipment before and after using ULV products* Cleaning of spray equipment when using ULV (ulta low volume = high concentrates, often 100% technical materials) products may present problems, since the presence of water must be carefully avoided. Before using ULV products after aqueous sprays have been used, thorough flushing with a solvent miscible with both water and the ULV formulation is required. Ethylene glycol, mono-alkylethers and related compounds have these required properties. (Quantick and Perry, 1981)

References

Anon. (1975) *Aerial Application of Pesticides Safety Manual.* Health and Welfare Canada, Health Protection Branch, Environmental Health Centre, Tunney's Pasture, Ottowa K1A 0L2, Canada.

Anon. (1978) *Aerial Agriculture Chemical Rating Manual.* Australian Bureau of Animal Health, Department of Primary Industry, Canberra, A.C.T. 2600, Austrialia.

Quantick, H. R. and Perry, I. C. (October 1981) 'Hazards of chemicals used in agricultural avaiation: a review.' *Aviation, Space, and Environmental Medicine*, 581–588.

World Health Organization (1975) 'Recommended classification of pesticides by hazard.' Extract from *WHO Chronicle* **29**, 397–401.

5
Selection of airstrips

Introduction

Most agricultural flying is done, for reasons of economy, from unprepared airstrips and ordinary grass fields near to the work in hand. These may be on the short side and with rough surfaces, and therefore they must be inspected carefully from the ground before use to make certain they are suitable. The following is a general guide and some suggested dimensions. It is, of course, not possible to list all the factors in the consideration of a suitable airstrip, and at the same time cover all aircraft types.

Width

A width of 100 ft (30 m) throughout the effective length will normally be sufficient. This may comprise:

(1) Central section, suitable for landing and take-off 30–35 ft (10 m).
(2) Adjacent sections, suitable for run-off and manoeuvring 30–35 ft (10 m) on either side.

Lateral clearance

A clearance area of 30 ft (10 m) would normally be required on each side of the strip throughout its length, in which there are no upstanding obstructions capable of damaging an aircraft while it is manoeuvring on the surface of the strip or flying at any height and wholly within the overall width of 160 ft (50 m) comprised of the strip plus the lateral clearance areas.

Longitudinal gradient

The maximum overall longitudinal gradient and any changes of gradient must be such that the aircraft can take off and land safely. It would be feasible that the gradient is such that only one way operations may be considered, i.e. downhill take-off and uphill landing.

Transverse gradient

The transverse gradient on the landing and take-off path must be no greater than that which will permit an adequate reserve of directional control of the aircraft to be maintained during landing and take-off.

Surface

The most desirable strip is one which is dry, smooth, and with short grass. Take note of the type of soil. Peat tends to increase the rolling resistance of the wheels, thus lengthening the take-off run, especially after it has collected surface water during rain. Clay likewise becomes easily water-logged. Chalk usually drains quite quickly, but when wet becomes very slippery and prevents effective braking.

If the grass is more than six inches deep, it tends to cling to the wheels and lengthens the take-off run, and if it is as deep as the wheels it may well make acceleration almost impossible. Clover and alfalfa are very slippery, especially when wet, and may seriously impair braking efficiency.

In the tropics, and occasionally elsewhere, a strip may be of bare earth without vegetation. In dry conditions there may be a considerable dust problem, especially if there is no wind to remove the dust, and attention will have to be paid to the adequacy of the air intake filter fitted to the engine, and to the difficulty of landing into the dust clouds. Inspect the strip carefully for holes, broken fence posts, ditches and so on. Make sure that it is not too rough – a good test is to drive a car over the field in a criss-cross pattern at 25 m.p.h. (40 km/h), and excessive bumpiness will soon be apparent.

Most of the above considerations apply also to landing – those concerning braking efficiency are most important – and it will normally be possible to land the empty aircraft on the strip from which it lifted its load. However, if possible the strip should also be suitable for landing on with a full load, and this will require a ground run as long as the take-off run with a good surface for braking. (It does not follow that if there is a take-off run of so many feet there is a landing-run of the same length – for example, the presence of tall trees at the downwind end of the strip may make an into-wind landing impossible without overrunning the field.)

The central 30–35 ft (10 m) of the strip over its length should be smooth; the 30–35 ft (10 m) on each side of the central area should be such that an aircraft running over it following a swing on take-off or landing would not suffer damage. The remainder should have no obstructions above ground level.

Approach and climb-out areas

The approach and climb-out path or paths must be at least 160 ft (50 m) wide for a distance of 800 ft (250 m), measured in a straight line from ground level at the nearer end of the strip. From this point it must be possible to maintain a minimum obstacle clearance of 50ft (15 m). A curved flight path may be used in achieving this clearance.

Length

As a general rule the length must be at least twice the distance taken by the aircraft to unstick, and where a low obstacle such as a hedge is to be cleared, it must be at least three times this distance. If an obstacle 50 ft (15 m) high has to be crossed the distance will be at least six times the ground run.

Situation

The strip must be as close as possible to the work to save 'dead' flying. Sometimes a short strip from which a reduced payload can be lifted, and which is very close, may be preferable to a longer one further away – but the exact calculation involves consideration of application rates and is outside our present scope. It is a good plan to select as high an airstrip as possible in hilly country – this is safer and saves time and fuel by avoiding climbing with payload.

Do not forget, when selecting a strip, to make sure that the surrounding country leaves ample room to manoeuvre when taking off and landing. In places where winds are liable to change frequently, choose a strip that can be used in as many wind directions as possible. The strip must be accessible to ground vehicles. It should not be necessary for these vehicles to travel on the strip: access to the loading area should be by a separate route.

There must be provision for a loading and turn around area. The loading bay should be located at the end of the strip from which take-off will normally be commenced. It should be to one side of the strip and should be as level as possible to minimise the risk of the loading vehicle damaging the aircraft and to facilitate accurate measurement of the load.

It is not sufficient for a pilot to accept, without further inspection, a strip which has been previously inspected or used. It may have deteriorated considerably in the intervening period. Even if it has been used very recently it should be carefully checked from the air before landing is attempted, to ensure that it is still safe – in particular, to ensure that animals have not wandered onto it.

The most important factor in the accurate selection of airstrips is the experience and judgement of the pilot, and his knowledge of the aircraft type and its capabilities. This experience can soon be acquired, but care must be taken in the meantime to play safe and select only the more obviously suitable fields, disregarding at the same time farmers and ground personnel who, without the knowledge of all relevant factors, may try to persuade a pilot against his judgement.

6
Airstrip organisation

Introduction

There will be many occasions where a pilot would be responsible for the airstrip organisation. The routine tasks could be performed by an 'airstrip supervisor', but only the pilot is able to judge clearances for taxying, manoeuvring, positioning for replenishing and refuelling.

The replenishing of the chemical load can be done in a number of ways and the success of the operation can rest on the smoothness of the loading team to perform this task. In the case of mechanical loaders for solids, the loader driver must exercise great care as loading anything up to 2 tons of chemical with the pilot sitting in the cockpit requires skill to position the vehicle without touching the aircraft structure, and to release the chemical at the right moment.

The importance of safety consciousness is paramount in these operations. The pilot is manoeuvring an expensive aeroplane with a spinning propeller which will not necessarily be stopped for a one minute replenishment of chemical. The loader driver must be able to position the loading vehicle as soon as the aircraft has stopped at the pre-arranged position. In the case of liquids, the loading crew is to be in position with the hose, and pumping should begin when proper connection is made. It can be seen that these actions need careful briefing and careful implementation before the team become proficient and operate smoothly, efficiently and safely.

Operations in remote areas often attract the locals to crowd around and watch something they may not often see, if at all, and this can offer its own problems. It is vital that crowds are kept at a safe distance from aircraft, spinning propellers or rotors, and also chemical containers, especially the empties, as they could be used for other purposes with fatal results.

There are many aspects in the organisation of the airstrip, and common sense together with a safety consciousness of each element in the operation that has to be performed will help give pilots the correct mental attitude in planning and implementing the operation.

Action before and after flying

Preparation of airstrip

Inspect the strip to make certain that it is clear for use, and that the weather or plant growth has not affected its serviceability since it was first selected. Direct the chemical tanker, or loading equipment and supplies to a convenient part of the field where flying will not be obstructed. Strain on the aircraft caused by continual taxying when loaded can be relieved by loading up as near as possible to the start of the take-off run. Sometimes, a strip will be long enough to allow landing and taking off in the same direction without back-tracking, in which case a great deal of time will be saved by loading up at the point where the aircraft rolls to a halt after landing.

Put fuel supplies out of the way of loading operations, erect the windsock in a visible and exposed place, and make sure that a fire-extinguisher and first aid kit are available and that everybody knows where they are. Finally, clear the strip of onlookers, especially children.

Before operations

Carry out the daily checks and pre-flight inspections required by the maintenance schedule and manufacturer's instructions. Special points to notice in agricultural work are:

Air filter (carburettor air intake) Low altitude operations require this to be cleaned or renewed far more frequently than normal, particularly in dusty conditions. Efficient air filtration is vital for reducing engine deterioration.

Fuel system The filter bowl must be inspected regularly for dirt and traces of water.

Airframe cleanliness Make sure the entire airframe is free of frost, ice, or snow, any of which may have sufficient effect on the aircraft's performance to prevent it from becoming airborne at take-off. Dead insects on the leading edges of the wings and tail may have a similar effect, and should be cleaned off.

The effect of glare is greatly magnified by a dirty or badly scratched windscreen. The importance of keeping windscreens clean and in the case of perspex screens particularly, taking care that they do not become scratched or crazed, cannot be over-emphasised.

Petrol, thinners, automotive polishes or similar solvents should never be used to clean perspex. Clean lighting kerosene may be used to remove deposits of those chemicals which resist ordinary soaps and detergents. Otherwise the latter should be the only cleaning materials used, and these should be completely flushed off with clean water after use. Even a chamois or soft rag can scratch perspex. Light scratches can be removed with proper perspex polish or with jeweller's rouge, applied with cotton wool. Frost should be removed with cold water – never with hot, as the sudden change in temperature can cause crazing of the perspex.

Agricultural equipment must be checked for correct operation before loading begins.

After operations

Drain all chemical from the system and clean the aircraft and its equipment to minimise the risk of corrosion. (See chapter 4, section on decontamination.)

Tying down

If the aircraft is to be left unattended on the strip, it must be secured against wind damage. (Many insurance policies exclude damage by wind to aircraft not firmly tied down.) It is always as well to pick a sheltered part of the airstrip for parking, bearing in mind however the danger of falling branches during gales. It is also wise to park out of sight of passers-by if possible.

The aircraft should be secured by each wing and by the rear fuselage to weights or corkscrew-shaped pickets. Avoid wooden stakes as these are easily dislodged should the ground become waterlogged, as generally happens in a gale. The wing ropes should be just slack enough to allow it to rock slightly in the wind. The wheels should be braked and chocked, and covers and control locks fitted. In high winds the aircraft is perhaps safest if placed tail to the wind, provided the tail is really well secured; in this position the wind, striking the trailing edges of the wings, produces no lift which might move the aircraft. In this case however controls *must* be securely locked, to prevent them from slamming back and forth.

Clearing the strip

Empty chemical containers must never be left lying about. They must be disposed of safely. In rare circumstances it may be possible to return drums to the manufacturer. Drums should first be rinsed thoroughly (and the rinsings added to the following spray load and applied to the target via the spray system). Selling for scrap is only a possibility after decontamination: rinsing usually with water, a detergent and an alkali. Where burial of containers is considered, ensure that burial takes place well away from livestock feeding areas, water courses and supplies. Rinsing is advisable before burial. Drums that have contained herbicides should never be used for other farm purposes and should be punctured after use to prevent re-use. Never burn containers that have held hormone-type herbicides or pesticides containing chlorates, arsenic or mercury. Pesticide containers should only be burnt in special incinerators as there could be vapour problems. Burning is a specialised method of disposal and should not be considered on site. Do not throw empty containers into ponds or streams, for danger of contaminating drinking water or poisoning fish. Areas of grass contaminated by spilt chemicals must be fenced off if livestock are to return to the field. The aircraft must be fenced to protect it if cattle are to be let in as they rub themselves against it. (This precaution is not necessary in the case of sheep.)

Refuelling

It is more difficult than ever in agricultural work to keep fuel supplies in good condition, and nowhere is it more important. The following points however will assist:

(1) Barrels, especially ones that are not full, can collect water by condensation if left standing for long periods – store in a lying position. A water-finding paste which indicates the presence of water by becoming discoloured is available.
(2) Hand pumps, hoses, cans and funnels must be kept clean and out of reach of agricultural chemicals. Hoses must of course be petrol-resistant, and all fittings should be of non-ferrous metal. Plastic funnels and cans must not be used; they may cause a discharge of static electricity and subsequent fire and explosion.
(3) Clean away dirt and chemical dust that settles near fuel filler caps. Owing to the dirt of agricultural work, tank vents are more liable to block, and, if not kept clear, will cause fuel starvation.
(4) Earth the airframe before refuelling
(5) Fuel should be filtered through clean chamois leather.
(6) Do not refuel and load chemical at the same time.
(7) Inspect the aircraft fuel system every day for signs of water or dirt in the filter bowl.
(8) Fuel is sometimes carried in the hopper for long ferry flights, and this gives the aircraft a considerable range potential. Great care is

necessary when filling the hopper with fuel, particularly in hot and dry climates, as the bonding of a fibre glass hopper may not be to the standard of regular fuel tanks. There have been cases of static discharge causing fire and complete destruction of the aircraft while filling hoppers.

Ground handling equipment

For handling spray liquids, chemical tankage is provided, usually mounted for mobility on a lorry or trailer. A pump is used for mixing the recirculating chemicals, and for pumping them into the aircraft. Many chemicals, mainly dispersible powders, need to be pre-mixed in a small tank before being diluted for use. Agitation is also necessary; it may be done mechanically by a paddle-wheel arrangement revolving in the tank and driven by the pump engine, or hydraulically by constant recirculation at a high flow rate. The liquid is filtered before being delivered to the aircraft. Figure 6.1 shows the diagrammatic layout of a typical tanker.

Hand loading of fertilisers and granules takes a long time and does not provide for screening of the material for lumps. Mechanical loaders are either specifically designed for the work, such as that shown in plate 6.1 or consist of a hopper mounted on a tractor or lorry, raised and lowered hydraulically with fore and aft movement provided by the driving of the vehicle. Using modern techniques the aircraft may be loaded in under a minute but care must be taken to avoid all risk of damage to aircraft

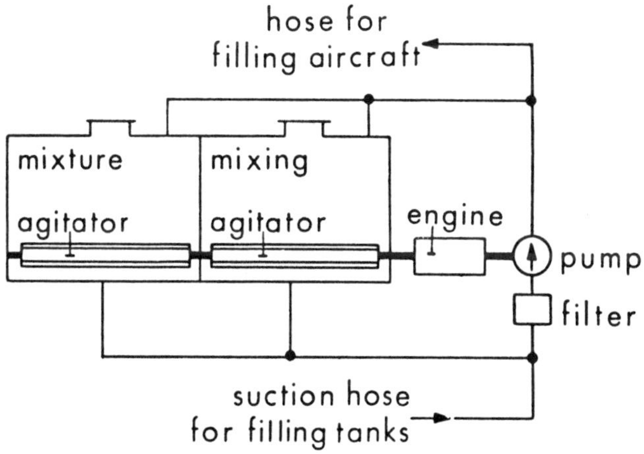

Fig 6.1 Diagrammatic layout of a typical ground tanking and mixing equipment

Plate 6.1 Mechanical loader specifically designed to load agricultural aircraft with fertiliser or granules (photo: Field Air, (Ballarat) Pty Ltd Australia)

through a collision caused by too much haste. The aircraft must not be taxied until the loading vehicle and personnel are clear.

A somewhat slower technique (usually used for a large multi-engined aircraft) employs an augur conveyor. A technique evolved in the U.S.A. using prepacked bags of material, of pre-determined volume, which are lifted over the hopper door and their load released into the hopper, may prove to be as quick as, and more economical than, existing methods.

Closed circuit pesticide transfer

Hand pouring of liquid pesticides, particularly the organophophorus concentrates, is potentially dangerous. In fact all pesticides should be handled with great care, as over a spraying season continued exposure even to very small splashes can lead to chronic poisoning (see chapter 4 on chemical safety aspects).

The state of California, U.S.A. (often the leader in safety legislation) ruled that, from 1 January 1977, hand pouring of liquid pesticides displaying the signal word 'danger' on the label shall be eliminated by the use of a closed mixing system. Soilserv Inc. U.S.A. were the first to receive state approval of their 'negative pressure system'. The chemical is sucked from drums into the measuring device rather than being pushed or pumped, as with a positive pressure system. A key element of the system is a control panel-board mounted on the basic unit. Values

Plate 6.2 Closed circuit pesticide transfer system in operation; this example is by Soilserv Inc. (photo: Soilserv Inc.)

on the board are colour coded to correspond with the various chemical containers used. Chemicals are taken from various sized containers up to 200 l drums through a device known as a 'multiprobe'. There is little chance of the hoses rupturing or cracking but, should this occur, the system shuts down and no chemical is transferred, only air.

Closed circuit systems are recommended for all liquid pesticides as not only a safety precaution in the long-term handling of pesticides and accidental contact, but in the interest of an environmentally clean and safe operation. Remember that adjuvants can cause skin irritations and distress even if the active material is relatively safe. Another closed circuit system is manufactured by Mid-Continent Aircraft Corp., U.S.A. Their system is called a chemical induction system, again meeting the stringent requirements of the state of California.

Safety equipment at the airstrip

There should at all times be a vehicle at the airstrip for emergency rescue should an accident happen on the airstrip or nearby. All ground crew personnel should be able to drive the designated vehicle and know how to use safety equipment which includes the location and operation of the fire extinguisher carried on the aircraft. Safety equipment should be kept in lockers on the vehicle which can be securely locked when not on stand-by. When operations are in progress, the lockers are unlocked but should not fly open when the vehicle is driven over rough ground.

Fire extinguishers There should be a small hand-operated extinguisher in the aircraft accessible to the pilot and accessible from the outside. There should be not less than two extinguishers on at the airstrip – one large capacity foam, and a regulated control extinguisher for small fires.

First aid kits There should be one small kit mounted in the aircraft with a notice indicating clearly its location, and one co-located with the fire existinguishers at the airstrip.

Crash equipment There should be a crash axe (approved design), crow-bar, bolt cutters and asbestos gloves (two pairs minimum) co-located with the fire extinguishers.

Washing facilities There should be washing facilities available, clean water and soap (a portable tent-shaped shower bath is compulsory in Italy).

List of telephone numbers of doctors, local hospitals, and local authorities e.g. police.

The above list is the *mandatory* minimum schedule. Contents of the first aid kit should contain at least the following items:

- Eye cup;
- Drinking glass;
- Flask of fresh water;
- 500 g salt;
- Large quantity of activated carbon in powder or tablet form;
- Large quantity of a demulcent, e.g., milk of magnesia or soluble starch;
- Atropine sulphate, in tablets or automatic self injectors;
- Blankets;
- Any special media necessary according to the nature of chemicals applied;
- Washing bowls/pails, clean fresh water;
- Towels;
- Soap;
- Sponges;
- Rubber gloves for the person treating the case;
- Spare clothing (clean overalls).

References

Mid-Continent Aircraft Corporation, Planemate Division, Drawer L, Hayti, Missouri 63851, U.S.A.

Soilserv Inc., P.O. Box 1817, Salinas, California 93901, U.S.A.

7
Operational flying and techniques

Introduction

Due to the fact that agricultural flying is generally executed at low level, the pilot has little time for his instruments and must rely mainly on his flying 'feel'. This chapter discusses a number of situations that may occur in low-level flight and tells the pilot how to foresee, recognise and avoid dangerous manoeuvres. In addition, a number of conditions are discussed that may be unfamiliar to light aeroplane pilots. Loading conditions are highly variable, requiring frequent retrimming in order to keep control forces approximately constant. The technique for take-off and landing on short fields and the influence of ambient temperature and field elevation on performance are reviewed. The main part of the chapter is devoted to the influence of wind, giving landing techniques in crosswinds, possible erroneous action in low-level turns with drift and the effect of wind gradient on aeroplane performance and amount of aileron required in a turn. The information given is mostly on a qualitative basis.

Flying for agricultural purposes differs in many ways from other commercial flights. Height is in general for the greater part of the flight very low, allowing very little room for error. Flying therefore requires the constant and utmost attention from the pilot. Because of the low level he has to concentrate mainly on the surroundings, leaving little time for the instruments, other than that required for occasional checks. Therefore a relaxed position and a highly developed feeling for flying are very important.

A second influence of the low level is the effect of wind and turbulence, which are much more noticeable near to the ground, especially the wind gradient, i.e. the change of wind speed with height above the ground. A further typical aspect of agricultural aviation is the highly variable loading conditions. Both weight and centre of gravity can vary considerably in a fairly short period of time, requiring constant adaptation on the part of the pilot.

Take-off surface

In typical operations the aeroplane is usually based at a temporary airstrip, the qualities of which are far short of a well-equipped air base. It will in general be on the small side. Usually a field length equal to three times the length of the take-off run will be adequate. The nature of the surface must be known, because a peat surface, for example, will increase the rolling resistance of the wheels and therefore also the take-off run. Some kinds of vegetation, such as tall grass, clover or alfalfa will have the same effect, as will a high moisture content of the soil. Furthermore it is important to know whether the chosen take-off surface has a gradient. To indicate wind direction and force, a wind sock should be situated in a suitable position. Adverse combinations like uphill gradient and tailwind should be avoided for take-off.

In the initial take-off the tail must be lifted off as soon as possible by pushing the control stick forward to avoid dragging the tail wheel, which otherwise could cause an appreciable resistance, especially at the rearward centre of gravity. As soon as some airspeed is attained the aeroplane should be brought in a somewhat nose-up attitude to enable the wing to relieve the weight from the wheels and so to decrease rolling resistance. On a take-off surface offering a higher rolling resistance the optimum attitude for minimum take-off run will be more nose-up. An extreme nose-up position however will cause drag and is therefore not advisable.

Some flap deflection will allow the pilot to fly the aeroplane off at a lower airspeed and therefore it requires a shorter field length. Some pilots do not deflect the flap until just before lift-off speed is attained, in an effort to minimise air drag during the take-off run. The reduction in drag at the lower airspeeds is not worthwhile though, as the action distracts the pilot during a critical phase of the take-off, and it is not recommended.

Sometimes it is convenient to land downwind. Even though the aeroplane is considerably lighter at landing than at take-off and also more manoeuvrable, a distinct danger exists of executing a ground loop especially as the aeroplane controls are not very effective in a downwind landing as soon as the airspeed has dropped and while the groundspeed is still high. Brakes must be used with care under all conditions but especially in humid weather as clover and alfalfa are very slippery when wet.

Loading

In loading the aeroplane, both the amount and the position of the load are important. A heavily loaded aeroplane requires a longer take-off run because the mass to be accelerated is greater, the rolling resistance of the wheels is increased and the minimum flying speed is higher. Because the aeroplane is also sluggish when manoeuvring and has little performance margin when heavily loaded, it is advisable to delay spraying small fields until a greater part of the load has been applied.

If the hopper is situated behind the pilot, the centre of gravity will be rearward at full load, requiring a forward control stick position to maintain longitudinal equilibrium. The pilot will have to exert a push force on the stick, which in many cases can be reduced or sometimes entirely eliminated by proper use of the elevator trim control. If the stick force cannot be reduced to zero the pilot must take care not to relax pressure on the stick because of the danger of inadvertently stalling the aeroplane.

An extreme rearward centre of gravity position is undesirable because the stability of the aeroplane will be marginal. This results in the variation of stick force with airspeed being very small – or even adverse – which makes the pilot's job very difficult because he has no clear indication of airspeed from his stick force. (Also recovery from inadvertent spins will be more difficult.)

As spraying progresses, the centre of gravity will gradually move forward, requiring a more rearward stick position and a pulling force on the stick to prevent the aeroplane from diving into the ground. It is desirable to retrim frequently to reduce this stick force to zero.

Cockpit drills and vital actions

The need for cockpit drills and vital actions is not lessened by the fact that a take off and landing is being made every four or five minutes. On the contrary, fatigue, monotony and the attitude that 'it's been going all right for hours, no need to check' have resulted in many accidents, arising from such things as attempting to take off with the fuel incorrectly selected, which would never have occurred if the pilot had got into the habit of performing simple routine checks. There is always time to perform these vital actions: in fact, the time involved in their performance is negligible once they become, as they must, as habitual and natural as opening the throttle for take off.

Taxying

The need for care when taxying assumes even greater importance than usual in the confined area of an agricultural airstrip. Remember that the aircraft takes longer to stop if the brakes are applied when travelling downhill; also the additional power required to maintain a given speed uphill may increase the tendency for some aircraft with conventional undercarriage to nose over if the brakes are applied hard. When taxying across the slope the same aircraft will have a tendency to turn uphill as the tail wheel tries to run downhill.

With aircraft having tricycle undercarriage, care must be taken to avoid taxying over loose stony surfaces at high r.p.m. Considerable damage to propellers can be caused by flying stones The practice of carrying out very rapid, tight turns on the ground, at high r.p.m. imposes excessive gyroscopic loads on the propeller, and is considered to have been a factor in the subsequent fatigue failure of several propellers in flight. Turns on the ground should be made slowly, with a large radius and with the lowest necessary r.p.m.

As a general rule, never taxy on any part of an airstrip unless you are absolutely sure that it is safe to do so – if necessary, make sure by walking or driving a vehicle over the area. Taxying should be done over a known route and at a speed adapted to terrain roughness. Lowering the tyre pressure may alleviate the worst bumps, (unless the aircraft has low-pressure tyres fitted, then the pressure is set in the operations manual). Taxying accidents are the most unnecessary of all types. They are so easily prevented by a little care and good airmanship.

Plate 7.1 Cresco Turboprop agricultural aircraft (photo: New Zealand Aerospace Industries Ltd)

Turns

Normally turns will not be executed until after the aeroplane has pulled away from the ground to give more room for manoeuvring. Care must be taken that the airspeed is not allowed to drop too much during the pull-up as in the following turn the stalling speed of the aeroplane will be higher due to the increased lift demanded from the wings to counteract the centrifugal force in the turn. We will now look closer at the aerodynamic principles involved in turning the aeroplane.

To make an aeroplane turn, a force must be applied towards the centre of the turn required. To impose this force on an aeroplane, the total air reaction must be inclined from the vertical towards the centre of the desired turn so that its horizontal component provides just enough force to make the aeroplane turn and keep it turning. This force is known as the 'centripetal force'. In a correctly balanced turn, the inclination of the reaction is produced by banking the aeroplane as shown in fig 7.1, where OW represents the weight of the aeroplane, and OL the lift it develops. The lift component is of course vertical in straight and level flight, but now is inclined to the vertical at the angle of bank. The vertical component OA of OL balances the weight of the aeroplane, while the horizontal component OC of OL provides the necessary centripetal force.

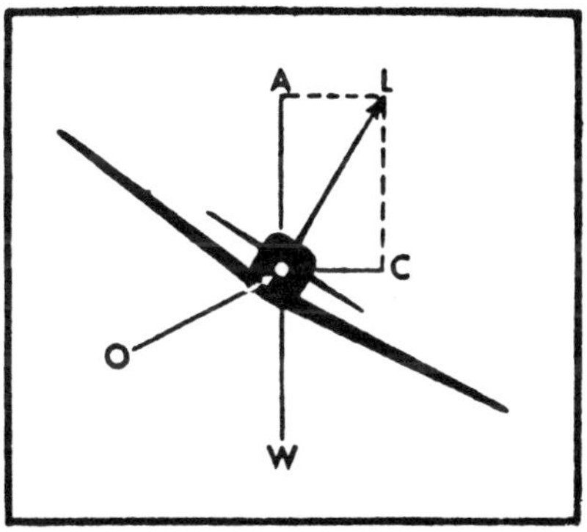

Fig 7.1 The correctly co-ordinated turn (I.C.A.O. 1968)

As the bank is increased, so must the total lift produced by the wings be increased to maintain height, and this increase in lift will also cause an increase in the stalling speed. One of the essential facts of flight that should always be in the forefront of the pilot's mind is *the stalling speed increases in a turn.* The increase follows a simple mathematical rule: it increases as the square root of the load factor, the factor by which the lift increases in a turn compared to the lift required for straight and level flight. This is illustrated in fig. 7.2. In C, with 60° of bank, the wings are producing twice as much lift as they were at A in straight and level flight. The stalling speed in straight and level flight is 60 kts (in this example), so with 60° of bank, the stalling speed will be:

$$60 \times \sqrt{2}$$
$$= 60 \times 1.414$$
$$= 85 \text{ kts}$$

Notice that in E of fig 7.2 with a load factor of 3.86, i.e. with the wings producing nearly four times as much lift as in straight and level flight, the stalling speed is nearly double its basic value, and as the angle of bank steepens further, the rate at which the stalling speed increases in a balanced turn rises very rapidly. At 80° of bank it would be 144 kts, at 81° it would have risen to 162 kts! An obvious point to remember from this is that an aircraft flying at low speed can tolerate only a relatively small angle of bank before the onset of a stall.

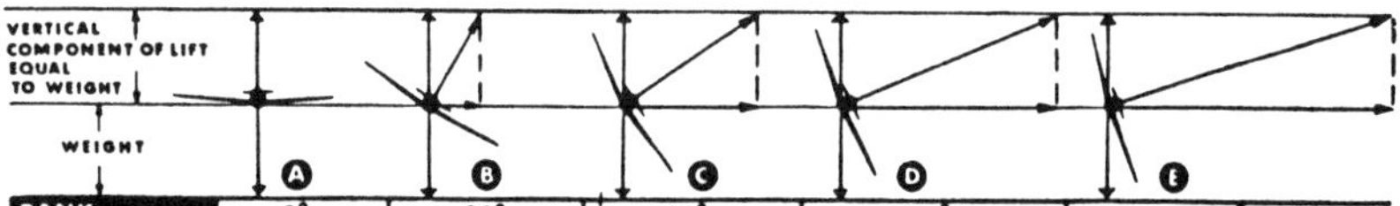

BANK	0°	30°	60°	70°	75°
LOAD FACTOR	1·0	1·15	2	2·9	3·86
STALLING SPEED	60 knots	64 knots	85 knots	102 knots	118 knots

Fig 7.2 Stalling speed as a function of angle of bank (I.C.A.O. 1968)

The danger of losing control increases if the aircraft should drop a wing while flying close to the stall with wings at a large angle of attack, as represented by the point X on the lift curve in fig 7.3. As the wing drops, the angle of attack of the down-going wing is increased, while that of the up-going wing is decreased, as shown in fig. 7.4. The result is that the aerodynamic condition of the up-going wing has come back to the point Z on the lift curve, while that of the down-going wing has moved past the stall to the point Y. Note that the up-going wing is now producing more lift than the down-going wing. The loss of lift on the down-going wing, together with its increase in drag, provide the elements necessary for *auto-rotation* and either a spin or a steep spiral dive may result.

Steep turns

An additional hazard is always present during a steep turn if the pilot's

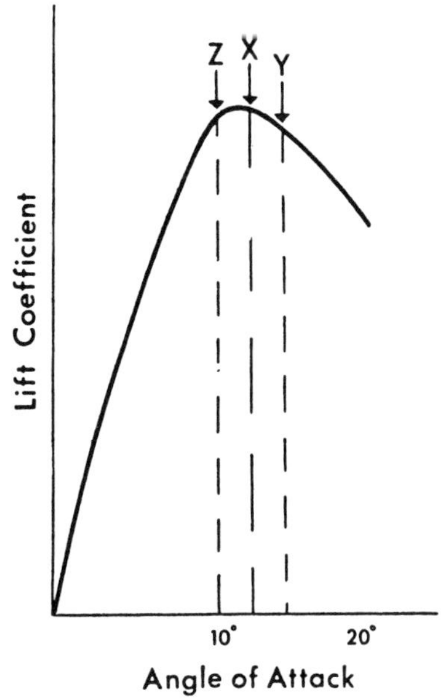

Fig 7.3 Coefficient of lift as a function of angle of bank (I.C.A.O. 1968)

attention is distracted. Because of the inherent directional stability of the majority of light aircraft, the nose will always tend to drop towards the lower wing. If this happens without being checked, the aircraft will enter a spiral dive, with an ensuing loss of height. To recover, if control is lost such as during a poorly executed steep turn, depends on whether the aircraft has been permitted to approach the stall or whether it has entered a spiral dive. If the onset of the stall is detected, for example, from the stall-warning horn or light, or from the sloppy feel in the

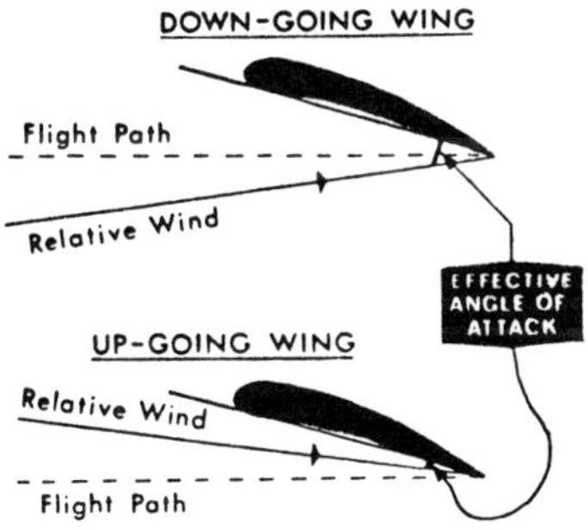

Fig 7.4 The elements of auto-rotation (I.C.A.O. 1968)

controls, or from airframe buffeting, the control column should be moved forward, full power applied, and the wings levelled. Because the recovery from a normal correctly executed steep turn requires the use of considerable top rudder, it follows that, if the aircraft is in a steep turn when a stall becomes imminent, levelling the wings will require co-ordinated use of rudder as well as ailerons. The application of power assists the recovery action by increasing the airflow over the wing and tail surfaces, thus decreasing the stalling speed and increasing the response of both rudder and elevator control. The use of power also has the beneficial effect of helping to accelerate the aircraft to a higher speed away from the stall, so decreasing the angle of attack of the wings.

The correct recovery action to be taken when the aircraft has been allowed to enter a sprial dive near the ground is a little different. Initially, power should be reduced to prevent the spiral 'tightening', the wings should be levelled, again with co-ordinated rudder and aileron, and the aircraft than eased out of the dive. At this point, especially if the airspeed is low, re-application of full power can aid recovery, as with the recovery from the stall, by improving control response and by enabling the aircraft to climb immediately.

All too frequently, throughout the history of aviation, pilots have found themselves in trouble when their attention has been divided between flying their aircraft and looking at something on the ground, or when they have been possessed by an irresistible spur of the moment urge to demonstrate their flying ability to lesser mortals watching from below!

The modern light aeroplane is usually very docile to handle in normal flight, even at the stall, but like its ancestors, it can still become a killer if control is lost during a turn at low altitude when the steep attitudes attained may make recovery impossible in the height available.

Common faults in turns

There are three ways to fly a turn of which the best is the normally co-ordinated turn, where rudder and aileron are so co-ordinated as to keep the slip indicator in its central position. If the pilot is sufficiently relaxed and comfortably seated, he will not need instruments; he will feel any lateral forces resulting from badly executed turns by 'the seat of his pants'. A skidding turn, see fig 7.5, results from too much rudder into the turn (bottom rudder), or too much counter aileron during the steady turn. The slip indicator will deflect towards the high wing, and likewise the pilot will feel himself slide out of the turn, if he has relaxed enough. In an open cockpit he will have an additional warning in that the wind will strike him from the high wing. Because of the aileron

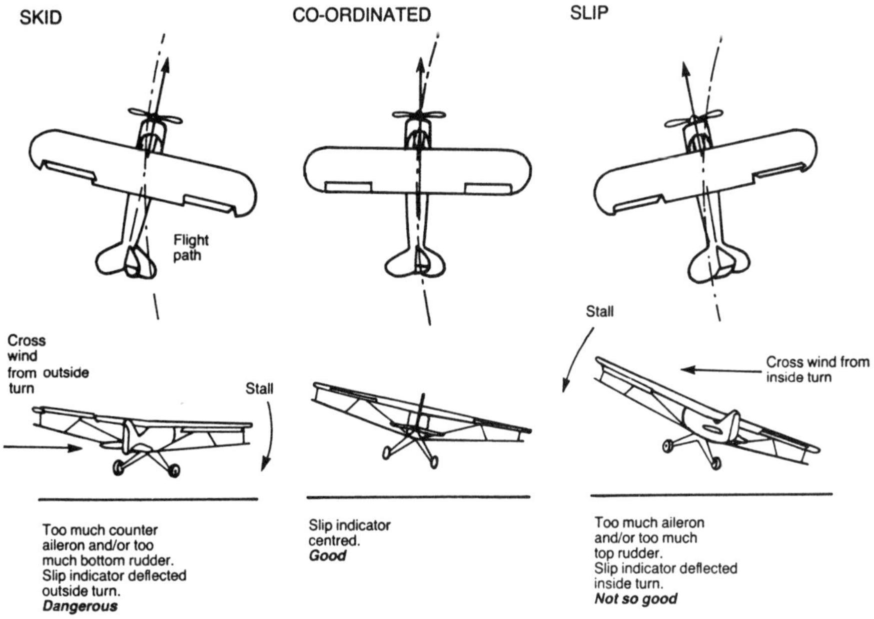

Fig 7.5 Faults in turns (Lucassen, 1959)

position in this type of turn the low wing will drop first in an inadvertant stall, causing the aeroplane to 'spin under'.

A slip results from too much bank or some counter-rudder ('top-rudder'). The slip indicator will deflect towards the low wing, the pilot will slide in the same direction and the relative wind will strike him from the low wing. In an advertant stall the high wing will drop first, causing 'spin over the top'.

In both cases of badly executed turns the airflow, having a lateral component relative to the fuselage, increases the air drag and therefore decreases the aeroplane performance, in extreme cases slowing it down to a stall. In general there will be little inclination on the part of the pilot to bank steeply close to the ground and therefore the skidding turn is the more likely of the two to happen.

Usually there will be little time to correct an improperly executed turn. It is very important, though, to know what manoeuvres can be dangerous and why. A most useful instrument is the stall indicator. This instrument is sensitive to the angle of attack of the wing and gives warning of an incipient stall independent from loading conditions or manoeuvres. It is therefore easier to interpret than the air speed indicator, because stalling air speed increases with aeroplane weight and steepness of bank. A recommended setting for the stall warning to start is 2 kts above the stalling speed in level flight with closed throttle. The transmitter part of the instrument must be situated outside of the propeller slipstream and care must be taken that it does not get contaminated with spraying fluid.

Acceleration

A fatigue factor which is probably less self-evident than most is *radial accelerative force,* or ***g**-force.* Quite apart from any aerodynamic considerations, it is undesirable to 'pull' more **g** than necessary in the end-of-swath turn. Certainly, a higher rate of turn may bring the pilot back on to his next run a few seconds sooner. But its penalty is increased fatigue. The mechanism of fatigue production by **g**-forces is not fully understood, but the effect is well recognised in military aviation, especially in low-level operations. Lower-rate, wider turns constitute intelligent flying in the average agricultural situation. Radical **g**-force is also important in agricultural flying because it can cause sudden disorientation if the head is moved rapidly while in a tight turn or pull-out from a dive.

The prime cause of at least two New Zealand agricultural accidents is reported to have been disorientation of the pilot when he suddenly looked downwards and to one side into the cockpit while in a tight turn. Pilots should train themselves against making rapid head movements while in tight turns. People responsible for cockpit design or modification can assist by making sure that emergency controls such as dump levers are so placed that large angular movement of the pilot's head from the normal position is not necessary.

Atmospheric influences

Temperature

A high air temperature results in a lower air density and, therefore, because of the lower mass flow through the engine, in a lower engine power. This is not apparent from the normal full power check on the engine, as the power required to turn the propeller is also less in this less dense atmosphere. Therefore there will be scarcely any r.p.m. drop, relative to an engine check on a cold day when the power is high. The lower power will be noticeable in the take off, because a longer run is required. A second reason for this longer take-off run is the higher true air speed that is required at low air density to develop the same aerodynamic forces for supporting the aeroplane. Therefore at the same lift-off speed as read from the air speed indicator ('indicated air speed'), which is sensitive to impact pressure, the true speed will be higher.

Barometric pressure

A lower barometric presure has the same effect as a high air temperature as discussed above. In general the day-to-day variations of barometric pressure are not worthwhile bothering with as far as the influence on true air speed is concerned. On a high-altitude airfield, however, the reduction in barometric pressure is significant and it will result in longer take-off runs. When – as often is the case – the air temperature is high as well, the combined effect may result in a reduction of the allowable load in order to maintain the safety margin.

Wind direction and force.

In order to discuss the effect of wind it is first assumed that wind direction and force are essentially constant. The effects of wind gradient and gusts will be discussed later. Of course both wind direction and force may vary greatly from place to place and in the course of the day, therefore the pilot should always make sure about local wind conditions.

In rectilinear level flight, the only effect of wind is to make the aeroplane drift. This can be especially difficult in take off and landing with crosswind. While headwind has a beneficial influence on the ground run required, a take off in 90° crosswind will require more than the zero wind ground run because of the increased air drag resulting from control deflections that are necessary to keep a straight heading.

If the direction of spraying can be chosen it is preferable to fly at right angles to the wind direction and to work upwind for every spraying pass. In this way groundspeed will be equal in both directions, and the pilot will not be flying through his own spray. It is more usual, however, that the shape of the field dictates the spraying method.

In landing it is very important to avoid a lateral displacement at the moment of ground contact, because of possible damage to the landing gear and possibility of a ground loop. There are two ways to avoid this, the first being a final approach heading into the intended direction of landing but slipping into the wind with the upwind wing low, the second being to approach the landing field heading into the wind to such an extent that the aeroplane travels in the intended direction of landing (fig. 7.6). Just before touch-down the aeroplane must be levelled out, and at the same time straightened out to avoid either landing on one wheel or lateral forces being applied to the landing gear.

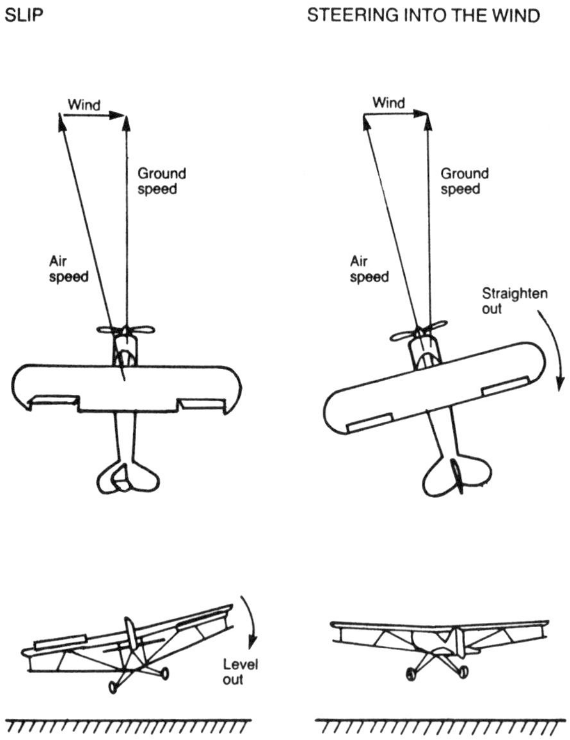

Fig 7.6 Landing with crosswind (Lucassen, 1959)

In a slipping approach the rate of descent is higher because of the increased drag; also because of the unfavourable airflow, the stalling speed is higher. During the approach rather larger control deflections are required but the touchdown is easier than in the second case, which calls for good judgement of the amount of rudder required for straightening out. In practice, a combination of both methods is used with an approach heading into wind and some slip shortly before touchdown.

Turns in wind

The case of a well-co-ordinated 90° turn from 90° crosswind will be examined. Turning away from the wind, fig. 7.7 shows that the groundspeed of the aeroplane increases while the wind drift gives the pilot the impression that the aeroplane is slipping into the turn. Therefore the pilot will have the erroneous inclination to counteract this apparent high speed and slip by pulling up and either giving some counter aileron deflection, or more bottom rudder. If he does this, however, the aeroplane will in effect start skidding, which is apparent from the slip indicator deflecting towards the high wing. Also the pilot will feel himself sliding that way. In fact a rather dangerous situation occurs in which the aeroplanc is skidding with too little airspeed resulting from the erroneous pull-up manoeuvre, leading to 'insipient spin under' in the extreme case. Therefore the pilot must ignore the visual impression he gets of the movement of the aeroplane by watching the ground and he should fly by 'feel'.

The opposite happens in a turn into the wind. The pilot will have the erroneous visual impression that the aeroplane slows down and is skidding out of the turn. He must resist the temptation to correct this apparent condition by pushing the nose down and either applying more aileron or some top rudder. Although the resulting conditions of high airspeed and slip are not dangerous, the co-ordinated turn will always enable the pilot to extract the maximum performance out of his aeroplane.

If the turns are executed at very low height, there will be some influence of the wind gradient; this will be discussed later. There is a rather widespread misconception that turning into the wind will enable the pilot to convert some of his kinetic energy into extra height, as the aeroplane apparently slows down, relative to the ground. Equally it is sometimes thought that it is necessary before turning away from the wind to sacrifice some height in order to pick up the apparent extra speed needed. In fact it is only the speed of the aeroplane relative to the ambient air surrounding it that matters. Therefore, if the wind speed

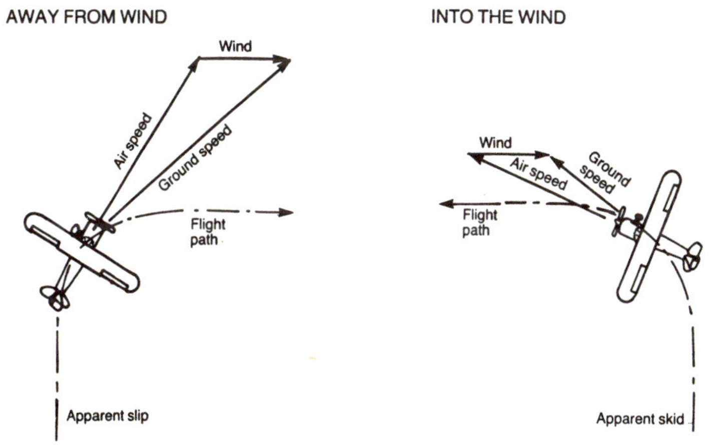

Fig 7.7 Turns away from the wind and into wind (Lucassen 1959)

is constant at the level of flight, the aeroplane will execute steady turns at constant airspeed and constant control settings while the groundspeed is varying widely without the pilot noticing provided he does not look at the ground. In hilly terrain, though, a level turn will take the aeroplane to different heights above the ground and in this case the effect of wind gradient will be noticeable.

Wind gradient

Generally the wind speed alters with the height above the ground, as is shown in fig. 7.8. The reason is that the airflow is slowed down near to the gound to essentially zero at ground level. This effect of wind gradient is most noticeable at heights below about 50 ft, and therefore it has to be reckoned with in agricultural aviation.

In a take-off into a head-wind, the aeroplane will rise into subsequent layers of air where the wind speed is higher. As the aeroplane carries its momentum while climbing, its airspeed will gradually rise. Conversely if the airspeed is kept constant by the pilot the rate of climb will be higher in head-wind than in still air because this increase in airspeed may be converted into extra height. So far everything is fine, but if after take-off a turn is initiated into downwind the aeroplane will be losing airspeed while climbing, because of passing into faster layers of wind with too low a momentum of its own. Because in turning downwind the groundspeed will increase (fig. 7.9), the pilot will have the erroneous inclination to pull up, which combined with the effect of wind

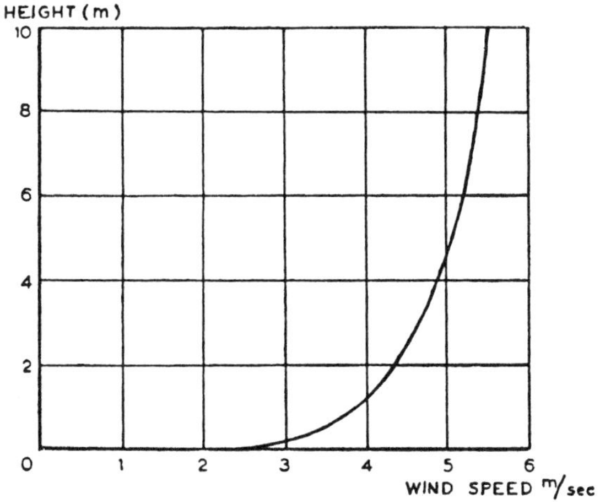

Fig 7.8 Variation of wind with height (wind gradient)

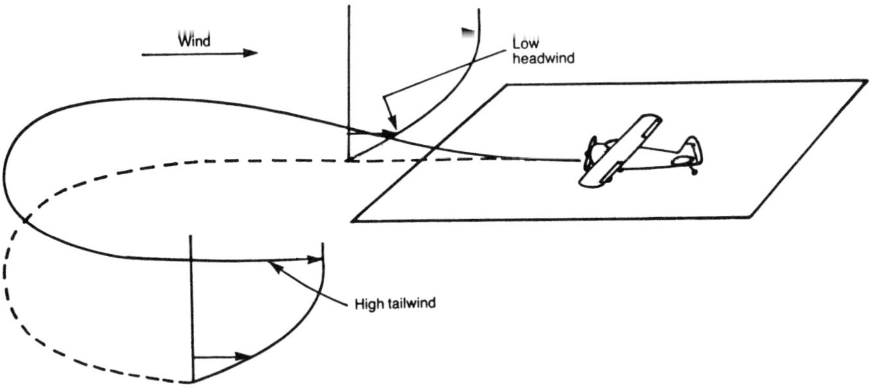

Fig 7.9 Take-off in a wind gradient (after Lucassen, 1959)

gradient may lead him into a stall. Therefore the airspeed must be *watched carefully* when turning downwind after take-off.

When flying horizontally *into wind* with a gradient, the aeroplane will be unstable with regard to flying altitude, because a disturbance upwards will carry it into a layer with greater wind speed, which increases the wing lift and therefore carries the aeroplane further upwards, increasing the disturbance. Likewise a disturbance downwards will result in loss of lift and a more pronounced descent (fig. 7.10). On the other hand flying horizontally *with the wind* will render the aeroplane altitude stable, as now an increase in altitude will carry the aeroplane in a region with more tailwind, cancelling the disturbance, due to loss of airspeed and wing lift.

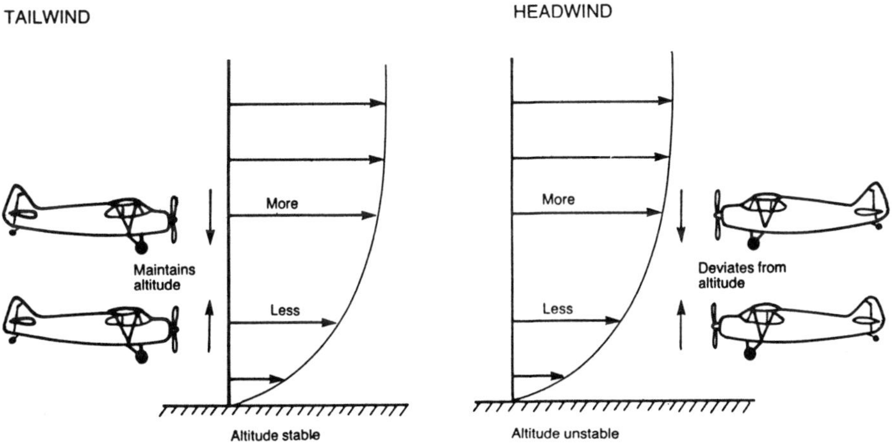

Fig 7.10 Level flight in a wind with a gradient (Lucassen, 1959)

The effect of wind gradient in climb has been pointed out at the beginning of this section. It must specifically be noted that the rate of climb at constant airspeed will be reduced when flying downwind. In the glide the rate of descent will be high flying *into wind* and low when flying *downwind*; this effect must be taken into account when approaching for a landing.

When turning at very low altitude the high wing will move through layers with a higher wind speed, reducing the airspeed over the wing when flying downwind and increasing it flying upwind. In the first case, a turn away from the wind, more aileron deflection will be needed to execute the turn, increasing the danger of stalling the high wing, which would cause spin over top. Because the wind gradient tends to flatten the turn if the pilot does not act, its effect is stabilising in roll.

When turning into the wind the opposite is the case: the pilot has to apply more counter aileron to prevent the angle of bank from steepening (fig. 7.11). In fig. 7.12 a summary of the wind influence is given. It appears that the adverse effects of wind and wind gradient on the required aileron deflection do not occur simultaneously in turns, but the combination of altitude and roll instability does occur when turning into wind. The most awkward situation results from turning down wind.

Gusts and turbulence

In general, gusts occur both in vertical and in horizontal directions. They are mostly caused by the wind striking large or small obstacles, or flowing over terrain with different vegetation and therefore different temperatures under the influence of the heat of the sun. Strong tur-

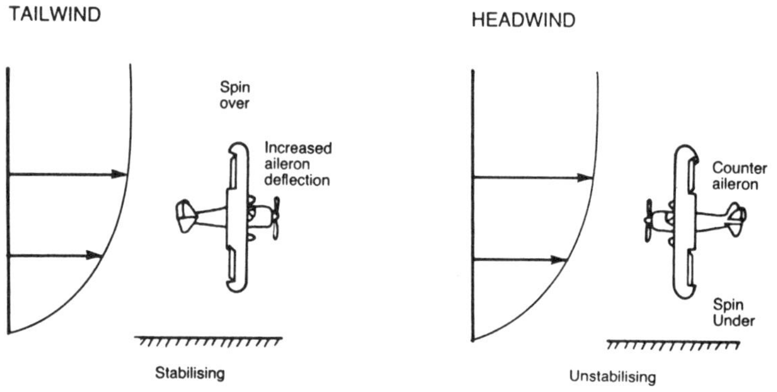

Fig 7.11 Turns in a wind with a gradient (Lucassen, 1959)

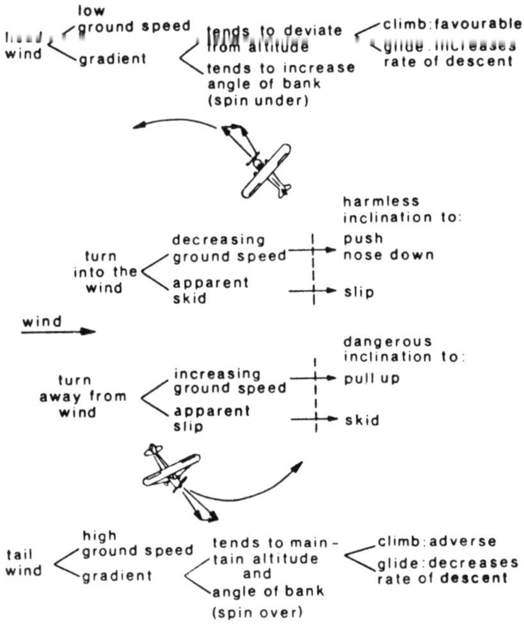

Fig 7.12 Summary of wind influence on turns (after Lucassen, 1959)

bulence often occurs downwind from a range of trees or other barriers (see chapter 9). In the event of strong downdraughts forming, they may severely affect the rate of climb.

There is an optimum airspeed in rough air. Too low is dangerous because of the possibility of a stall in an up-gust. Too high is uncomfortable because the gust loading increases, and may in extreme cases overload the aircraft (see chapter 1). Wind gusts in the direction of flight can have the same effect, while lateral gusts tend to throw the aircraft off course.

Obstructions

For the most part, obstructions other than wires can be fairly easily seen. One notable exception is dead trees and dead branches of an otherwise green tree. Another is the obstruction – perhaps a pole or tree stump – exactly lined up, along your line of flight, with a more distant object whose range is either known, by reason of its position relative to a major feature (e.g. one post of the boundary fence) or can be fairly accurately assessed because of its known size (e.g. building or large tree). If you allow your eyes to remain focussed on the obvious distant object it will effectively camouflage the nearer one.

A careful inspection prior to commencing treatment will locate each individual obstruction, and if you know where to look the least conspicuous object becomes more readily visible. Once seen, avoidance of an obstacle becomes a matter of concentration, alertness and judgement – and you will impress nobody by cutting it so fine that it looks more like luck than judgement. The wire strike hazard is treated in greater detail later in this chapter.

Plate 7.2 Cessna Agwagon 300; the pilot has as excellent field of view forward and downwards (photo: Cessna Aircraft Co.)

Most operations are at a height of less than 15 ft (5 m) and this means that the pilot regularly encounters trees, wires, etc., standing a good deal higher than the aircraft's height above the ground. These must be negotiated safely, but at the same time the correct operating height must be reached quickly and held as long as possible, and the airspeed during the run must be constant, or uneven application may result. The sequences of action will now be considered. Note that in gusty conditions extra margins of height and speed should be left.

Descending over an obstacle to commence run (see fig. 7.13)

At 1, approach at a low but fully controllable speed in level flight, a few feet above the obstacle. If flap is used for this manoeuvre it is assumed that the same flap setting will be used throughout the spray

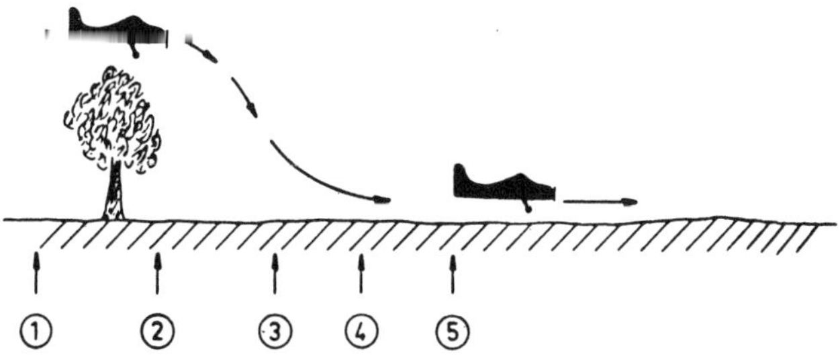

Fig 7.13 Descending over an obstacle

run. If flap would not be used for the spray run then it should not be used over the obstacle, because the subsequent retraction will present a hazard to the pilot flying at the spray height.

At 2, lower the nose, simultaneously reducing power to prevent a speed increase. At 3, while rounding out, give if necessary a burst of power to check the rate of sink. Remember that particularly with a load on board the aircraft may tend to continue sinking even after it has reached a level atitude, in which case the angle of attack will be high and there will also be a danger of stalling. Allow for this by rounding out soon enough. The power required may be considerable; anticipate it slightly, and make a smooth movement of the throttle. The danger to be avoided is that of letting the wheels touch the crop, which could have sufficient drag to stop the aircraft.

At 4, settle quickly down to the correct height and speed. The power applied in 3 may be excessive for level flight; adjust it. At 5, operate the spray control.

Climbing over an obstacle at the end of run (see fig. 7.14)

This can be done by utilising the excess energy to zoom over the obstacle. However it is only by experience of the aircraft type that the

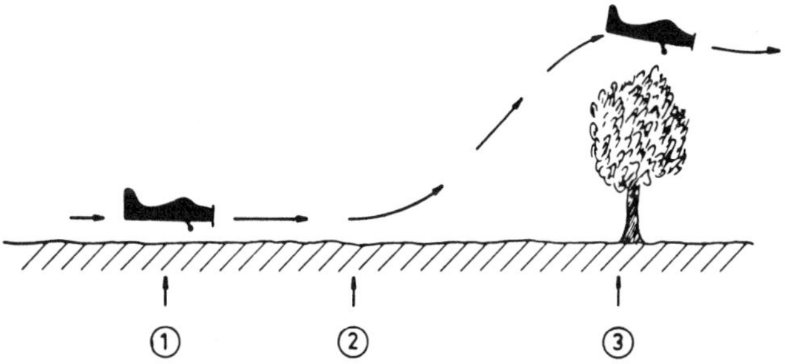

Fig 7.14 Climbing over an obstacle

pilot can judge how large an obstacle can be tackled in this way at ranging all-up weights. The application of full power and the commencing of the climb must be made in ample time, and once clear the nose must be held down until speed lost during the climb has been regained.

At 1, apply full power in plenty of time – about 200 m before the end of the run. At 2, shut off the spray and then pull the nose smoothly up into a climb. At 3, level out immediately the obstacle has been cleared; maintain flying speed by keeping the nose down as long as is necessary.

Note that when the obstacle concerned is a dwelling-house, runs must be made in the opposite direction, so as to descend over it; this avoids the necessity of flying towards the house at low level, with, in case of misjudgement or engine failure, the chance of hitting the house.

Flying parallel with a line-obstacle

The most difficult part here is to judge the distance of the wingtip from the obstacle; accurate judgement comes only with experience, and in the meantime the pilot must of course maintain a safe clearance. In most jobs it will be necessary to place the spray or dust as close as possible to the obstacle – sometimes even to place the chemical beneath the overhanging branches of trees. This can partly be done by relying on the way in which the wingtip vortices spread the chemical out behind the aircraft – to an ultimate swath width of perhaps twice the wingspan or more. However this may not in itself produce an adequate dosage of chemical at the edge of the field. Wind can assist in drifting chemical into awkward places.

Gaps between obstacles

It is often useful to fly through gaps in, for instance, a row of trees. Take care to check for drift – otherwise at the last moment the wind may displace the aircraft from its intended path. See also that no electric wires cross the gap – their poles may be hidden by the trees.

Slopes, contours, undulations

Where the ground is mountainous or steeply undulating the important consideration is that the aircraft must never be placed in such a position that the gradient is greater than its rate of climb. It may be necessary to make all runs downhill. This wastes time where a number of runs have to be made to disperse one load, as the aircraft has to make a climbing circuit of the area before each run. A further disadvantage, with fixed output rate equipment such as used for spraying, is that the output rate will be reduced below the calibrated figure, since the aircraft's speed will be higher, or, if power is reduced, the output of the pump will be less owing to reduced slipstream, in the case of a wind driven pump, or reduced engine r.p.m. where the pump is engine-driven. This objection does not apply where the pilot has control over the hopper-door opening, as with dusting or fertilising installations.

It may be possible to depart from the normal application height at a point some way down the slope into a gully, returning to the correct height at a point on the up-slope the other side, from which the aircraft's performance will enable the remainder to be safely and correctly treated. The effectiveness of the treatment of the lowest part of the area may be impaired by this method and it is not particularly desirable where a high degree of accuracy is required, as in spraying.

An alternative method is to fly along the rising ground – sometimes referred to as 'contour flying', although the aircraft may not, in fact, be strictly following the contours because of the need to maintain a straight path. Since the materials dispersed tend to drift downhill, it is preferable to start this type of treatment at the bottom of the slope, each run being progressively further up, to avoid flying back through the drift. In addition to the obvious risk of contamination with toxic chemicals, this may also reduce visibility by obscuring the windscreen.

The pull-up and inital part of the procedure turn should be made towards the high ground if possible. In this way the aircraft will never be headed at a sharper angle than approximately 45° towards it. If it is done the other way, a sudden downdraught encountered while the aircraft is heading at right angles towards the high ground, in a tight turn, can leave it in an extremely dangerous position, unless the initial 45° turn is prolonged by a period of straight flight to enable a gentle turn onto the next run to be made.

'False horizon effect'

A pilot becomes accustomed to maintaining the nose of the aircraft in a given relation to the horizon to achieve the desired performance at a given weight and power setting. In hilly country it is possible for the ground ahead of the aircraft to be sloping upward without the pilot realising it. In effect, this displaces the horizon vertically upward. The nose/horizon relationship normally appropriate to straight and level may, under these circumstances, place the aircraft in a climbing attitude, with a corresponding loss of airspeed and manoeuvring performance. In the extreme case an unexpeced stall may result.

The approach to hilly country

This should always be made at an oblique angle so that a turn away can be quickly made if doubt arises as to whether the aircraft will outclimb it. Make sure that there is always an 'escape route' available if, for some reason, the aircraft performs less well than anticipated.

Dumping of the load

The need to dump a load may be precipitated by poor judgement, miscalculation, unexpected meteorological variations or a combination of these and other factors. This is an emergency procedure and is almost certain to present the pilot with the need for quick decision. It is important that the pilot should know the time and distance that will be covered by the aircraft before appreciably better performance of the aircraft will result from dumping. Although this will be demonstrated during training it will not be possible completely to simulate emergency conditions. Operationally, an additional margin should be allowed for possible failure of the aircraft to respond as expected after dumping.

The only safe rule is 'if in doubt, dump'. There will nearly always be an element of doubt as to whether it will be necessary to dump, but by the time the doubt is resolved, it may be too late – even if you get away with it, the margin will certainly be far too small.

Forced or crash landing areas

It is obviously impossible to plan every operation so as to remain within gliding distance of a suitable area. However, it should be kept in mind as a deciding factor when there are several possible alternative treatment plans. Pre-knowledge of the exact location of such areas may save those few vital seconds of indecision which can make the difference between a successful forced landing and an expensive prang.

Position of the sun

The glare from the rising or setting sun has been the cause of several accidents and is a real danger. Fortunately, in the early morning or late evening when this hazard is greatest, wind strength is usually at a minimum and the treatment can be so planned as to give consideration of this problem precedence over considerations of wind (fig. 7.15). The effect of glare is greatly magnified by a dirty or badly scratched windscreen. (See chapter 6, section on airframe cleanliness.)

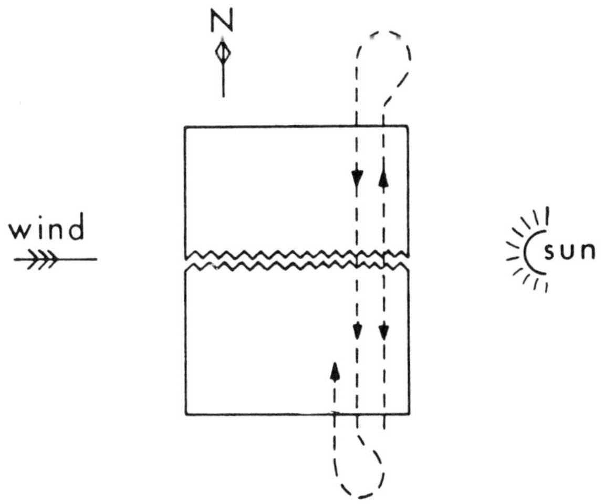

Fig 7.15 Do climbing turns towards the sun (if necessary) and descending turns away from the sun; beware of glare if any dirt (pesticide) is on the windscreen

Approach and landing

Up to date information on the condition of an airstrip should be obtained before a landing is attempted. However, *it is very unwise to accept information from a person unfamiliar with aviation.* A very careful pre-landing inspection should be carried out. It is not feasible to lay down a procedure that can be followed in each case but the following principles should be kept in mind:

(1) Inspect the strip and surrounding area from a height sufficient to clear all possible obstacles. Check the strip for obstructions, noting particularly whether there are any animals in the same field and their reaction to the noise of the aircraft.
(2) Confirm wind velocity if possible.
(3) Check strip surface condition from low altitude. Decide landing direction. (Don't come below possible power line height until certain all wires in the vicinity have been noted. Remember that, in undulating country, there may be wires spanning the gullies at a considerable height.)
(4) Make dummy approach to assess wind gradient, approach and overshoot areas. On 'one way' hill strips there will be a point on the approach after which a go-round should not be attempted. Assess where this point occurs.
(5) During inspection, speed should be low enough to allow time for assimilation of all ground features – but maintain an adequate

margin of speed and control for any sudden evasive action. Use flap and power intelligently and as recommended for the aircraft type.

(6) Having decided to land, *do not drag it in low and slow* – the wind gradient may get you. Also there could be a power line some way out in the approach area which you've either failed to see or decided, rightly, would be no hazard to a normal approach. So make a normal approach, aiming to touch down in the first 50 m.

(7) Don't stand on the brakes if the gound is wet. A locked wheel has no sense of direction – and very little braking effect.

Take-off and landing on steep slopes

Very good acceleration can be obtained by taking off down a steep hill, and the run required will be extremely short. There are no special difficulties attached to this. Landing requires care; the three-point attitude for touch down is considerably steeper than in a normal landing and the round-out must be prolonged by using power to bring the nose right up to the required postition without a premature stall. After a little practice on gentle slopes, pilots will find that quite steep slopes can be tackled; however it is inadvisable to stop the aircraft on a steep slope, or to allow it to run in any direction except directly up or down the slope, and loading must be done in a reasonably level area.

The procedure turn-around

The operational flight manoeuvre which causes more problems to application pilots than any other is the procedure turn-around at the end of the swath run. There are numerous misconceptions about the turn-around, like 'how it should be done', and the time it takes to complete. It may be well to state that the procedure turn-around is a necessary event which has boundary limits which the application pilot dare not violate (Galipault, 1966).

Essentially there are two methods: the classic procedure turn (fig. 7.16) (sometimes called the standard procedure turn), and the 'round robin' procedure turn. The classic procedure turn is the more normal method where the pilot either uses natural or artificial markers, or a minimum of two human markers. For the round robin method, an additional two human markers are needed, or a more sophisticated fixed marking system or, indeed, electronic track guidance. The round robin is a quicker method of reversing the aircraft track.

The classic procedure turn is now analysed. The incorrect turn illustrated in fig. 7.17 shows that it is obviously desirable, in nil wind con-

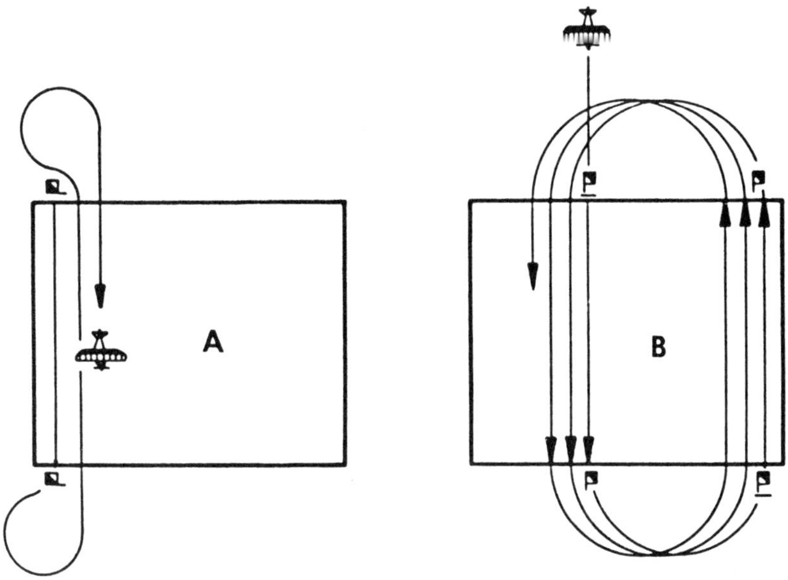

Fig. 7.16 Procedures for reversing the aircraft track: A, the 'classic' procedure turn; (B) the 'round robin' procedure turn (F.A.O. 1972)

ditions, to make the initial turn away from the direction of progress across the treatment area. This will reduce the distance by which the aircraft must be offset in order to be able to make a safe rate of turn back onto the next run, and will therefore reduce the time spent in the procedure turn. The initial pull-up (a to b) should be made with the wings level, to avoid the possibility of striking an obstacle – or even the ground – with the downgoing wing. From b to c the climb is maintained and the aircraft turned through approximately 45°. At c a level turn is commenced in the opposite direction, the aircraft rolling out of the turn at d. From d a straight descent is made to start the next run at e.

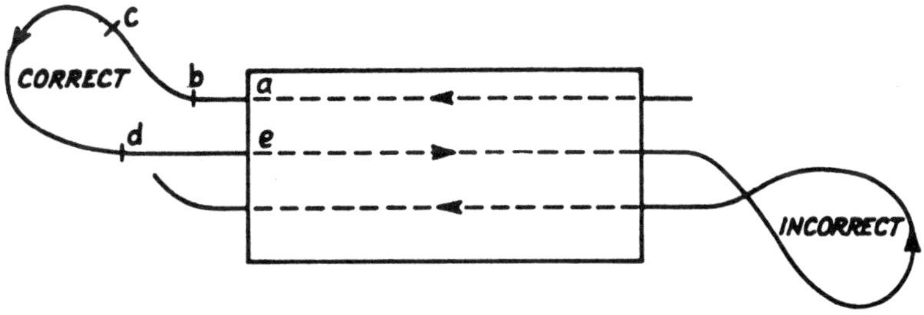

Fig 7.17 The classic procedure turn – correct and incorrect procedures

During this descent power is adjusted as necessary to achieve the desired applicating speed at the beginning of the turn.

Additional power may be required for the pull-up and/or the turn itself, depending on height of obstructions, load remaining, aircraft type, etc. If power is to be added for the pull-up, the best sequence is to apply power first, then cut off the spray/dust and initiate the pull-up. In some aircraft, partial flap may be used to decrease the radius of turn (from c to d) if required. In general, it is highly doubtful if the few extra seconds which can be saved by pulling the turn as tight as possible, are worth the price which must be paid in terms of reduced safety margin, increased physical effect, the cumulative fatigue induced by constant *g* loadings and reduced engine life resulting from continual applications of high power.

The initial turn should be made down wind as shown in fig. 7.18 (a) to take advantage of the drift assistance in off-setting the aircraft to the point from which the reversal of turn can be made. Fig. 7.18 (b) shows the effect of making the initial turn upwind. It can be seen that it will be necessary to fly upwind for a longer period in order to avoid placing the aircraft in a position from which a dangerously tight turn will be necessary to bring it back onto the required path. The effect of continuing drift during the reverse turn may very well result in the aircraft overshooting and being forced to make a violent correction during the final run in.

Sufficient height should be gained in the procedure turn to take the aircraft above all obstructions. A turn 'right on the deck' has been known to become even more spectacular than the pilot intended. A reasonably steep approach from point d (fig. 7.17) will obviate the possibility of collision with an obstacle which may have been noted during the pre-treatment inspection but dismissed or forgotten as being unimportant owing to its distance from the boundary of the treatment area. Airspeed must be carefully controlled during this latter stage, to ensure

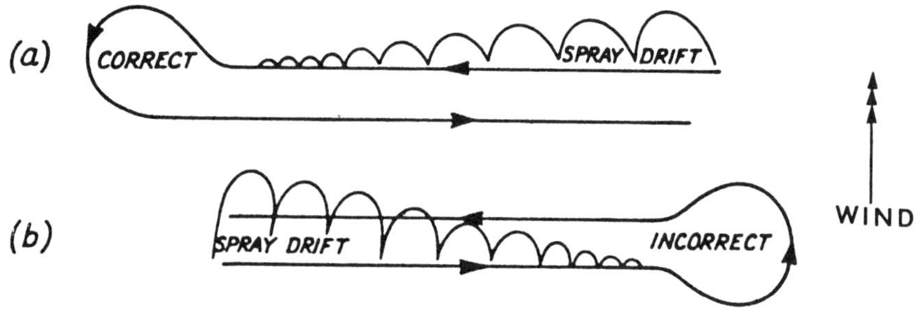

Fig 7.18 Effect of wind on the procedure turn

that each spray run is commenced at the speed required for correct and uniform application. This will obviously be easier if the procedure turn is executed at a uniform height regardless of whether there are any apparent obstacles to be avoided or not.

Most application pilots know the consequences of attempting to minimise the radius of turn to that theoretically possible for the aircraft under given conditions. The minimum radius turn is basically defined by the maximum amount of lift which can be produced for the given flight conditions. In order to gain this lift the aircraft must operate in very close proximity to the aerodynamic stall. Therefore, the following is a review of some basic aerodynamic relationships before considering the geometry of the procedure turn-around.

The maximum normal acceleration that an aircraft at a given airspeed can maintain without stalling (A_s) is determined by the relationship:

$$A_s = \frac{C_L \, dS}{2W}(V^2) \qquad (1)$$

where C_L is the coefficient of lift, d is the air density, S is the wing area and W is the weight of the aircraft and where the term

$$\frac{C_L \, dS}{2W}$$

is a function of the design characteristics, weight of the aircraft, and the air density; and where V is the airspeed of the aircraft. Turning acceleration (A_T) is determined by the expression

$$A_T = (A_N{}^2 - 1^2)^{1/2} \qquad (2)$$

where A_N is the acceleration perpendicular to the plane of the wings (as shown in fig. 7.19). The radius of turn (R) is determined by the expression

$$R = \frac{V^2}{A_T} \qquad (3)$$

To prevent the aircraft from stalling, the acceleration normal to the wing must be less than the acceleration to produce a stall. Thus, the amount of **g** pulled in the turn must be less than the maximum amount of lift produced by the wings.

Therefore the minimum radius of turn (R_{min}) achievable at a given airspeed is

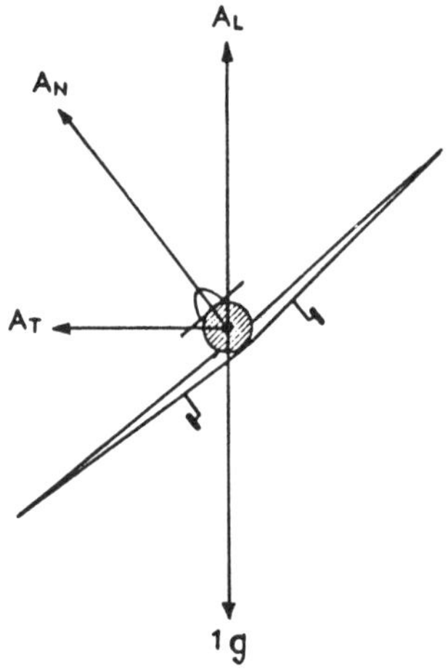

Fig 7.19 Accelerations

$$R_{\min} = \frac{V^2}{\left[\left(\frac{C_L \; dS}{2W} V^2\right)^2 - 1^2\right]^{1/2}} \qquad (5)$$

or

$$R_{\min} = \frac{1}{\left[\left(\frac{C_L \; dS}{2W}\right)^2 - \frac{1}{V^4}\right]^{1/2}} \qquad (6)$$

The relationships in equation 6 give several clues about how the procedure turn should be flown.

Any historical notions about the validity of manipulating airspeed to minimise the turn radius should be dispelled. As noted in equation 6, a reduction in velocity has very little beneficial effect on $R_{\min}$. More directly, control of airspeed requires that the pilot look inside the cockpit at a rather inaccurate airspeed indicator when he should be looking outside. Most experienced applicator pilots will infrequently check the airspeed indicator to verify that all is going well in the turn.

The term $(C_L \, dS/2W)^2$ in equation 6 does, however, give important information about turning performance. The coefficient of lift (C_L) may be thought of as a measure of the quantity of lift being produced for a given angle of attack. It can be seen by reference to fig. 7.20 that for a given aerofoil shape the lift coefficient increases *with angle of attack* up to a maximum point and then falls off. The maximum point corresponds to the aerodynamic stall.

The aircraft wing must show its lift behaviour along this curve. That is, unless the configuration is changed by deflecting flaps or some similar device, for every angle of attack there will be a single lift coefficient produced. The wing will stall when it reaches an angle of attack corresponding to the maximum lift coefficient. With the aircraft weight, wing area, air density, and airspeed held constant, note that a minimum turn radius is obtained when the lift coefficient is maximum. Of course, this places the aircraft very close to the stall region, and the incipient stall may result if the pilot misjudges the amount of elevator deflection required to keep the angle of attack near maximum.

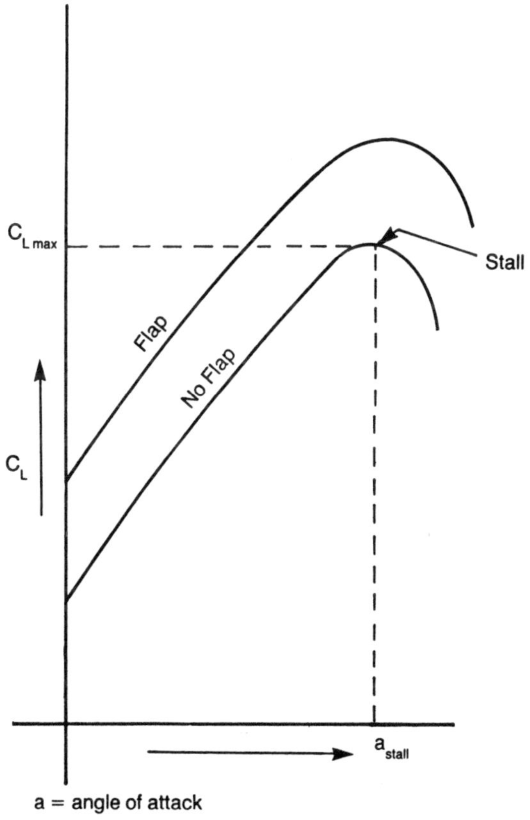

Fig 7.20 Coefficient of lift versus angle of attack

On the point of stalling speed in level and turning flight, the maximum lift coefficient is denoted by C_L, returning to equation 1 to extract the equation for lift:

$$L = \frac{C_L \, dSV^2}{2} \quad (7)$$

and compute the stalling speed, V_S. For simplicity, it is assumed that the stall occurs from a level flight situation, where the lift produced by the wing can be considered equal to the weight of the aircraft, therefore substituting W for the L. Inverting the equation and solving for the stalling speed leads to the following form:

$$V_s = \sqrt{\frac{2W}{dC_{L\,max}S}} \quad (8)$$

From this equation it can be seen that as the weight increases, the stalling speed must increase. Further, the actual stalling speed (not indicated) will increase with decreasing air density or higher flight altitude. It should be kept in mind that this is for the constant angle of attack at $C_{L\,max}$. Note again that the stalling speed varies with weight and that the only thing constant about stall is the angle of attack at which the stall occurs. There are several other factors in addition to the weight which affect the stalling speed, for example aircraft centre of gravity location, amount of power applied, and maneouvres.

Since angle of attack is the only variable which directly affects stall, it can be stated that, in general, anything which affects angle of attack will affect the proximity to stall (equation 1). It is now possible to return to equation 6 and state that the most important variable in minimising the turn radius is angle of attack (or the coefficient of lift), while all other factors act to vary the stall speed. Also, as bank angle is increased, the aircraft wing senses that a greater load is present for it to support. Thus, to maintain a given altitude in the turn more lift must be produced; this is most easily done by increasing angle of attack. However, as indicated, there is a limiting angle of attack prior to stall. Couple these factors with air updrafts, and the applicator pilot finds himself in a difficult position of determining the best radius of turn to minimise the chances of entering an aerodynamic stall.

Now there is a relation between the procedure turn-around and the angle of attack, it is possible to describe the goemetry of the manoeuvre. Perhaps the most important segment of the turn-around manoeuvre is execution of the initial turn. When terrain and obstruction permit distribution, the swath runs are made with a crosswind condition. Therefore, to assure that the turn-around can be made within some limiting angle of bank (usually 60°) the first turn at the pull-up should be made downwind. The pull-up should bring the aircraft at least 50 ft above ground level and 25 ft above the highest obstacle in the turn. The amount of heading change from the end of the swath run to the turn back to the new run will vary according to the aircraft's performance characteristics, the direction and speed of the wind, and obstructions within the turning area (fig. 7.21). For example, a 90° crosswind to the swath will normally require only 45°–60° change in heading before starting the turn back. However, with a tail-wind on the swath run the first turn may require a 60°–90° change in heading (fig. 7.22). Likewise, many pilots find it necessary to roll out of the first turn to a 'wings level' attitude and constant altitude for a few seconds, before making the turn back onto the new swath. This is usually done when the first turn must be made into the wind.

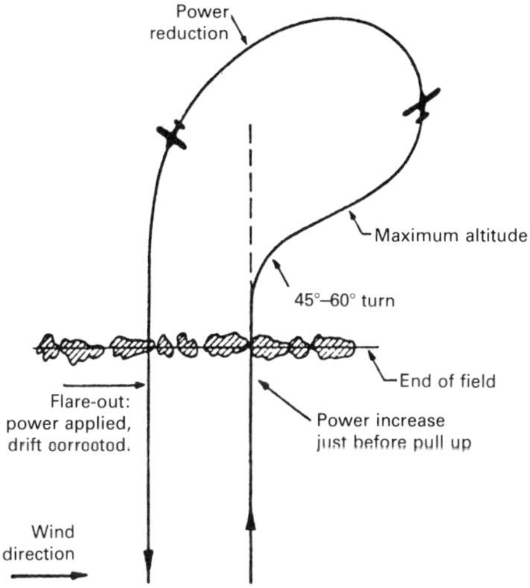

Fig 7.21 Procedure turn with 90° crosswind (Gaulipault, 1966)

As the pilot rolls the aircraft into the second turn, he should keep it at the desired altitude until it is apparent that the turn can be successfully completed. It is vitally important that the pilot maintain co-ordinated flight throughout this phase of the turn manoeuvre. He should not make a 'snapped' reversement turn. The reversement turn should be stopped at the angle of bank that will most nearly maintain a constant radius of turn back to the next swath run. The best way to assure that altitude is held is by keeping the aircraft's nose properly referenced on the horizon.

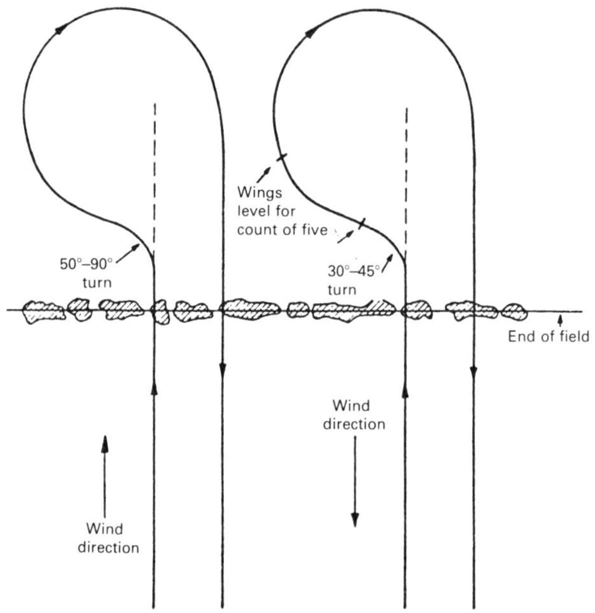

Fig 7.22 First turn with headwind (right) and tailwind (left) (Gaulipault 1966)

When the aircraft has reached a heading of about 90° to the next swath run in this turn, the pilot should start a power reduction in order to lose altitude without overspeeding onto the new swath run (fig. 7.21). The angle of bank maintained throughout the remainder of the turn should be tight enough and steep enough to prevent a speed increase without a stall, and still line up for the next swath run. Altitude should be maintained until the pilot has rolled out of the turn and is ready to descend to the flareout point. If, after completing the last turn, the pilot finds himself poorly aligned with the new swath, he should climb and begin a new turn-around rather than adversely skid the aircraft onto the centreline.

A portion of the turn-around which has contributed to numerous accidents is the flareout onto the swath run. After completing the roll out from the final turn, the pilot should push the aircraft's nose down and descend to the flare point. The nose-over should not be so abrupt that negative *g* forces cut off the engine's fuel supply. The nose-overs should be rapid and firm enough to place the aircraft in the proper position for flaring out. During the descent the aircraft will normally accelerate to swath speed. Power adjustments to swath speed should be completed during the descent.

Power should not be changed from just prior to starting the flareout until the actual flareout is completed. The purpose of not changing power here is to prevent any sudden changes or disturbances of the airflow over the wings. It is well to remember that sudden accelerations or decelerations of the propeller chop up the airflow over the wings and can result in stalls or sudden losses of altitude. Also, if the aircraft is trimmed for a nose-up attitude, sudden power blasts lower the tail and put the aircraft in a nose-high attitude.

Pilots have frequently misjudged the proper point of flare and the amount of elevator deflection required at the flare point. This occasionally results in the aircraft striking the ground obstructions, or becoming entangled with the vegetation being treated. Similarly, if the swath run is made into a strong cross-wind (six knots or more) consideration must be given to making a drift correction at the time of flareout. These factors, coupled with changes in aircraft weight, centre of gravity location, and stability and control changes due to ground effect, require the pilot to be very alert. Fatigue may significantly downgrade the pilot's ability to control the aircraft accurately throughout the turn-around manoeuvre.

The most critical factor in minimising the turn radius under the varying conditions described, and to maintain a safe margin above the stall is to keep the pilot informed of the angle of attack. It is therefore strongly recommended that aircraft used for continuous low-level operations, particularly considering the very wide range of aircraft weight (i.e. disposable load) should have an angle of attack indicator. The advantages of employing such information far exceed its cost. The savings are manifest in greater assurance of safety, keeping a safe margin from aerodynamic stall while allowing the pilot to operate close to it. This device is easily installed and requires very little preventive maintenance. The displayed information about angle of attack is easily read and can be placed in the 'head-up' field of view.

New application pilots should be required to receive dual instruction on the procedure turn-around with emphasis on the effects of the many flight variables involved. This should include doing the manoeuvre at different aircraft weights and centre of gravity locations, also in varying wind conditions and obstruction distributions. Only then should the pilot practise the manoeuvre and then only at a safe height. Emphasis should be placed on the recognition of and recovery from the incipient stall.

As proficiency increases, power adjustments will be made at only two places, that is, at the start of the pull-up, and the end of the reversed turn. Proficiency must also be gained in operating the dispersal equipment at the correct times.

The problem of collision with wires

Wires, cables and high tension lines are probably the greatest hazard facing the aerial application pilot today and this applies to all applicator pilots, whether inexperienced or highly experienced.

Although the hazard is not the same in all countries, there are many areas (e.g. industrial) where new cables are being strung, or where new townships require electric power. The overhead power lines supported by towers with cross-trees are probably the quickest and cheapest method in the distribution of electric power. This is an important point to remember: 'has a high tension distribution system been installed since the last spraying season, right across a former clear and unobstructed area?' Where is it in relation to the crop to be treated, or the landing strip, or the route to either? These distribution systems can be installed surprisingly quickly.

From Australia, where comprehensive agricultural aviation statistics are available, during the period 1973 to 1978, wire strikes accounted for some 20% of agricultural aircraft accidents, in which the aircraft was substantially damaged or destroyed. They also accounted for 40% of all fatalities and 36% of all serious injuries, so it can be seen that the chance of surviving a wire strike accident is considerably lower than any other type of aircraft accident. Indeed, as 17% of all wire strikes result in fatal injury and 22% in serious injury, a pilot involved in a wire strike has a one in three chance of being killed or seriously injured.

From a representative ten wire strikes:

- Two involved wires of which the *pilots were unaware*.
- One involved *misjudgement of wire clearance* or other obstructions not noticed in the treatment area inspection, and when evasive action was taken, the aircraft struck the wire.
- Seven out of this ten happened when the pilots *forgot a wire they had previously located* (Freeman, 1979).

From the U.S.A. the total of all helicopter wire strikes during 1979 averaged 7 helicopters per month. Over 21% of the total helicopter fatal accident rate is attributable to wire strikes (agricultural operations are included in the total). (*Rotor and Wing international*, 1980.)

The wire strike problems will now be looked at in greater detail. Whether the preliminary treatment area inspection is done from the ground or from the air, wires are reasonably easy to see. From the ground they are quite conspicuous, since they are seen against the background of the sky. Under such conditions of high contrast, the eye has a remarkably good resolving power and wires can be seen from quite a long way off. From the air, up to about 500 ft, the wires themselves are not especially conspicuous, but the regular pattern of the poles or towers can be seen fairly clearly and the position of the wires deduced. At the spraying height neither of these conditions prevail. The background of the wires – trees, land, etc. – provides poor contrast while the poles may be hidden by trees or be so far to the periphery of the pilot's visual field as not to be noticed. Therefore the wires become inconspicuous, and also their vertical extent is not easily determined.

A primary cue to distance judgement is thought to be the apparent size of known objects. A wire is definitely small in diameter and of indefinite length and so is highly unsuitable for this kind of estimation. By contrast, a tree is a very much better object on which to base these judgements. Unless bare of leaves it is fairly conspicuous and, while there is no standard size, there is little difficulty in judging whether it is a small tree close or a larger tree further away. Another cue to distance is the gradient in texture in the ground surface between the observer and the object. A tree is planted at a definite point in the ground surface whereas a wire is not related to any definite ground point unless a pole is visible close to the place of intended crossing. The poles not only provide range information but their tops also definitely determine the maximum height of the wires. However, both height and range information can only be provided by poles which are not too far towards the periphery of the pilot's vision.

Where the wires are positioned along a fence or road, or line of trees, etc., excellent range information can be provided by these features, but of course, no cue to the height of the wires, nor any positive reminder of the presence of wires.

From the foregoing, it can be seen that pending universal use of reliable and unambiguous electronic warning devices to inform the pilot where the wires are (and probably what to do) practical methods in assisting pilots in the form of reminders must be devised, and where necessary, artificial range cues provided.

Wire location

During training, greater emphasis must be placed on working around wires, particularly wire location with indications of wire runs by poles, insulators, cross-trees and dwellings. Ensure that the trainee pilot realises that indications are not good enough on their own and that he must locate the actual wire. If in doubt, he must fly over the pole to locate the wire.

The importance of treatment area inspection must be emphasised strongly. Ground inspections are sometimes not possible and often of doubtful value in determining pole runs and wire dispersement. Aerial inspections are preferred as the perspective is right and the chances of a pole being hidden from view are less, because it is possible to see other poles along the wire run. The aerial inspection must start as the aircraft approaches the treatment area and continue into the area, and must be thorough. Nothing must be left on the basis of 'I think that's where it goes', the pilot must be 100% certain, and if he is not, then he must look again.

The pilot must make proper use of all visual clues. The most obvious are the pole runs associated with the wire run. Cross-trees on the poles indicate supplementary wire runs and the angle of the cross-tree, in relation to the main run, will indicate the angle of the supplementary or spur wire. As a general rule, in an area where domestic power supply is available, dwellings and other buildings could have power connected and no attempt should be made to begin a treatment until the wires supplying the buildings in the treatment area have been located. Also, visual clues are only indications of wire runs and the wire itself must be located.

Misjudgement of wire clearance

Misjudgement of wire clearance usually results from two factors. Firstly, the pilot pulling up too late to clear the wire either at the end of a run or during the run where it is not possible to fly underneath. To avoid this problem, pilots must ensure that before attempting to climb over a wire which does not have a good reference point with which to judge the distance from the wire, some other point must be selected at which the pull-up is initiated to give adequate clearance. The same applies to letting down over a wire. Two areas where use of this technique is advisable are when approaching a wide span remote from poles or when crossing a wire at an angle to the flight path. It can also apply when approaching wires strung at different levels, for the highest wire always looks the farthest away.

The second factor, which results from misjudgement of clearance, is where the pilot finds the wire he intends to pass under is lower than he thought or has an obstruction underneath. The former is easily dealt with because it is obvious during a proper inspection of the treatment area that a wire has either adequate clearance or suspect clearance. When clearance is suspect, the aircraft should be flown at spraying height, parallel to the wire, and the *clearance physically checked*. Obstructions beneath the wire should be located during inspection. Strong emphasis should be placed on inspecting the surface below the lower levels of the wire run for obstructions and undulations. The fence alongside the spraying run is another area where the pilot is likely to encounter obstructions encroaching upon his flight path. When an obstruction is located under a wire during a spraying run, it is usually a small one (otherwise it would have been seen during the inspection) so to avoid it yaw the machine and flat turn slightly.

Wire strikes where the wire has been located but is subsequently forgotten

This problem involves the highest proportion of strikes, deaths and serious injuries and yet is the hardest to solve. However, it *can* be solved. Firstly during training and supervision, the future agricultural pilot must be made aware that one fatality in four involves striking a wire that has already been located and so while it is essential to locate wires, it is even more essential to remember them, and the only way to remember a wire is to dismiss all irrelevant matter from the mind while engaged in treating an area and concentrate on the job in hand. Easily said, but very hard to practise. It is extremely important, and new pilots can be trained to do it. The budding agricultural pilot can also be trained to carry out an extra 'check wires' or 'check obstructions' check, before carrying out clean up runs. This is the main area of wire strikes and results from relaxation, mental overload (and these two can go hand-in-hand) together with orientation of the treatment area and obstructions changing through 90° or 180°.

The problem of mental overload is uppermost in the case of the experienced pilot. Individuals vary as to the mental load they can tolerate but all must reach saturation some time and the addition of one more factor will drop two or three items out of their memory and not necessarily the unimportant ones.

The foregoing looks at the three main occasions when pilots are liable to strike wires. The first two can be eliminated by good training and a thorough treatment area inspection. The third case is more difficult and, from the statistics, the most dangerous. The fact that experienced pilots have also come to grief in this situation points to a revision in procedure.

The preparation for treatment of areas that have wires close to, or over the area needs extra careful planning. The treatment area inspection, as already discussed, must include planning by the pilot of the approach and departure routes to and from the area (safety lanes). The area must be divided up into segments and each segment planned and treated separately.

The segments are areas which are well defined with natural boundaries, or to be marked out, and which command an individual procedure, i.e. one segment will be assessed as safe to continue under the wires, another segment will stop short and will be marked accordingly. The procedure will be the same for each run, i.e. pull up straight ahead, or pull up and turn right, or pull up and turn left. Standard procedure for each segment will allow the pilot to time each run and he will know as he progresses accross the area, either by his stop watch or instinctively, when he is due to pull up. Besides, he will be looking for the marker at virtually the same moment on each run. If the first run is towards the pole or pylon, he may have a distance cue, and as he progresses towards the middle of the span of wires when distance clues may not be available, he will have confidence in the marker being a safe distance to commence his pull up. If the wires are other than 90° to the direction of the runs, marking in the same manner will be necessary. It may be safer practice to start with the shorter runs first and continue with subsequent longer runs. The pull up would be followed by a turn away from the wires.

It would be advisable to treat these segments 'flight by flight' and not change a procedure during a particular flight; in other words, each action at the marker will be the same. The layout of the segments, the division of the segments and the direction and order in which they are flown must be planned immediately after the treatment area inspection. The pilot must have a sketch map on as large a scale as necessary upon which the salient features are marked, including of course the position and run of the wires. Also the pylons, and all other major features to a minimum distance of 1.5 km outside the treatment area, including the entry and exit routes.

The segments are marked in such a way as not to be confused with an adjoining segment, i.e. they are colour coded. The position of the markers on the ground and the segment divisions are decisions made by the pilot. Only the pilot knows what he considers to be a safe distance to pull up in front of a line of wires, or where the procedure is safe to change from pulling up to going underneath. The markers themselves must be distinctive. They must be sufficiently closely spaced to ensure that at least one is positively visible to the pilot on each run. They must also be of such a distinctive and standardised shape and colour that the pilot cannot confuse them with natural objects in the environment and can instinctively relate them to the procedure he has planned for this segment. White plastic translucent cones have been shown to be satisfactory.

Where human markers are used to enable the pilot to line up on his runs, they may be placed to perform the additional function of reminders. However, if they are also to perform this function, it is essential that they use some different coloured flag or two flags instead of one, for instance. The pilot must know that these markers are *reminders of a procedure*, and must not just revert to flying straight on (unless the procedure planned is to fly under the wires). Distinctiveness and standardisation are important. It would be advisable to do a preliminary run (at a safe height) to see that the markers are correctly placed and to provide a reminder of where all the obstructions are placed before going down to the spraying height.

As long as the pilot is reminded that a wire is present it does not follow that he is obliged to see it, and it may not be possible anyway at the spraying height; what is important is the action necessary when seeing the marker. It is more important to see the markers than the wires because action in initiated at or near the markers. As already explained, even seeing the wires does not mean the pilot is going to miss them. When replenishing at the airstrip, use the sketch map to update the procedure which will be used on the next segment. A moment or two in reflection on the next procedure will be worth while because the constant awareness of the wires will keep the mind focussed on their proximity.

Letting down over wires can be as hazardous as pulling up too close, so the return run presents its own problems. Pilots (including helicopter pilots) have hit wires on the descent into the area. If there is a big span of wires supported with cross-trees, it may be wise to consider the return run as a ferry flight back to the original start line and fly on the markers. It is not safe to let down with wires anywhere in front of the aircraft because it is not possible to know how far they are away. Markers placed for a safe pull-up can be considered safe to let down provided the pilot can be positive that he has passed completely over the wires. This may only be possible at or near the pylon. It will be very much more difficult away from this reference.

The point to remember on this procedure is that letting down towards the marker on a return run assumes the pilot, after safely crossing over the wires, can position his aircraft at the correct speed and height, and also commence spraying at the same line where it was stopped on the forward run. This is possible, as the markers should be far enough away from the wires. Some overhead distribution systems are very big indeed, and it would be possible to turn the aircraft without climbing over them, but they may be safe to fly under. Again, the positioning of the markers is the decision of the pilot who will know how much room he needs for his procedures.

It may also be a point to remember that the pilot who decides the marker positioning also flies the segment. It does not follow that another pilot would decide on the same position, or indeed the same procedure.

The foregoing is an approach to this very important area, particularly the case when wires are forgotten. It is most important that the pilot considers *each* flight and what the procedure will be at the markers. It is suggested that even if a segment is only two or three runs, the pilot lands and considers the next segment because by definition (in this chapter) the next segment requires a new procedure. This sort of approach may look overdone, but a pilot who has worked near his maximum flight time limitations for a few months in the spraying season is more able to fly blocks of similar procedures than to have to change the procedure in flight when, during a lapse, because of the re-orientation of the obstacles, he may *turn the wrong way*.

Do not worry about a low productivity rate in these segments. The objective is to plan and execute the application programme in such a way that the pilot has a precise plan of action on each flight, and memory does not become the weak link in the programme.

Clean-up runs

The segments where a pull-up procedure has been planned and completed would also require clean-up runs. This is another area of high accident potential. The best attitude to this aspect is to treat the clean-up runs as a totally new programme. The pilot has worked his way across a treatment area segment by segment, and as his procedure could have been different for each segment, he would have foregotten the reasons why the procedures were changed; furthermore, he had time to think before each segment was treated to allow for any special circumstances. The orientation has now moved through 90° or so. The clean-up run may be the last item before stopping work for the day and there could be an overwhelming tendency to do this quickly, particularly after a very demanding day flying towards, underneath and over the top of wires. If possible, re-cap with the sketch maps to see if there were any obstructions adjacent to the wire runs. If necessary, fly the clean-up runs at a safe height in the first instance before dropping down to spray them. Treat each clean-up run as a complete procedure with the same mental attitude as all the other runs. Leave the area by the exit route.

Some items of equipment will now be considered which are becoming available for the aerial application pilot for safe flying in the close proximity of high tension wires, and as safety measures when wires are accidentally struck.

Cable warning system

Recently, an electronic cable warning system, manufactured in the U.K., has become available for light aircraft including helicopters. The system is able to identify high tension wires and indicate to the pilot the orientation of the wires in relation to the aircraft heading. It does not mean that all wire strikes are a thing of the past, because pilots are still striking wires with this device fitted and working. It has been established that pilots have reported the system giving sufficient warning to avoid a wire strike where otherwise a strike was probable.

The detection range of the system can be up to 1600 m. Typically, detection of a power cable of about 500 m would give 10 seconds' warning time to the pilot of an aircraft flying at 100 kts. Apart from the cockpit display, there is an audible warning. (British Aerospace PLC, U.K.) For the aerial application pilot, such a device could be used to monitor the wires that the pilot is already aware of, but may not necessarily see. It can be considered as an additional safety device, but does not mean any change in the planning and execution of spraying operations in the vicinity of high tension wires as discussed.

Wire strike protection system

For those occasions when a helicopter pilot is confronted with wires (for any reason) and he is not able to avoid them, or does not see them, a wire strike protection system (WSPS) is available from Aeronautical Accessories Inc., U.S.A. It is essentially a wire cutter mounted on the top and bottom of the cockpit area. It protects virtually 90% of the frontal area (fig. 7.23). For the aerial application helicopter and, indeed, any helicopter which is engaged in low level operations, this system should be a mandatory standard fitting (Rotor & Wing International 1980).

Agricultural aircraft cable cutter

There is a development in Australia where a cable cutter using a cutting blade driven onto an 'anvil' by a propellant charge has demonstrated the ability to cut stranded steel cables up to 2.36 mm in diameter. Such a system is a one shot device and must be rearmed if used (Smith 1977).

To sum up procedures to cope with the hazards of wire collisions:

(1) Better training for new pilots. A thorough planning of spraying op-

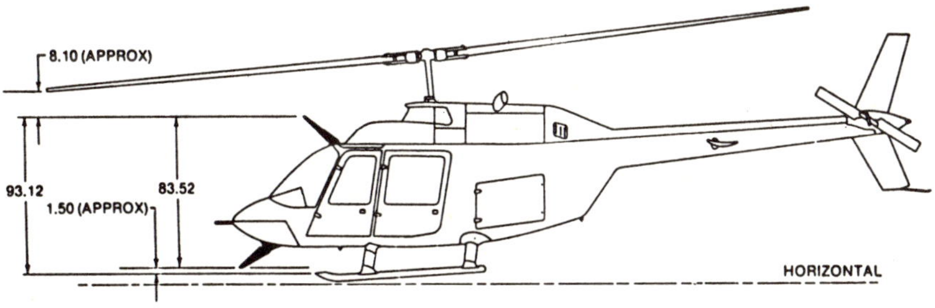

Fig 7.23 Wire strike protection system; Bell 206 in this example

erations in the vicinity of wires, including the principles of 'marking' as a reminder of a procedure. Actual in-flight training in the recognition of the different types of wires and their location. Planning of entry and exit routes to the treatment area.

(2) A thorough treatment area inspection to include the areas under and close to wires, particularly when the wire is low. Preliminary planning of the direction to spray and range cues to be used. Planning of position of supplementary markers to be used. Preparation of sketch maps.

(3) Thorough briefing of ground party, marker positioning, decisions of segment boundaries (and procedure changes) followed by flight inspection before spraying.

(4) Treat clean-up runs as a totally new programme, with their own treatment area inspection. There are NO short cuts in these procedures.

(5) All pilots to be made aware that distractions from the job in hand resulting from mental overload cause wire strikes (and other accidents).

(6) Do not let familiarity make you casual in your approach to wire location and avoidance. Maintain standards and always have a healthy respect for wires.

(7) To conclude, it is worth noting that if a safety helmet is not worn, and a wire is struck, the chances of survival are almost halved.

Density altitude

We all know that an aeroplane will not take-off in as short a distance on a hot day as it will on a cold day. Also that at a high altitude airfield, a take-off will require a longer ground run than at an airfield at sea level. These effects on aircraft performance are essentially a result of two factors, *pressure altitude* and *temperature*.

In order that an aircraft may take off, it must produce lift. This lift is generated by the wings, and requires forward speed. To establish this speed, the propeller, which is an airfoil, must exert the necessary thrust. Power developed by the engine must be sufficient to generate this thrust by turning the propeller.

The density of the air in which the aeroplane flies is an important factor in regard to performance. Both the propeller and the engine utilise the air around the aeroplane: the engine to produce the power, and the propeller to generate the thrust. Anything which affects the density of this air necessarily alters the performance of the aeroplane. Density altitude is determined by pressure altitude and temperature. When we refer to pressure we are referring to the weight of a column of air. If we measure this column at sea level it will weigh more than a measurement taken at 8000 ft, because there is less air in the column at 8000 ft altitude. The other factor which bears on air density is temperature. A given volume of air will be less dense when heated.

When the air density is reduced, power will fall off in an unsupercharged engine. The propeller loses efficiency both from the loss of power from the engine and from the fact that the propeller blades will not take as much 'bite' out of less dense air. Since the propeller is not pulling or thrusting at maximum force, it will take longer to obtain the necessary forward speed to produce the required lift. Also the wings will require a higher speed to produce the same lift in less dense air. Consequently, the take off will require more time and more distance.

It is not sufficient to say that an aeroplane will take-off in a given number of feet on an airfield at 5000 ft elevation, even if the pressure altitude is also 5000 ft. (These elevations would only be co-incident in the 'international standard atmosphere'.) Density altitude may be thought of as performance altitude. Since both pilots and aeronautical engineers must have a basis for comparison, arbitrary temperatures have been assigned to specific altitudes; in fact all the parameters in an atmosphere have been defined and called the 'international standard atmosphere' (ISA). If the temperatures are the same at given altitudes as those which exist in the ISA atmosphere, then pressure altitude and density altitude would be the same (as already mentioned). However, this is rarely the case, and a correction must be applied to obtain the density conditions.

For example: in the ISA condition the temperature at sea level is 15° C (pressure is 1013.2 mbs or 29.92 ins). If the temperature observed was +31°C then the correct reference would be listed as ISA+16°C. This is the normal way temperatures are referred to in performance charts. As the ISA lapse rate is assumed to be 2°C per 1000 ft (below 36000 ft) the temperature in the standard atmosphere at 3000 ft elevation is +9°C. If the observed temperature was +31°C, then the temperature reference would be ISA +22°C.

How to establish density altitude. For example: an aircraft is to operate from an airfield with an elevation of 1800 ft, and air temperature is 30° C. What is the ISA temperature that must be used in the performance charts, and what is the density altitude?

ISA temperature at 1800 ft is 11.4°C (15°C - the lapse in temp of 3.6°C for 1800 ft)
Observed temperature is 30° C
Temperature reference is ISA + 18.6° C

Set the altimeter to standard pressure 1013.2 mbs or 29.92 ins, and take the pressure reading in the ISA atmosphere, which is say 2000 ft.

Refering to table 7.1, for a pressure altitude of 2000 ft and where the temperature is 30°C the density altitude is 4100 feet.

The precise performance figures would have to be extracted from the appropriate aircraft performance manual, but the order of magnitude of performance reduction would, for the above example, be as follows:

(1) 55% increase over the normal take-off distance.
(2) Rate of climb reduced by 35%.

Table 7.1 Density altitude tabulation (I.C.A.O., 1968)

Pressure altitude	C 15° F 59°	20° 68°	25° 77°	30° 86°	35° 95°	40° 104°	45° 113°	50° 122°
S.L.	0	550	1 100	1 650	2 200	2 750	3 300	3 850
1 000	1 200	1 750	2 300	2 850	3 400	3 950	4 500	5 050
1 500	1 850	2 400	2 950	3 500	4 050	4 600	5 150	5 700
2 000	2 450	3 000	3 550	4 100	4 650	5 200	5 750	6 300
2 500	3 050	3 600	4 150	4 700	5 250	5 800	6 350	6 900
3 000	3 650	4 200	4 750	5 300	5 850	6 400	6 950	7 500
3 500	4 250	4 800	5 350	5 900	6 450	7 000	7 550	8 100
4 000	4 900	5 450	6 000	6 550	7 100	7 650	8 200	8 750
4 500	5 500	6 050	6 600	7 150	7 700	8 250	8 800	9 350
5 000	6 100	6 650	7 200	7 750	8 300	8 850	9 400	9 950
5 500	6 700	7 250	7 800	8 350	8 900	9 450	10 000	10 550
6 000	7 300	7 850	8 400	8 950	9 500	10 050	10 600	11 150
6 500	7 950	8 500	9 050	9 600	10 150	10 700	11 250	11 800
7 000	8 550	9 100	9 650	10 200	10 750	11 300	11 850	12 400
7 500	9 150	9 700	10 250	10 800	11 350	11 900	12 450	13 000
8 000	9 750	10 300	10 850	11 400	11 950	12 500	13 050	13 600

(1) Set altimeter to standard, 1013.2 mbs or 29.92 ins. Altimeter will now read pressure altitude.
(2) Take the outside free air temperature (in the shade).
(3) Find the pressure altitude in the appropriate column.
(4) Read to the right of pressure altitude figure until intersecting the temperature column corresponding to the temperature taken; this is the *density altitude figure*.

References

Anon. (1983) 'Cable warning system', British Aerospace Dynamics Group, Bracknell, Berkshire, RG12 1QL, U.K.

Anon. (March 1980) 'Wire Strike Protection System (WSPS).' *Rotor and Wing International*, 28–29.

Anon. (1966) *Agricultural Pilot Manual*. Issue no. 3. Department of Aviation, Australia.

Anon. (1978) *Handbook for Agricultural Pilots*. 3rd impr. I.A.A.C. Cranfield, 82–85.

Eggspuehler, J. J. *ed*. (1963) Special Flight Instructor Course for National Trades Association. Department of Aviation, the Ohio State University, U.S.A.

F.A.O. (1972) 'The use of aircraft in agriculture.' Agricultural Services Bulletin 16.

Freeman, C. J. (1979) 'The problem of power lines, their location and avoidance by aircraft engaged in agricultural operations in Australia.' *Agricultural Aviation* **4** (4), 183–186.

Galipault, J. B. (1966) 'Agricultural aviation safety: the procedure turn-around.' *Agricultural Aviation* **8** (1), 14–18.

I.C.A.O. (1968) 'Safety in aerial work part 1 – agricultural operations.' I.C.A.O. Circular 85–AN/71

Lucassen, L. R. (1959) 'Flight techniques for fixed wing aeroplanes in agricultural aviation.' *Proceedings 1st I.A.A.C. Congress*. Cranfield, U.K., 15–18 September.

Smith, W. R. (1977) 'Development of a cable cutter for agricultural aircraft.' *Agricultural Aviation* **18** (1), 12–14.

8

The helicopter in agriculture

This chapter has been up-dated from the third edition by Dr Carrol M. Voss, in particular, the section dealing with the flying and turning techniques. It is incorporated with his kind permission. (Dr Voss is President of Ag-Rotors, Inc., U.S.A. This chapter deals only with those aspects of aerial agriculture peculiar to helicopter operations.

Introduction

The helicopter, together with its predecessor, the autogyro, represent a unique branch, the rotary wing family, in the evolution of powered aircraft, and is of special interest to agriculture. Historically some of the advantages of rotary wing aircraft in the field of crop protection were recognised some forty years ago, when the use of an autogyro to spray arsenicals for control of cankerworm on fruit trees in the U.S.A. was found to halve the cost of application in comparison with the use of a ground sprayer.

The properties of slow speed flight, ability to execute tight turns and land and take off with safety in small fields were considered by Potts in 1939 to be the chief advantage of the autogyro. Particular value lay in the treatment of small broken woodland areas. For large flat areas, the fixed wing aircraft's greater speed and load carrying capacity were judged preferable. Subsequently the helicopter with motive power supplied to the main rotor, and the resulting torque stabilised by a small tail rotor, has more or less supplanted the autogyro, the advantages of vertical take off and landing (VTOL) and superior flying qualities proving paramount.

The structural and aerodynamic characteristics of the helicopter have improved over the last thirty years, particularly in the last decade with military experience and new materials technology. The limitations of performance – payload/range – have mostly been overcome and the range of machines currently operating extends from a single-engine aircraft of 134 kW and 300 kg payload to twin engine machines of 820 kW and 8000 kg payload. While there has been a small resurgence of interest recently in the autogyro with the development of simple, lightweight, one-man machines, the payload so far has proved very marginal, although this type of machine is finding favour in some countries with a limited ULV application. Like fixed wing aircraft, there is now a generation of helicopters specially designed for aerial application.

The helicopter can demonstrate distinct advantages in certain areas. Advantages and disadvantages can vary depending on the job in hand, the type of application and other factors. Some of the advantages are:

- *Customer satisfaction and public relations* Due to its vertical take off and landing capability, a helicopter can operate from the fields to be sprayed and the farmer can actually witness the entire operation of loading, mixing and dispersal of chemicals or seeds, etc. This could result in good customer satisfaction and public relations.
- *Landing strips* In this era of shortages there are countries where maximum land must be put to cropping, and it is difficult to spare acres or hectares of arable land for use as airstrips every 20 or 30 km or so. Helicopters can operate from the edge of a field or a pond or even from a pad on the top of a loading truck, and no land need be

Plate 8.1 Helicopters have the ability to operate from very small landing pads; in this case from a specially equiped loading truck; Hughes 300 helicopter (photo: I.A.A.C.)

prepared for landing as in the case of a fixed wing operation. This is particularly true in some of the rice growing areas of the world.

- *Ferry time* Unproductive ferry time between loads can be minimised, if not completely eliminated. If loading is planned such that an even number of swaths can be sprayed, the helicopter lands back for replenishing on the same side of the field without even ferrying across the field being treated (fig. 8.1).
- *Spraying speeds* A helicopter does not have a stalling speed (at least compared to a fixed wing lifting surface) and can operate from zero airspeed to its maximum operating airspeed. It is possible to spray at very low airspeeds – 20 to 25 m.p.h. (32 to 40 km/h) – for the very heavy coverage which is not possible with fixed wing aircraft.
- *Turning time* Due to its maneouvrability, a helicopter can turn around in a shorter time than a fixed wing aircraft. It is also capable of performing in-field turns when there are high trees or obstructions at the end of the field which can be covered in the clean-up runs. This results in an increased work rate and productivity.
- *Spray distribution* A large mass airflow is created by a helicopter which flows down through the rotor and to the rear. This airflow can be utilised to disperse the spray droplets through the crop, including the under surface of leaves. This is true of liquids and dusts. However, at the higher speeds the distribution patterns become similar to fixed wing aircraft, i.e. at speeds above 40 km/h, although downwash velocities appear to be greater than in comparable weight fixed wing aircraft. At speeds approaching 100 km/h, significant asymmetry occurs in the rotor wake which requires the use of an asymmetric nozzle layout to give an even distribution (Parkin, 1979).
- *Spray gear* Spray gear for helicopters is driven mechanically, hydraulically or electrically with power derived from the engine directly or

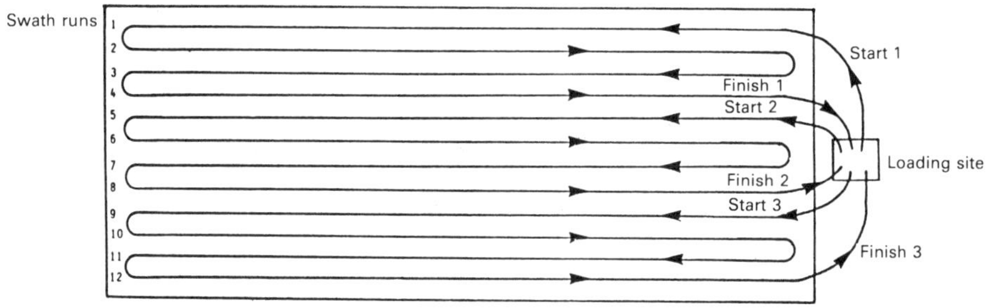

Fig 8.1 An even number of swaths per sortie keeps the ferrying (dead flying) to a minimum (Voss, 1980)

Plate 8.2 Bell 47-G-2A equiped with boom-and-nozzle gear (photo: Ag Rotors Inc.)

indirectly. Helicopter engines operate at constant speed and hence pump speeds are maintained constant, irrespective of airspeed. This is not the case with airspeed driven windmill powered pumps, which are more common on fixed wing aircraft.

- *Contour and hill flying* When operating in mountainous terrain it is naturally advisable that swaths be laid along the contours (for fixed wing aircraft as well). Care must be taken here, especially at the lower speed levels and when hovering, as the ground cushion will be affected by the inclined ground. Sufficent height and clearance must be maintained to ensure that there is no possibility of the rotor or spray boom coming into contact with the inclined ground. It is much easier for a helicopter to maintain constant speed should the aircraft have to depart from the contour level. Obviously, if a fixed wing aircraft flys downhill, the increasing airspeed produces a fall-off in the application rate.
- *Special operations* A helicopter is capable of special operations utilising its rotor downwash and slow flying capabilities, e.g. frost control, which is done over orchards. The helicopter can break through inversions forming over orchards by driving the warmer air above the inversion level to the lower levels and helping to prevent frost damage to fruit. Flying at 75 to 100 ft in an inversion temperature difference of about 8° C caused an increase of nearly 4° C at the 1.5 m level. The effective 'swath width' was in the order

of 75 m. It seems that the optimum flying speed is about 40 km/h (A.S.A.E., 1976; Miller *et al.*, 1971).

- *Emergency landings* In theory, a helicopter can land on practically any surface in an emergency; it does not need a specially prepared strip or relatively long clear area. However, provided the helicopter is flying fast enough, or is high enough to establish auto-rotative descent, a safe landing can be performed unless the pilot is so unlucky as to alight on very rough ground. Damage to the main rotor or tail rotor, should they strike the ground or obstructions, could be substantial.
- *Obstruction clearance* Because of the generally superb visibility from helicopter cockpits, pilots would have more reaction time available to avoid obstructions; maneouvrability also helps in taking evasive action in the face of obstructions.

Some of the disadvantages of the helicopter are:

- *Costs* Helicopters are costlier to operate per hour compared to similar weight fixed wing aircraft.
- *Maintenance* Due to the complex power chain, drives from the engine to the main rotor, the tail rotor, the control systems, etc. require a greater maintenance effort at the main base and in the field, and add to the cost of operating.
- *Loading and C of G limits* Most helicopters have small C of G variation limits, and loading becomes critical. It is also greatly affected by changes in air temperature and humidity.

Operations, performance and flying techniques are now looked at in greater detail.

Performance

Altitude, temperature, humidity and weight all affect helicopter performance. The effect of increased altitude and/or temperature is to reduce air density and this affects both engine and rotor performance. The effect of humidity is to reduce the weight of the air taken in by the engine, i.e. an increase in humidity decreases the density of the air. The effect of an increase in any or all of these variables is to cause a drop in engine power. Since general practice is to allow only comparatively small variations in rotor r.p.m. the upper limit being set by the maximum engine r.p.m. (except where free turbines or tip jets are used) and the lower limit by the maximum permissible coning angle, the speed of the rotor blades is substantially constant. Thus the effect of reduced air density is to reduce lift since lift is proportional to density in a given set of circumstances. To obtain the same amount of lift despite a lower density, higher blade pitch angles must be used. The higher angles cause a less favourable lift/drag ratio, since the blade angle of attack moves away from the optimum angle, and increases the danger of over-pitching in hovering or very slow flight. If the engine power is also reduced this danger is greater. In extreme conditions of low air density and high humidity it may be impossible to hover. Even if it is possible to hover very close to the ground (maximum ground effect), if full power is already being used to do this, there is no extra power available for transition to forward flight and the helicopter will strike the ground as soon as it has moved off the ground cushion.

Weight must be considered in conjunction with performance. At constant rotor r.p.m. a decrease in weight requires a lower pitch angle setting and therefore gives less drag and decreases the power required. The weight a helicopter can safely carry is therefore dependent upon the power available from the engine under any given set of circumstances.

It is not unusual for a helicopter to operate at various heights in the course of daily operations. An example would be for a helicopter to be loaded at a base at sea level (A) and to off load at a landing pad 2000 ft above sea level (B) ten minutes later. The problem then arises as to the maximum load that can safely be carried. If the helicopter was loaded to its maximum all-up-weight permissible under the existing conditions at A it may be too heavy to hover with full power under the existing conditions at B.

Take-off and landing areas

Selection of take-off and landing areas is subject to several considerations. When taking off the aircraft may be loaded to its limit, and consequently need a considerable cleared area to permit translational flight to be established. Naturally this area should be situated as close as possible to the area to be treated. This will mean that a lighter fuel load may be carried which will allow a heavier payload. An area which is considered safe for take-off under heavy laden conditions should prove to be more than ample for all landings.

Hovering and ground effect

The magnitude of the ground effect depends on the efficiency with which the ground surface tends to return the downward slipstream in an upwards direction. Ground effect is reduced as rotor distance from the ground increases and also when the nature of the ground surface is such that it tends to dissipate the downward flow, e.g. bushes, long grass, crops. Care must be exercised when hovering over sloping ground as the return airflow from the ground is deflected laterally and ground effect may be lost completely.

Re-circulation has a detrimental effect on performance and may be experienced in some circumstances; hovering in a small deep depression in the ground or a small forest clearing are ready examples. A particularly dangerous situation occurs when hovering close to a tall obstruction such as a hangar wall where re-circulation may be experienced on the side nearest the obstruction. The lift is reduced on that side and the helicopter tends to tilt and move in the direction of the obstruction.

Operational planning

Ground inspection – treatment area

Prior to flying to the area to be treated the pilot should inspect the area from the ground and draw a plan showing boundaries, obstructions, contours, etc. Particular care should be taken with respect to all types of overhead wires which create a hazard very difficult to see when airborne. The plan of the treatment area should be carried by the pilot in the aircraft throughout the entire operation so that reference may be made to it as required.

Flight inspection – treatment area

The first flight over the area to be treated should be made at a reduced all-up-weight. Prior to commencing the treatment the pilot should thoroughly inspect the area from the air and annotate his plan with any further information that may be gained. The knowledge gained from the ground and flight inspections should then be utilised to plan the operation as a whole. This particular operational planning is a most important phase and should not be neglected.

The pilot's plan should make use of the following considerations:

Purpose of treatment

Crops of a certain nature may be beaten down by the downdraught from a helicopter's rotor. Other crops may be more sturdy. In the first case the pilot must be particularly careful to avoid hovering over the crop. In the second case the damage caused by prolonged hovering may be only slight, but it should be avoided where possible. Penetration in these cases must also be considered. By reason of the strong down-draught a helicopter will achieve penetration of a crop which may not be possible by a fixed wing aircraft.

Restricted area operation

When operating into corners surrounded by high obstructions consideration must be given to how this area may best be treated. The use of quick stops may be employed in some cases. However, the undesirable features of prolonged hovering must be considered. It is advisable to treat these restricted areas at the commencement of the operation as most pilots have more alertness at the commencement than at the completion of this type of work. Greater safety will be achieved in this way. In the event of the pilot's plan requiring flight over obstructions he must ensure that the margin of safety is kept at a relatively high level.

Effect of wind on planning operation

Usually agricultural operations will be carried out crosswind. Care must be taken therefore that the aircraft is tracked correctly between markers to ensure that the swaths are correctly overlapped. In cases where it is necessary to lay swaths into wind or downwind care should be exercised with speed selection in each direction so as to ensure that coverage remains constant.

Manoeuvring turns

The basic techniques involved in agricultural flying with helicopters are similar to the fixed wing techniques. The ferry flight, field survey, entry into the field, swath runs and pull-up or exit from the field involve the same basic techniques. Maintenance of height, speed and direction during a swath run are also the same as for the fixed wing aircraft. These techniques are covered in the chapters on fixed wing aircraft. Swath turns in helicopters are slightly different from fixed wing and are now treated in more detail.

Right hand turns

These turns are based on the zero wind condition: wide turns. As the end of the field approaches, the entry for clearing the barriers is started with aft cyclic and climb power in sufficient proportions to clear the barriers and gain height (50–100 ft). After the barriers are cleared, apply forward cyclic to regain lost airspeed with a slight left turn (to give room for the turn). As airspeed is acquired, start the right turn with aft and right cyclic. This is done so as to start the right hand turn and also to get the helicopter in a climb attitude. This is necessary so that when the helicopter has reached the peak of the climb it has also the steepest angle of bank applied for that turn. This is done so that centrifugal force will be thrown upwards minimising the load factor which is applied to the helicopter. If this is done correctly the centrifugal force will work for the pilot, counteracting the force of gravity; it is possible to hit a position of zero ***g*** forces where the pilot will feel weightless. It will also be necessary while the helicopter is in the turn to apply right pedal to keep the nose of the helicopter tucked in the turn; power is maintained throughout the turn (this is done so that the effects of torque can be used by the pilot to help turn the nose of the helicopter towards the field). At this stage, the cyclic must be adjusted as necessary to maintain groundspeed. If the airspeed is allowed to get too slow, power settling could occur while in the turn. As the turn is being completed, aft cyclic will be necessary to slow the helicopter down, and down collective will be used to start the rate of descent. At this stage the helicopter will be facing into the field and adjustments with the cyclic and collective for entry will be necessary.

If the entry approach is to pass over barriers, then prior to arriving over the barriers the helicopter must be slowed down with aft cyclic until the airspeed is 15–20 knots slower than the swath speed, and use up collective to maintain height. If the approach is clear of barriers, and there is no wind, then the approach should be continued down on the collection and speed adjusted to the swath speed, or swath groundspeed if there is a wind, for the two will not be the same. This is very important, so that the helicopter will be at the correct height and groundspeed as it passes over the first crop.

When approaching over barriers, it should be made certain that the barriers are actually behind the helicopter prior to starting the descent into the field. Many accidents have been precipitated by pilots lowering the collective for entry into the field too soon, which causes them to strike the obstructions.

On entry into the field, it will be necessary to apply a little forward cyclic when lowering the collective. This is done so that the angle into the field will not be too shallow.

Left hand turns

These turns are based on zero wind condition: wide turns. As the end of field approaches, the entry for clearing the barriers is started with aft cyclic and climb power in sufficient proportions to clear the barriers and gain height (50–100 ft). After the barriers are cleared, apply forward cyclic to regain lost airspeed with a slight right turn (to give room for the turn). As airspeed is acquired, start the left turn with a slight aft and left cyclic. This is done so as to start the left turn and get the helicopter in a climb attitude. This is necessary so that when the helicopter has reached the peak of the climb it has also the steepest angle of bank applied for that turn. This is done to reduce the ***g*** forces and disc loading.

As the helicopter starts to turn through the half-way point it will now be necessary to apply forward and left cyclic. At this stage, the power can be reduced by lowering the collective; the power is reduced so that torque will be reduced, helping to turn the nose of the helicopter towards the field. After the collective is lowered, aft cyclic can now be applied to slow the helicopter down as it comes around to the field. Entry is made the same way as with the right hand turns, and with the same precautions. Through the last part of the turn it may be necessary to use a little pedal to help keep the nose tucked while turning.

It should be remembered, however, that these turns are *not pedal turns*, they are primarily *cyclic turns*, since cyclic is azimuth control. Pedals are used to assist in the turn by keeping the nose of the helicopter tucked while turning. The use of pedals will increase as the turns become steeper.

Safety

When planning the operation the pilot should give consideration to his actions in the event of an engine failure. He should annotate his plan with all suitable areas for auto-rotative landings. Care must be exercised at all times to ensure that the aircraft is flown in such a manner that an auto-rotative landing may be executed at any stage of the operation. If a dumping device is fitted to the helicopter, the pilot should not hesitate to use it in any emergency.

To obtain maximum gliding range the forward speed should be maintained above that required for minimum rate of descent in autorotation. Pilot's handling notes will indicate optimum rotor r.p.m. and airspeed combinations for maximum range.

Once within range of a suitable forced landing area, airspeed should be reduced to that required for minimum rate of descent. 'Engine-off' technique for the final stage of the descent will vary with helicopter types but the aim, if possible, is to achieve a zero groundspeed and a zero rate of descent at touch-down. This will not always be possible and the combination can be varied to suit the situation.

References

Ag-Rotors Inc., P.O. Box 578, R.D.1., Gettysburg, Pennsylvania 17325, U.S.A.

Anon. (1978) *Handbook for Agricultural Pilots*. 3rd edn, I.A.A.C. Cranfield Institute of Technology, Bedford, U.K.

A.S.A.E. (1976) 'Helicopters as frost protection devices.' *Transactions A.S.A.E.* **19** (4) 672-674, 677.

Miller, M. *et al.* (1971) 'Helicopters for frost protection.' *California Agriculture*, 2-4.

Parkin, C.S. (May 1979) 'Rotor induced air movements and their effects on droplet dispersal.' *The Aeronatucial Journal*, Royal Aeronautical Society, 183-187.

Potts, S.F. (1939) 'Spraying woodlands with an autogyro for control of Gypsy moth.' *J. Econ. Ent.* **32**, 381–387.

Voss, C.M. (1975) 'The helicopter's contribution to agricultural aviation at present and in the future.' *Proceedings of 5th International Agricultural Aviation Congress, Stoneleigh.* I.A.A.C., 223-228.

Voss, C.M. (1980) Private communication.

9
Micro climatology

Introduction

Pilots holding a commerical pilot's licence (usually the minimum qualification for agricultural flying) would already be familiar with synoptic meteorology as it affects route and forecast terminal weather. What may not be so familiar are certain of the dynamics in the lower atmosphere which affect the low flying aircraft.

Experienced agricultural pilots develop a natural awareness of the probable turbulent flying areas related to topographical features, and where to expect changes in drift, and so on. This awareness is developed by experience. Additional information is included from recent studies, notably by Fujita (1983), on low-level wind shear and outflow phenomena associated with thunderstorms and squalls.

For the new agricultural pilot, a study of this chapter should enable an understanding of some of the orographic induced wind effects and convective outflow effects, and for the experienced pilot, probably some consolidation of his experiences.

Shelter effects

This section is taken from a publication by Oke (1978). The use of a barrier to provide shelter from the wind is an old and well-developed procedure. The barrier may be a line of trees (a shelter belt) or any other arrangement of trees, bushes, hedges, soil embankments, stone walls or fences. The principal aim is to reduce the horizontal wind speed near the ground in areas open to damaging or otherwise undesirably strong winds. Such areas include coastlines and open prairie landscapes, where frictional retardation is weak because of small terrain roughness, or locations open to topographic or other local wind systems possessing undesirable features, i.e. strong and/or cold katabatic winds. The objects of protection could be sensitive agricultural crops, among others. The climatic effects of sheltering are not restricted to the simple reduction of wind speed.

Figure 9.1(a) shows the mean *streamlines* as airflow encounters a solid barrier placed across its path. Figure 9.1(b) is a general classification of the flow zones which result. Even before the air reaches the obstacle it begins to react because of the pressure build-up ahead. The bulk of the flow is forcibly displaced up and over the barrier. Immediately above the barrier the streamlines are forced to converge as the same mass of air attempts to 'squeeze' over, causing an acceleration or jet, but once over it is able to expand again and decelerates accordingly. This is the flow found in the *displacement zone*. After crossing the barrier the room available for expansion suddenly increases but the fluid cannot immediately react to fill it. The flow therefore separates from the barrier's surface and its organisation breaks down into a much more turbulent condition in the low pressure or *wake zone* which extends downwind from the barrier. Immediately behind the barrier the pressure is low and thus tends to 'suck' air into a semi-stationary lee eddy or vortex. This part of the wake is known as the *cavity zone*. The large lee eddy structure is dissipated into the smaller turbulent eddies of the wake zone, before finally settling down and reassuming conditions similar to those of the upwind flow. Within the wake the

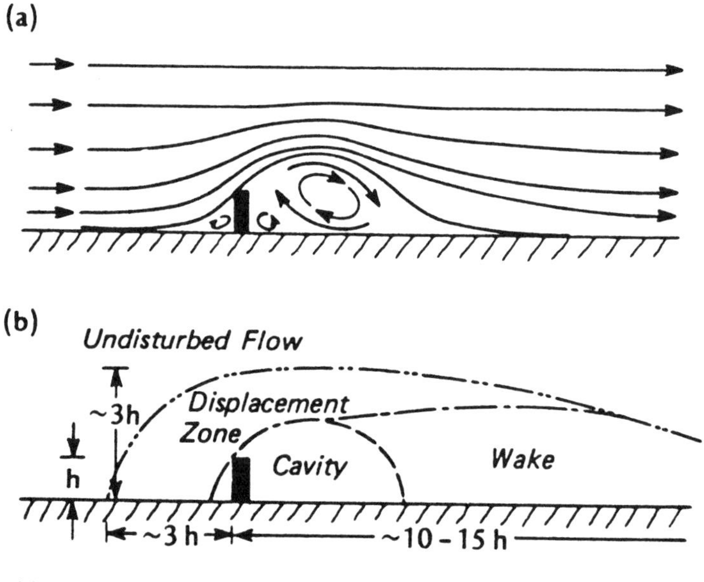

Fig 9.1 (a) Streamlines; (b) generalised flow zones associated with typical pattern of airflow induced by a solid barrier placed normal to the flow; dimensions expressed as multiples of the barrier height, *h* (Oke, 1978)

separation of the flow lessens the force of the wind on the ground and the near surface wind speed is decreased – this is the sheltering effect.

In order to be able to compare the effects of different-sized barriers it is common to represent horizontal and vertical dimensions in terms of the barrier height (h). In these units the barrier is seen to affect flow to at least 3 h above the surface, and to the same distance in front of the barrier (fig. 9.1(b)). The distance of influence downwind of the barrier depends upon the density of the barrier, defined as the percentage ratio of the open area of the barrier as viewed normal to its axis, to its total vertical area (i.e. a totally impermeable barrier has the maximum density of 100%). The distance of downwind influence is usually judged in terms of the percentage reduction of horizontal wind speed compared to the upwind (open) value of the same height. The effect of barrier density upon the distance of downwind shelter is illustrated in fig. 9.2 from measurements at a height of $\simeq 0.25\ h$ in the vicinity of shelterbelts. If the barrier is very dense the reduction in wind speed is seen to be considerable immediately to the lee because there is little or no penetration, but the wind regains its former value relatively quickly because the strength of the cavity is intense and the faster moving air above is quickly drawn in.

A dense barrier to the surface wind can be seen to extend its influence to about 10–15 h downwind. As may be expected the low density barrier provides the least protection near its base because it allows considerable throughflow, but its recovery is slower than the high density one because the air passing through provides a 'cushion' in the cavity zone and the flow assumes a more even aerodynamic shape. The point of 90% recovery occurs about 15-20 h from the obstacle. Thus it emerges that the medium density barrier provides the best overall shelter by combining maximum retardation compatible with aerodynamic 'cushioning' in the lee. The effects of such a barrier extend to about 20–25 h based on the 90% recovery criterion, but reduced wind speeds may even be observed as far as 40 h downwind.

The above relationships apply to the ideal case of flow normal (in the crosswind direction) to a long barrier. If the angle-of-attack of the flow is oblique then the area of shelter is proportionately reduced until with parallel flow the shelter is negligible, except due to friction on either side of the barrier itself. At the ends of a barrier the wind tends to curl around and form turbulent vortices which encroach into the sheltered area. Equally if there are significant gaps in the barrier the wind will jet through giving speeds *greater* than the upwind flow. If the width of the barrier is significantly larger than h then throughflow is virtually eliminated. Therefore the pattern of wind speed in its lee conforms more to that of a high density barrier (fig. 9.2).

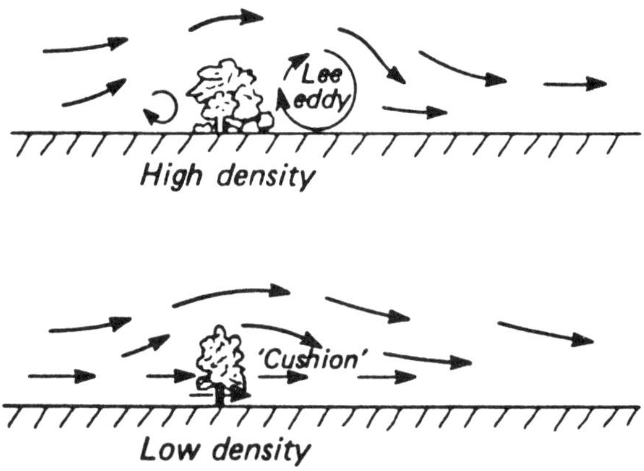

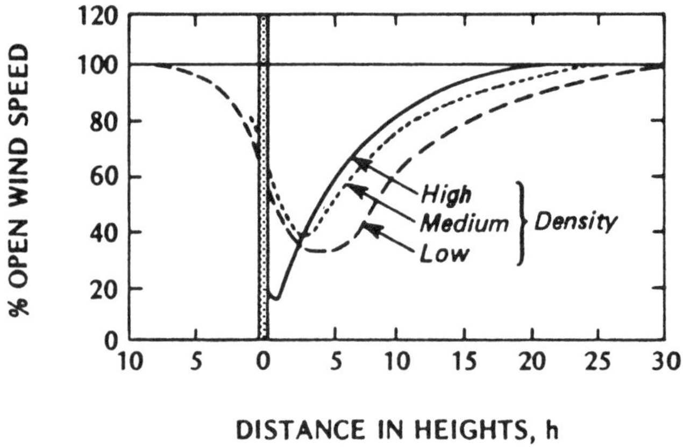

Fig 9.2 Wing speed reduction in the vicinity of shelterbelts with different densities (after Nägeli, 1946)

Dust devils

These are phenomena usually observed over very dry dusty or desert areas during daytime, and with a slack pressure gradient. Surface temperatures of 50° C are quite common and in extreme cases can reach at least 70° C. Both immediately above and below the surface, temperatures drop sharply, producing very steep lapse rates. Differences in the order of 30° C have been measured in southern Arabia in the lowest 50 mm over a sandy desert. This is equivalent to an environmental lapse rate 55 000 times greater than the dry adiabatic. It is not surprising to find the lower atmosphere over a desert to be convectively very unstable.

Such conditions lead to the development of special instability phenomena such as miniature whirlwinds known as 'dust devils'. If there is sufficient dust available, a column of rotating dust can be seen rising often several hundreds of feet. At the surface, considerable activity can be seen, and larger particles of dust and even small stones can be lifted. Fortunately, the pilot can see the column of dust and avoid flying into it. A hazard exists when the 'dust devil' tracks over a dust-free area, e.g. a lava bed, or grassy area, and becomes temporarily invisible.

Land and sea (lake) breezes (from Oke, 1978)

Land and water surfaces possess contrasting thermal responses because of their different properties and energy balances, and this is the driving force behind the *land and sea (lake) breeze* circulation system encountered near ocean or lake shorelines. Compared with most land surfaces a water body exhibits very little diurnal change in surface temperature. These land–water temperature differences and their diurnal reversal (by day the land is warmer than water; at night the land is cooler than water) produce corresponding land–water air pressure differences. These in turn result in a system of breezes across the shoreline which reverse their direction between day and night (fig. 9.3). The thermal breeze systems of this type are best developed in anticyclonic 'warm clear' weather, because almost cloudless skies and weak synoptic-scale winds permit the maximum differentiation between surface climates. Increased cloud or stronger winds modify or obliterate these local winds. Note that both the land and sea breezes are really the low-level portion of a complete circulation cell.

The daytime sea breeze circulation (fig. 9.3(a)) has a greater vertical and horizontal extent, and its wind speeds are higher, than the night land breeze (fig. 9.3(b)). This is because by day the solar forcing function is in operation and instability is greatest. Commonly the sea breeze blows at 2–5 m s^{-1}, extends inland as far as 30 km, and affects the air flow up to a height of 1 to 2 km. On the other hand the land breeze is usually about 1–2 m s^{-1} in strength and smaller in both horizontal and vertical extent. During the sea breeze the cooler more humid sea or lake air advects across the coast and wedges under the

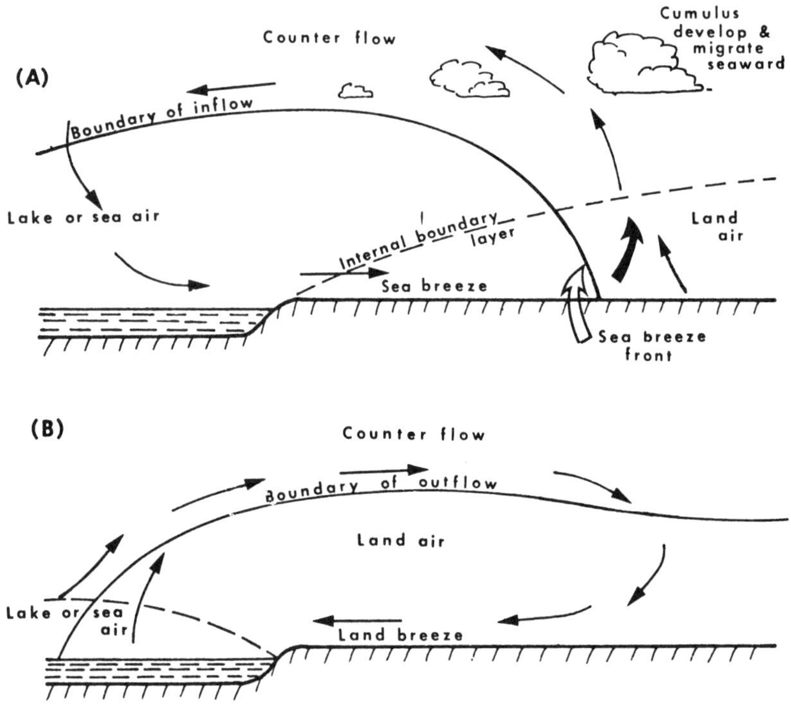

Fig 9.3 Land and sea (lake) breeze circulation across a shoreline: (a) by day; (b) by night (anticyclonic weather) (after Oke, 1978)

warmer land air. The advancing *sea breeze front* produces uplift in what is already an unstable atmosphere over the land. The front is therefore commonly associated with the development of sea breeze cumulus clouds which are caught up in the counter flow aloft and are carried seaward where they are dissipated, because they have been removed from their moisture source, and because over the water the air subsides, and warms adiabatically.

The lowest layer of sea or lake air which is advected across the coast is modified by the 'leading-edge effect'. The stable marine air is warmed over the land producing a more unstable internal boundary layer which grows in depth with distance from the shore.

Artificial rain

The release of precipitation from a cloud does not in general take place until after ice particles have formed in its upper part. This has led to attempts at rain-making by the introduction of material into a non-precipitating cloud intended to facilitate the production of ice crystals. The method often used has been to 'seed' a well-developed convection cloud with solid carbon dioxide dropped from an aircraft. The low temperature of this substance, less than − 65° C, cools the air coming into contact with it so that ice crystals are formed and precipitation may be initiated. Other attempts have been made to release precipitation by introducing large water drops into the lower part of a convention cloud (the coalescence theory); the drops might be expected to start the rain process when carried by the updraught into the higher parts of the cloud. Clouds have also been seeded with silver iodide crystals produced by burning the substance upwind of the area to be seeded.

While some success has been achieved with these and similar methods, the results so far have been by no means spectacular; limited falls of rain have been initiated only in favourable situations which were near to the point of giving rain naturally. The experiments have not yet become of economic importance.

Mountain barrier influence on airflow

The most important influence is the production of standing waves or standing eddies which have in the past caused many accidents because of their vertical currents, the *severe* turbulence that they can sometimes generate, and their effect on the accuracy of pressure altimeter readings.

Visible evidence of mountain waves and eddies

The vertical motion set up in an air stream crossing a hill, mountain or ridge very often gives rise to orographic clouds with distinctive features. These clouds, being related to orographic features, move very slowly, if at all, although the winds at their level may be strong. An indication of the wind speed at cloud level may be assessed by following identifiable cloud 'filaments' as they form and move from one end of the 'stationary' cloud to the other.

Lenticular clouds

These are stationary lens-shaped clouds which form in bands parallel to the mountain. The most windward of these clouds sometimes occurs above the ridge or a little upwind. Under favourable conditions when the terrain is dominated by one long ridge, several other clouds occur at regular horizontal intervals with clear or thinner cloud in between.

Two or three bands are commonly seen, but as many as ten or more have been observed at one time extending 80 km downstream from the ridge. The lenticular shape, regular spacing, and stationary position are indicators of standing waves, and are often the only clue that such waves exist.

These clouds may occur at different levels simultaneously, the lower ones looking much like ordinary strato-cumulus, the higher layers like lenticular alto-cumulus, and above that even cirrus-like enormous pennants flying from invisible masts (fig. 9.4(c)).

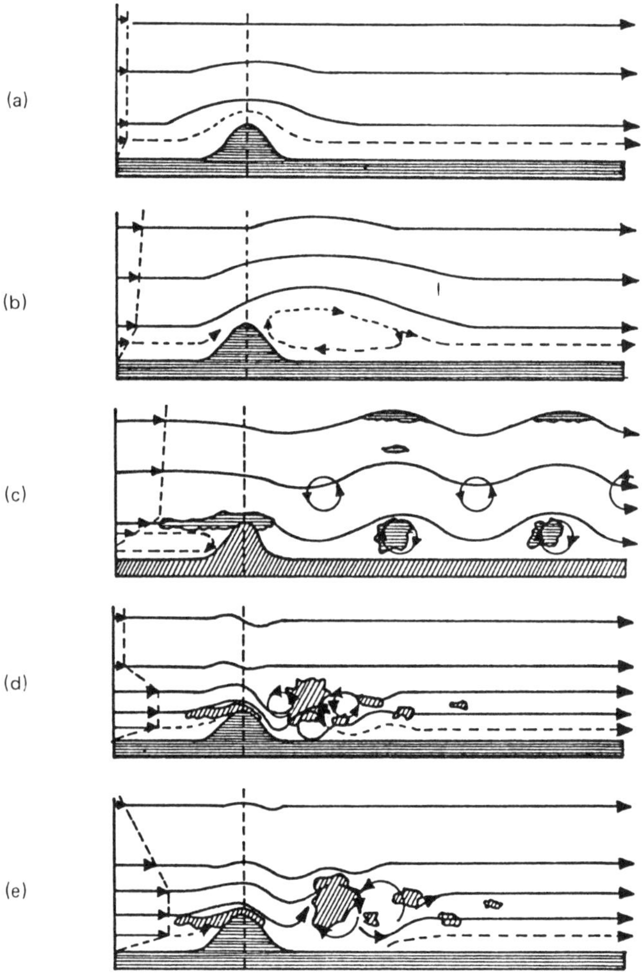

Fig 9.4 The formation of lenticular clouds and rotor clouds

Rotor clouds

These appear in the form of a stationary roll, sometimes immediately in the lee of the mountain, sometimes at varying distances downwind. From the air it looks like a line of cumulus clouds. The base of the cloud is generally near or below the ridge line, while the top may be considerably higher than it. Unlike lenticular clouds, the rotor cloud shows evidence of strong and sometimes violent turbulence; it appears to rotate, the upper part moving forward while the lower part moves backward toward the mountain. Sometimes a succession of rotor clouds appear at regular intervals downwind.

Rotor clouds develop in standing eddies which form on the lower layers under the crests of the mountain wave. These eddies are not unlike the small scale effects described as occurring in the lee of an impenetrable wind break (fig. 9.4(d) and (e)).

Cap cloud (fohn wall)

This is a low hanging cloud with its base near or below the ridge top level, and its relatively smooth top only a few thousand feet above the ridge. The major portion of the cloud is on the windward side where precipitation may fall from it. The leeward edge remains stationary and when viewed from downwind resembles a bank or a wall with fibrous fingers reaching partway down the lee slope.

Vertical current

From the viewpoint of aviation, vertical current is one of the most important aspects of these waves, particularly downdrafts. In Tasmania, wave downdrafts exceeding 1500 ft/min (8 m/s) have been recorded, and it is believed that much stronger waves exist. When waves are present, downdrafts generally occur immediately downwind of the ridge, indicated by the downward 'curling' and the dissipation of the cap cloud. If an aircraft flying upwind towards the ridge is caught in a downdraft, it might descend into the cap cloud and not gain altitude in time to clear the ridge. A further danger is that sometimes the waves are extremely smooth, even if the rate of sink is considerable. There may be no sensation of height change, indications being given only by instruments.

Turbulence

Mountain waves can range from extremely smooth flying conditions to the turbulence more violent than any in most thunderstorms. Of importance in aviation is the fact that the smooth and turbulence areas are often in close proximity, and there can be a rapid transition as smooth flow suddenly breaks down into turbulence throughout the vertical extent of the wave.

The most common and most important of the severe turbulence mechanisms is the area of *rotor clouds*. In standing eddies from a ridge approximately 4000 ft above surrounding country, vertical velocities up to 50 kts have been recorded (Australia) and changes in vertical speeds giving vertical accelerations of 2 to 4 *g*. Violent sharp-edged gusts can exceed 24 kts, and experienced pilots have reported complete loss of control for short periods in rotor clouds. Also aircraft have suffered structural failure.

The most dangerous situation is when lack of moisture prevents cloud formation, or when the sky is completely overcast by a thick layer of low cloud, and no prior visual evidence is given of the existence of turbulence by typical cloud formation.

Low level wind shear

Low level disturbances that may emanate from below convective cloud bases can vary from mild turbulence to violent downdrafts as high as 7500 ft/min (38 m/s). These phenomena will be looked at in more detail; however, as it will be seen later, studies over very recent years are only just showing how certain of these mechanisms behave, and indeed it is now becoming possible to measure some of the parameters and issue warnings to pilots about to make an approach, or commence a take-off. This is of course a facility only available at some major airports. The agricultural pilot often operates far removed from such facilities, and meteorological warning services, apart from which he would not necessarily use radio while actually spraying. He must of course be aware of the weather patterns and meteorological tendency for his area, and in tropical latitudes there could be appreciable thunderstorm activity during the late afternoon.

It is unlikely that the agricultural pilot would be crop spraying if thunderstorm activity is expected over the treated area within a few hours; however, certain types of application do not depend on a rain-free target area, i.e. aquatic larviciding, certain granular applications, fertilising (solid not liquid foliar) bait application, etc. The pilot is then concerned about the build-up of thunderstorm activity as the day progresses. Furthermore, ferry flights could take place at the end of a mission to a new area, and it must be remembered that the agricultural pilot would not necessarily have any homing aids to approach a new temporary airstrip. The danger of looking for his airstrip near or underneath large convective cloud build-ups must be appreciated. Pilots low flying in visual contact and in the vicinity of any convective cloud build-ups should avoid flying under *any* downward pointing filaments of cloud, or tongues or rolls of cloud as these outline the local downdrafts. For the well-developed cumulonimbus build-ups, low flying under these conditions is particularly hazardous.

Investigations in recent years into the phenomena of wind shear at low levels, particularly in the U.S.A., have revealed the intrinsic hazard to aircraft flying adjacent to or through vertical or horizontal wind shear. Aircraft have come to grief in these situations over the years, but it seems that an accident at Kennedy Airport, U.S.A., in June 1975 where a Boeing 727 settled onto the ground during an ILS approach in a thunderstorm, prompted a detailed investigation into the meteorological conditions.

Although the agricultural pilot would not necessarily perform IFR ILS approaches, the phenomena of low-level wind shear from advancing squall lines should be understood, as the effects can take place a surprising distance ahead of storms. Furthermore, the agricultural pilot is flying continuously at low level and the risks of encountering these effects are consequently increased. This section will also look at the mechanism of a rarer event the *microburst*.

The following section is taken mainly from Mr Peter Garrison's paper, 'Shear determination', which appeared in Flying *(1983), and is reproduced with the kind permission of the author.*

Referring back to the Kennedy Airport accident, simulations of the flight path of the aircraft led to the conclusion that it had encountered vertical gusts so powerful that it could not climb through them to remain on the glideslope. The idea of intense localised vertical gusts close to the ground was not entirely new, but in the aviation world Theodore T. Fujita (Professor of Meteorology at the University of Chicago) coined the terms *downburst* and *microburst* to describe them and, very soon, many airports attempted to install wind-shear detectors scattered about the airport, and a buzzer in the tower that would go off when local differences in wind velocity exceeded certain limits.

Towers began issuing warnings of possible wind shear to pilots who, while duly alarmed, were not too clear about what they were supposed to do about them. It was in spite of just such warnings, and perhaps because of the pilots' uncertainty about their implications, that another Boeing crashed at New Orleans (in July 1982).

The following is after an article in *Flight International* in 1984:

The pilot may not know the severity of this type of disturbance.

He will be using what information he has to avoid severe shear, and what skill he has to escape from an unexpected encounter. The obvious way to familiarise pilots with severe downdraft, or shear, and even microbursts, is training on a simulator; however, a vital input in shear training is a realistic profile of change in wind vector along any flight path.

American Airlines Training at Crawley, England now offer such training based on a realistic variable intensity model of a microburst. It simulates situations from very low to very high downdraft and outflow which are not limited to the effect of horizontal wind component change alone, or two dimensions only.

Once the theoretical aspects to account for the Kennedy accident were investigated, it was possible to explain a number of other airline accidents and near accidents by various sorts of wind shear scenarios, and so the development of wind shear prediction techniques and detection equipment became a priority of the F.A.A. (U.S.A.).

The problems of detecting wind shear, let alone predicting it, are considerable. It cannot be seen, and a huge volume of air must be searched if all major airports are to be protected. Nevertheless, progress has been made in both ground-based and airborne detection systems. At the same time, disagreement and uncertainty persist as to the exact nature and frequency of hazardous wind shears, and what pilots can do about them.

The term 'wind shear' refers to the 'shearing' or scissor-like action of two air masses moving in relation to one another. One can see this type of motion easily in water: often a rapidly moving current in a stream is contiguous with a pool of still or slowly eddying water. Their boundary is a narrow turbulent shear zone. A trout swimming across the shear zone would have the impression of being shoved to one side, whichever direction it was headed.

An aircraft flying across a shear zone in air has the same feeling of being shoved; the pilot terms it hitting, or being hit by, a gust. Gusts are sudden and brief; however, a shear zone may be several hundred feet thick and free of turbulence, and the pilot may experience it only as an inexplicable change in his airspeed or in the vertical speed needed to stay on the glideslope.

The shears encountered in cruising flight have their hazards, but it's when wind shear is encountered close to the ground, during an approach or on take off, that a crash may be the result.

Wind shears are of two general classes: horizontal and vertical. The two types are not separate and independent, but from the pilot's standpoint they present different problems and require different reactions. Horizontal shears are present just about everywhere, but they can ordinarily be ignored; the velocities and rates of change are small

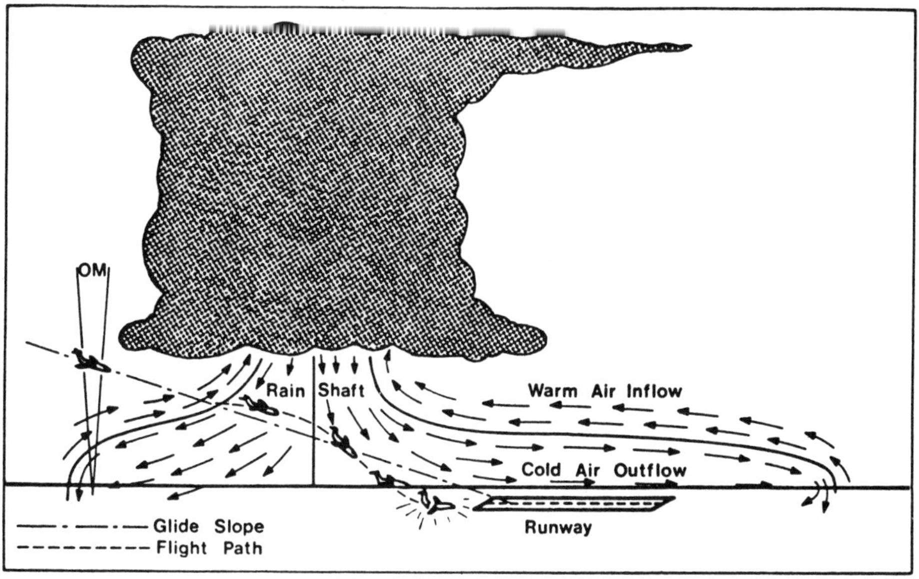

Fig 9.5 Typical wind shear associated with thunderstorm (with acknowledgements to *Aviation Safety Digest*, Australia)

enough to permit pilots and aircraft to adjust to them more or less automatically. It sometimes happens, however, that the velocities at the surface and a thousand feet above it may differ by 40 knots or more. An aircraft descending through the velocity gradient has to adjust its airspeed and vertical speed noticeably to maintain a certain desired approach slope. A groundspeed adjustment of 40 knots over a period of 20 seconds, which could easily be required, involves an acceleration as great as that during the take-off roll. A greater adjustment may be beyond the aircraft's capacity.

If there is a strong headwind during the beginning of the descent and it decreases rapidly with height the pilot, who has set up an abnormally low rate of descent and high power, experiences a mysterious slump in his airspeed combined with an increase in his rate of descent. The nose drops, and he begins to settle below the glideslope. In the opposite case, where there is a tailwind at altitude and no wind or a headwind on the ground, the reverse occurs; the tendency is simultaneously to gain airspeed and to rise above the glideslope. In either case, the appropriate reaction is a combination of a power change and an elevator movement intended to trade speed for altitude, or vice versa. The situation becomes hazardous only if it occurs so close to the ground that the proper adjustment to vertical speed cannot be made quickly enough, or if the aircraft is so heavily loaded or draggy that it can't make rapid airspeed accommodations. These conditions tend preeminently to exist in airline jets, and they are the aeroplanes that have the most serious problems with wind shear. A dramatic instance of the disproportion that can exist between wind shears and aircraft performance was seen in a 727 accident at Denver in 1975. The aircraft started to take off with a quartering headwind of 10 to 20 knots; it then flew into a tailwind estimated at 60 to 90 knots. Obviously, it could not make up the difference quickly enough; in five seconds the airspeed decreased from 157 to 116 knots and the crew was unable to keep the aircraft aloft.

So far we've talked only about horizontal shears. A more serious and only recently appreciated aspect of the problem is vertical shears. These occur mostly in the company of convective storms; horizontal shears are also common in the vicinity of fronts. The terms 'downburst' and 'microburst' refer to sinking air masses of small diameter – less than 10 km in the case of a downburst, and less than 2.5 km in that of a microburst. The smaller the worse, because the velocity gradients within the burst are steeper, and on encountering the burst the pilot and aircraft have less time to make adjustments. The effects of a vertical gust upon an aircraft are distinct from those of a horizontal shear; sudden changes in rate of climb or descent, or in position with respect to the glideslope, are unaccompanied by changes in airspeed. Only the angle of attack and the vertical velocity change.

In 1982, the U.S. National Center for Atmospheric Research conducted a study of air movements in the vicinity of thunderstorms. The project had the acronym 'JAWS' (joint airport weather studies). Airborne and ground-based instruments recorded vertical velocities in excess of 4000 ft/min, 2000 ft above the surface. Since downbursts don't penetrate the ground, their velocity becomes horizontal as they near the surface, spreading radially from the centre of the burst. The relationship of vertical velocity and height, which is of vital interest to pilots, has not been established, although it is thought that 2000 ft/min at 1000 ft and 400 to 600 at 200 ft might be good figures for a severe downburst.*

* Locally, these speeds could be greater. The following parameters are used in the microburst model in the American Airlines DC-10 simulator at Gatwick (U.K.) (*Flight International*, 1984).

Intensity	100%	50%
Core diameter	8 000 ft	6 000 ft
Vortex-ring height	1 800 ft	1 000 ft
Horizontal diameter	20 000 ft	12 000 ft
Height band	5 000 ft	2 500 ft
Max vertical speed	7 500 ft/min (38 m/s)	3 800 ft/min (19 m/s)

The whole microburst can be programmed to come down at up to 40° to the vertical – another observed phenomenon.

A study conducted at Oklahoma City using an array of three-dimensional wind-measuring instruments on a 1500 ft tall tower failed to reveal extremely high vertical velocities, suggesting that the vertical gust danger may not be so great at low altitudes after all. A greater hazard in the neighbourhood of a thunderstorm cell may be the horizontal shearing action between air flowing outward from a downburst on the surface, and air a few hundred feet above the ground flowing back into the cell.

An alternative theory to account for the Kennedy accident and other encounters like it, proposed by Jim Leurs, of the University of Dayton, involves the assumption that extremely heavy rain, by the combined disruption of laminar flow on the wings and the transfer of momentum of falling raindrops to the aircraft (Leurs is talking about downpours of four inches per hour or more), could produce the necessary rates of sink. Partisans of this hypothesis argue that unless the possible influence of rain is taken into consideration, the reconstruction of hypothetical downbursts from profiles of wind shear accidents is meaningless; but as yet there is no experimental verification of the effects of heavy rain on aircraft.

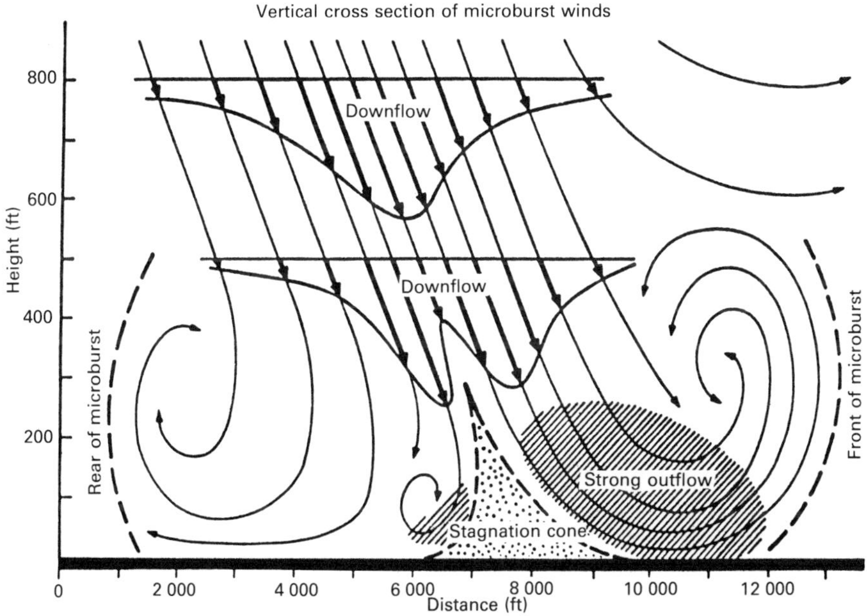

Fig 9.6 Vertical cross-section of microburst wind (with vertical scale exaggerated ten times). Downflows split either side of the stagnation zone near the microburst impact point. Outflow speed is several times faster than downflow speed at 300 ft above the ground (Fujita, 1983). (Reproduced with the kind permission of Pan American World Airways, Inc.)

Rain certainly affects the performance of small aircraft by making some go slower, and may also produce changes in pitch trim. Canard aircraft show the most drastic effects; almost all experience noticeable pitch trim changes in rain, and one type is reported to become unable to maintain altitude, regardless of power or pitch attitude. But whether the flight dynamics of something the size of a 727, or for that matter of a Citation, can be seriously affected by rain has not been determined. So far as momentum transfer is concerned, one would expect lighter aircraft, with their relatively larger ratio of projected surface area to mass, to be more strongly affected than larger ones.

Efforts to detect wind shears have taken several forms. One JAWS experiment used widely distributed arrays of ground-based sensors to measure the velocity, pressure, temperature and moisture content of the ambient air; whenever cool, moist air was found to be flowing outward from some location in all directions, it could be inferred that a downburst existed above that point. Doppler radar, which can sample the radial component of the velocity of parcels of air over a large area and up to a certain altitude, can provide the same type of information. In either case, extensive processing is required to reduce the raw data to usable form, and practical systems for real-time detection and warnings do not exist. The wind shear detection systems currently in use on airports report only variations in wind velocity on the surface, not with altitude or in a vertical direction – hence the extreme vagueness of tower warnings of possible wind shear.

Airborne systems under study include nose-mounted Doppler radar, which can give a few seconds' advance warning of a shear or turbulence encounter; devices that use inertia sensors to identify wind shear encounters while they are taking place and alert the pilot; and systems that compare groundspeed and airspeed to isolate the wind component and display it to the pilot.

A four-year study, concluded in 1979 and conducted for the F.A.A. by a group of contractors that included Douglas Aircraft, Collins Radio and N.A.S.A., developed prototypes of approach instrumentation for transport aircraft. All this equipment, which remains in the prototype stage at the moment, did prove to be successful in dealing with a variety of wind shear profiles, including one representing the Kennedy accident. From the point of view of the general aviation pilot, however, its practical application seems remote, because the required data sources and flight monitoring systems are found in only the most elaborate general aviation aircraft. More pertinent to everyday experience is the question of how great a danger wind shear really is, and what steps one can take to cope with it.

In visual conditions, the pilot of any but the most cumbersome and heavily loaded aircraft has little to fear from wind shear on landing, because the approach starts at a lower altitude, the average VFR approach is steeper than the ILS glidescope, and less time is spent close to the ground. Approaches are usually made from a traffic pattern, and the combination of a rapid descent and several turns to final masks the effects of shears. Random turbulence presents the usual hazards, for instance in the vicinity of a convective storm or a squall line, and there is always the possibility of stalling out of a short-field approach with a rapidly diminishing head-wind near the surface, or on an approach to a field surrounded by trees, where the wind suddenly slackens below treetop height.

For single-engine aircraft whose stalling speeds are required to be below 61 knots, if the wind is 30 knots at 3000 ft and eight knots at the surface and the approach speed is (as usual) about 20 knots above the stall, then a 5-knot extra speed margin is sufficient and a 10-knot margin ample. In any case, a light aircraft has no difficulty in making rapid airspeed adjustments.

If a thunderstorm cell is near the airport/airstrip, it is wise to delay the approach or take off until it has passed by.

For heavy aircraft and ones that take time to accelerate to their best climb speed, the greatest hazard of wind shear is not on the approach but on take off. The recent accident at New Orleans seems to have been caused by a wind shear, with the assistance of a tall tree just beyond the end of the runway. On initial climb there is no margin of power to call upon; if the aircraft begins to sink, there is no remedy except to get it cleaned up as quickly as possible. Either a downdraught or a rapidly increasing tailwind with altitude can rob you of climb. But an increasing tailwind with altitude is hazardous mainly if there are obstacles ahead, since it affects you only to the extent that you gain altitude.

An encounter with sink, or with inability to climb, immediately after take-off calls for self-control and presence of mind. If the loss of climb is due to local downdraughts or wind shears, you will eventually be able to climb; the important thing is to keep good control of airspeed – don't let it bleed off while unconsciously pulling the nose up – while waiting to fly out of the disturbance, which is bound to be of limited horizontal extent.

It has been suggested that wind shears may account for the reputed danger of making a turn to downwind after take off; the danger, the theory goes, is not in the turn downwind but in the rapid climb into an increasing tailwind. The visual disorientation produced by a downwind turn at low altitude may play a role as well. (See chapter 7, fig. 7.9: take-off in a wind gradient.)

Perhaps the future will bring precise methods of wind shear detection or prediction, or cockpit instrumentation to automate the correct reactions to it. But at present wind shear is the sort of fickle danger against which few precautions can be taken, other than to inform ourselves about its nature, to learn to recognise the conditions in which we are likely to encounter it, and to rehearse in our minds how it will feel and how we should react to it.

The downburst defined

Initially the concept of the downburst (a strong downdraught which induces an outburst of *damaging* winds on or near the ground), which originated after the analysis of the Kennedy airport accident (24 June 1975) was regarded as controversial. It was because only a handful of meteorologists at that time could visualise that a downdraught descends to as low as 300 ft (100 m) above the ground before spreading out violently. On the contrary, the downdraught, as revealed by the Thunderstorm Project (1946–47), was *assumed* to lose its downflow speed long before it reaches the ground. Therefore, an aircraft flying beneath a downdraught should not be affected by either downflow or strong outflow winds as long as its flight altitude remains close to the ground.

The gust front on the other hand, has long been regarded as the inducer of the wind which *endangers* aircraft during lift off and landing operations. In the context of the generalised planetary scale, a gust front is a *mesoscale*, 2–216 nm (4–400 km) front of the cold air which rushes out from beneath thunderstorms.

Fujita and Srivastava of the University of Chicago as co-investigators operated the NIMROD (Northern Illinois Meteorological Research On Downbursts) project in 1978 by using three Doppler radars, and twenty-seven automated surface stations. Approximately fifty downbursts were recorded during the forty-five days of the project operation. One of the Doppler radars recorded a peak outflow of 62 kts (32 m/s) located only 100 to 150 feet above the ground.

The JAWS (joint airport weather studies) project in 1982 was operated jointly by the University of Chicago and the National Center for Atmospheric Research with Fujita (U of C) and McCarthy and Wilson (NCAR) as co-investigators. The purpose of this project was to determine the scale, life and structure of downbursts. Of the numerous downburst winds recorded, 190 were less than 2 nm in size (3.7 km) being classified as *misoscale*, 130 to 13 120 ft (40 to 4000 m) disturbances.

Based on the NIMROD and JAWS researches, the downburst is now sub-classified into *macroburst* and *microburst*. The definitions are:

Macroburst A large (mesoscale) sized downburst. An intense macroburst often causes wide-spread tornado-like property damage. Damaging winds lasting 5 to 20 minutes, could reach 150 kts (77.25 m/s).

Microburst A small (microscale) sized downburst with peak winds lasting only 1 to 5 minutes. A microburst induces dangerous tailwind and downflow shear which cannot always be detected by ground-based anemometers.

Note: 84% of the JAWS microbursts produced no rain on the ground (dry microburst) and 48% of the NIMROD microbursts were dry. Conversely, the wettest microburst in JAWS produced 0.24 inches (6 mm) in 4 minutes, or 3.6 inches (9.14 cm) per hour rate. In NIMROD, the wettest was 0.58 inches (1.47 cm) in 4 minutes, or 8.7 inches (22.1 cm) per hour rate. Furthermore, there is no general rule on the strength of a microburst comparing its wetness or dryness. The strongest JAWS microburst was a *dry* example. (After Fujita, 1983.)

References

Anderson K. W. *et al.* (1978) 'Wind-shear in Australia.' Published in *Aviation Safety Digest* 106/1979. Aeronautical Research Laboratories, Department of Defence, Melbourne, Australia.

Anon. (1966) *Agricultural Pilot Manual.* Department of Civil Aviation, Australia.

Anon. (29 September 1984) 'Microburst explored.' *Flight International* **126** (3927), 812-816.

Fujita, T. T. (1983) 'Microburst wind shear.' SMRP Research Paper 199. Department of the Geophysical Sciences, the University of Chicago, IL 60637, U.S.A.

Garrison, P. (1983) 'Shear determination.' *Flying* **110** (2), 77-81.

H.M.S.O. (1977) *Handbook of Aviation Meteorology.* London: H.M.S.O.

Nägeli, W. (1946) 'Weitere Untersuchungen uber die Windverhaltnisse im Bereich von Windschutzanlagen.' *Mitteil. Schweiz. Anstalt Forstl. Versuchswesen, Zurich* **24**, 659-737.

Oke, T. R. (1978) *Boundary Layer Climates.* London: Methuen and Co. Ltd.

10
Flagging and track guidance

Introduction

In all aerial spraying operations, the area to be treated is covered by spraying successive swaths of a width appropriate to the particular technique used; these may vary from little more than the boom span of the aircraft to more than 100 m. Each swath must therefore be marked out so that the area is covered without any gaps which might render the treatment ineffective or any double coverage which would be wasteful and possibly damaging. The method of marking used is governed by the particular operation. In some cases, swaths many km in length may be used and these present very different problems to spraying a single field which is crossed in a few seconds.

There are four main methods of track determination available to the agricultural pilot. These are:

(1) The selection of natural markers.
(2) The use of artificial markers.
(3) The use of human markers.
(4) Electronic systems:
  (i) self-contained, using on-board references
  (ii) using external references.

Selection of natural markers

It is impossible to lay down any rules on this point. Each pilot will have his own method of recognising natural features – what may be obvious to one pilot may be just part of the background to another. Obviously two large trees in an otherwise open field will be selected by all pilots. However, if the rest of the area is covered by similar trees it may be necessary to select two that have distinctive shapes, colours or heights. There are, of course, countless other natural and artificial features available – dams, bends in creeks, patches of bare ground, gates, power poles, etc.

One feature can be used for more than one swath – it is quite easy to judge one swath to one side, one over the top and another on the other side. It is very easy, though, to become 'mesmerised' by a particularly prominent feature and to imagine that one is accurately judging a second, third and maybe more swaths to one side of it. In fact they are almost certainly becoming progressively narrower until one suddenly realises that the last two have been over the same place. The reaction to this is usually to make the next one excessively wide. The only correct method is to select a fresh set of markers for each run – if possible making a tentative selection for the next run.

Many pilots find it comparatively easy to choose markers which they can recognise again on the next run. Very often, however, a particular feature may appear completely different when it is approached from the opposite direction, i.e. after a procedure turn. Unless the crop has distinctive rows to give heading indication, or the field is a regular shape with natural markers, the judgement by the pilot is soon compromised by misleading cues, e.g. spraying across row crops, or at an angle other than 90° to the direction of the rows. Flying towards distant markers often tracks the aircraft in a curve concave to the direction of the wind. It soon becomes necessary to provide additional cues to the pilot to maintain constant swath spacing.

Artificial markers

These can take the form of semi-permanent markers placed at the ends of the treatment area and spaced at the appropriate swath interval for the type of application. If the swath run exceeds a few km, or the treatment area is undulating, additional intermediate markers would probably be necessary.

There is no hard and fast rule as to what these markers should be, availability of local materials being the deciding factor. The objective of markers is that the pilot should be able to identify them at the height he is flying, and see them *in time* to initiate corrective procedures when lining up after a 180° turn, and be able to maintain track towards the marker further along the swath or at the other end of the field.

Semi-permanent markers can take many forms – flags, at least 1 m square of a material that contrasts with the crop, or boards of a similar size mounted above the crop with brightly coloured card attached; 'dayglow' treatment (fluorescence), if available, makes good reflectors in sunlight. Semi-permanent markers are probably the most economic.

There are, however, a number of disadvantages with semi-permanent markers. Flat boards can be blown over, or turn edgewise to the direction of flight. They may also have to be adjusted in height as the crop grows. Fluorescent paint deteriorates in a few weeks. Flags may also blow over, or get wrapped around the pole; also souvenir hunters may find other uses for them. One big disadvantage is that the positioning assumes a given wind direction, and semi-permanent markers do not allow for large wind deviations.

Another form of artificial marker is the 'Automatic Flagman' manufactured by North American Industries Inc. This is a device fitted to the aircraft that enable the pilot to 'eject' a paper streamer weighted at one or both ends depending on the crop. This is a most useful device as it allows the pilot to mark his progress over large areas of mono cultures. The paper streamers come in different lengths from 2.4 to 4.5 m in length; they are available in white or fluorescent orange. The weighted end is chipboard. One version uses weights at either end allowing the streamer to drape over tall crops, trees and forest. The pilot uses an eject control wired to the control stick. A 'magazine' holding the flags is mounted on the top surface of the aircraft wing

Plate 10.1 Model 6 Automatic Flagman dispenser mounted on the lower starboard mainplane of an Ag-Cat (photo: North American Industries Inc.)

(the lower wing in bi-planes) and ejects the flags near the trailing edge. Magazines hold 100, 180 or 280 flags. There is also a helicopter mounting available.

A U.K. operator found the best arrangement to be a combination of fixed markers at one end of the field, and the Automatic Flagman at the other end where the line may be difficult to determine. Good judgement is necessary in dropping the flags as the accuracy of the swath width is vital. Some disadvantages of the Automatic Flagman are shown when they are used in crosswinds with marked turbulence. The distribution pattern would be variable, even if ejected at exactly the same height. Some crops would swallow up the streamer when waving in windy conditions. Some agricultural machinery would object to digesting quantities of paper and chipboard. However, it is the only system that can be completely controlled by the pilot and is, in the main, cost effective when considering other methods and labour costs.

Flying towards fixed or semi-permanent markers can sometimes be confusing after only a few swaths, particularly when concentration is necessary if flying in close proximity to obstacles. A system described by a U.K. operator uses sets of three markers in alternate contrasting colours. This arrangement is reproduced in the cockpit as a set of beads on a wire and after a little practice, providing the pilot remembers to move one bead each time he completes a swath, 100% accuracy can be achieved.

It must be emphasised that markers must have sufficient visible surface area to be immediately discernible by the pilot who is a considerable distance away, moving fast and with little time to pinpoint its location while aligning the aircraft. It is preferable that they should be recognisable by colour from adjacent fields, where markers may be positioned for other purposes.

It is worth mentioning that trees can be fixed markers with streamers or tapes (paper – to degrade) pulled or placed on the tree tops by some means. Crossbows, catapults, even stone throwing have been used to assist in this way and perhaps in the future there will be a simple mechanical 'tree-top' marker available. However to achieve any significant improvement to distribution accuracy, other methods should be utilised.

Balloons and 'kytoons' are both inflatable devices which have limited applications, usually for specific treatment projects especially with very tall crops or trees. (Kytoons are orange-coloured dirigible balloons 1.8 m long filled with helium, manufactured by W. R. Grace & Co., Cambridge, Mass. U.S.A.) Both may also be used for positional guidance over long distances to the required area or reference points in featureless regions for electronic guidance systems. They can be large and raised to considerable heights. However balloons are very unstable when tethered, hence the development of kytoons.

Plate 10.2 'Kytoons' helium-filled and ready to be deployed at either end of a plot in mountainous country (photo: Jerry O'Neal)

Both have similar disadvantages to field markers and additionally, due to instability and susceptibility to bursting, they will also be only directly overhead of the tether point, i.e. for ground reference, in zero wind conditions. However they are an inexpensive means for specific guidance although the supply of hydrogen or expensive helium gas in bottles can cause additional logistic and labour efforts. Provided there is a continuous wind it is conceivable that *kites* of the stable box or controllable types could have specific use as reference markers. With these devices the raising of passive reflectors may aid in the future development of advanced guidance systems consisting of a self-contained onboard aircraft electronic package relying on easily moveable fixed (ground) reference points for their function.

In spraying large areas of forest or tsetse bush, the problem of maintaining a proper spacing of successive swaths is very much more difficult. Each swath may be so long that a flag or marker board cannot be seen from beginning to end of the run. Furthermore the height of the forest may be such that no mobile marker of the board type can be raised from the ground to be seen above the tree tops. Some very ingenious permanent markers have been devised in forestry work, such as explosive cans of white paint detonated in the tree tops. More simply, white sheets have been spread in the trees. Any such method, used with a long swath, is at the double disadvantage of being seen at a very small angle by the low-flying pilot and having a poor level of contrast to the general background.

A system of permanent markers used in a successful tsetse eradication scheme in Rwanda has been described by Buyckx (1962). The area treated consists of a plateau broken by lakes and swamps with small narrow closed valleys cutting into the plateau. These valleys are filled with bush in which *Glossina morsitans* bred. White boards 120 cm high and 80 cm wide were wired onto poles 10 m high and set at intervals along alternate swathes, each being given a Roman numeral I, III, V, VII, or IX. The pilot then flew up and down the swathes as shown in fig. 10.1. This method was successful as a way of dealing with a number of narrow isolated strips of bush so scattered that several ground marker parties would be needed to mark for a single sortie. The permanent marking also made it possible to operate when ground parties would have been bogged down in wet weather.

Permanent markers are more difficult to use in the spraying of a large continuous area since the pilot may have difficulty in seeing the markers at a considerable distance and will find it even more difficult to choose the correct one if there is a long row of them. In forest spraying this has been overcome, when using large aircraft, by having a flying controller who circles above the spraying aircraft and guides

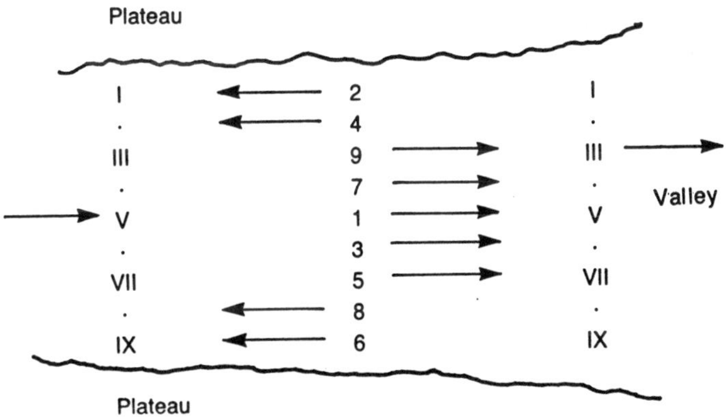

Fig 10.1 Flying technique evolved by Buyckx (1962) for spraying small valleys. The aircraft enters over marker V to spray swath 1, turns to enter swath 2 over marker I and continues to spray swaths in the order given by the Arabic numbers leaving the ninth swath over marker III to the right. In long valleys three or four rows of markers may be sent out to ensure accurate swath spacing

the pilot by VHF radio. This is an expensive solution to the problem and one which is beyond the reach of most.

Whittam (1962) has mentioned smoke as a possible marker. This was tried and found to be quite visible at two miles under favourable conditions. Shell diesoline was fed from a pressure retaining knapsack sprayer at a pressure of 0.35 kg cm^{-2} into the exhaust manifold of a Land-Rover. A controlling jet drilled with a number 60 drill (0.014 in) was found to give a suitable rate of flow. In operation the sprayer was turned on as the aircraft started its run toward the marker and closed again as it passed overhead. The excess oil in the exhaust system was then sufficient to produce smoke to guide the aircraft through its turn before the return spray run. Opening and shutting the throttle of the Land-Rover caused the smoke to be emitted in a series of puffs which were rather more conspicuous than a continuous stream. For use in areas of tall bush, the exhaust extension should be carried up at least 6 m which may prove unwieldy on rough ground. The smoke cloud also provides a good guide to meteorological conditions.

Aldis signalling lamps have been used successfully, for example for tsetse control in Tanzania (Miller and Chadwick, 1963). It was necessary for the signaller to stand on top of a vehicle in order to keep the aircraft in sight above the level of bush. It was also necessary to keep flashing the lamp at the aircraft while the pilot was turning to line up for the swath, as of course he was using the light as the only reference for the start of the run. A further signaller was positioned at the far end of the run, which was 6.5 km away. The poor visibility in early morning spraying in Tanzania made it difficult to see the white-painted top of the ground support vehicle; however, there was no problem seeing the Aldis signalling lamp. The maximum error on passing over the second signaller was half a swath, about 25 m. Miller and Chadwick also used high intensity xenon flash tubes as used in aircraft dinghies, but this tube did not have the power or the flashing repetition rate that is necessary for the pilot to use the light for lining up and maintaining track. It was probably not very good for the purpose for which it was designed, but it could use a small battery.

The use of high intensity lights for pilot guidance has been employed successfully in the past (Whittam, 1962). It was found from trials of brightness evaluation of different light sources that the light emitted by a xenon gas filled flash tube could be seen from a distance of 8 km in broad daylight. The tube can be flashed sixty to eighty times per minute, which is recommended for maximum attractiveness. It can be operated from the 12 volt electrical system of a motor vehicle. In the same trials, the tube was mounted onto a special telescoping mast to raise it to a useful height above ground. The mast was pneumatically operated. A small gasoline engine driven compressor and air storage tank was attached to the mast base. The complete assembly was easily installed in the back of a small truck. The mast when telescoped could pass under most highway bridges or wires and trees. When extended, the light was nearly 10 m above the ground. Since it was not guyed, it had to be telescoped down each time the vehicle was moved; however, this was no great problem as the mast could be raised and lowered in less than 30 s. A much simpler mast arrangement could be made and operated by hand if the maximum height need not be more than 4.5 to 6 m.

Plate 10.3 High intensity xenon flash tube mounted on a pneumatically operated telescopic mast; the flashes can be seen up to 8 km in daylight (photo: U.S.D.A.)

Smoke has already been mentioned as an aid to track guidance and another possible solution may be in the sequential ejection from the aircraft of smoke generators. Although this is not a new idea, a British pyrotechnics company is undertaking a feasibility study, in the light of recent developments, which may overcome the severe hurdles inherent in this concept.

The Agri-flag system is a pilot-operated device from the U.S.A. This is a novel approach and would have certain obvious limitations, but there are also specific utilisations, particularly in fertiliser and herbicide application. The system consists of a winch and battery unit, a flag and light mounted on a 'traveller', and a radio transmitter installed in the aeroplane or helicopter. The winch drum contains 915 m of cable, and the flag unit is capable of traversing rough ground, mud and low brush. To facilitate handling by one man, the winch and battery power unit are mounted on separate bases, each with a stout fibreglass cover for protection. Handles on each cover make it easy to unload the two units and place them in position together. Two colour-coded plug-in cables connect the power to the winch unit in a few seconds.

One man and pick-up truck can place several machines operating in the same area. For average sized crops, one Agri-flag is sufficient, while on long runs, particularly at night, two may be required. Ten radio frequencies are provided, with a selector switch on the transmitter housing.

To operate the Agri-flag system, the winch and battery units are placed in position at the upwind side of one end of the crop to be treated. The flag unit remains on the truck while the cable is attached to the rear of the truck for driving to the downwind side of the crop. There, the flag unit is placed in position and the cable attached to it. If desired, the blinking yellow light is turned on. A half-minute stop at the winch unit, to set the swath measuring mechanism, completes the preparation of the Agri-flag for operation.

As the pilot approaches the flag, near the end of a swath, he actuates the winch unit with the switch on his control stick. While he completes the swath and makes his turn-around, the flag moves exactly one swath width and is ready for the next run (after Transland catalogue).

Aritifical fixed and semi-permanent markers are many and varied, and there are certainly other approaches being used. Apart from purpose-built equipment, considerable scope for ingenuity and innovation is available, the nature of the crop or terrain to be treated and the availability of local materials being the guiding factors.

Human markers (or flaggers)

The first essential is, of course, that the markers should be so positioned as to be visible to the pilot. They should either wear clothing or carry flags of a colour which is visible against the background, and should be placed on the highest ground available and clear of trees, etc. They may be used to mark the centre of each run – in which case their initial position will be half the swath width (plus or minus an allowance for drift) from the starting boundary, and they will move the full swath each time.

When fairly long runs are involved, they should be placed some distance in from the ends of the field and should be briefed to start moving to their next position as soon as they see that the aircraft is lined up on the run, each marker starting to move when the aircraft is within a few hundred metres of him. In this case centre markers can be safely used. When the runs are short there may be insufficient time between the aircraft lining up and reaching the marker's position for the marker to move clear of the aircraft's path. One method, in this case, is for the marker to plant a flag to mark the run, move clear until the aircraft has passed over it, go back and collect the flag, pace out the next swath, plant the flag again and once more move clear. Time, again, may preclude this method.

A better method is to use wingtip markers. The normal method here is to place them, initially, the full swath width from the starting boundary, again allowing for drift. They will thus be marking the leading edge of the swath and will be clear of the aircraft (and also of chemical drift if the job is started on the downwind side) or, at the worst, will only have to take the first few steps towards the next mark to get clear. If operational considerations make it essential to start to job on the upwind side, and wingtop markers are to be used, they should be placed, initially, on the boundary fence, and should continue to mark the 'trailing' edge of the swath, in order to keep them clear of spray drift. As they will then be unable to start moving to their next position until after the aircraft has passed them, this is not an entirely satisfactory method. It may be thought that it is more difficult for the pilot to line up accurately on wingtip markers, but after a very little practice it is no problem, since it merely involves aiming, on each run, at a point a constant distance to one side of the marker. Where they are used to mark the leading edge of the run, the first aiming point of each job is exactly half way between the boundary and the marker, which provides a frequent check on estimation of the correct distance.

The pilot's responsibility for ensuring the safety of the markers from injury by the aircraft or contamination by toxic chemicals must always take precedence over all other considerations.

There exists a contamination hazard to flagmen working continuously within an unhealthy environment. For all agrochemicals have to a degree some aspect to which lengthy exposure should be avoided – be it toxic active ingredient, solvent or solid particle, liquid drop or vapour. Suitable protection is thus essential as appropriate. Training is a must so that confidence exists beween pilot and marker, particularly in that the latter understands what the pilot wants and how he does the job.

The first consideration thus involves stimulating an awareness by markers of the importance of wearing protective clothing, decontamination and the other safety practices and procedures appropriately recommended for the particular treatment. Where highly toxic material is dispersed they should also have regular medical checks, based on time

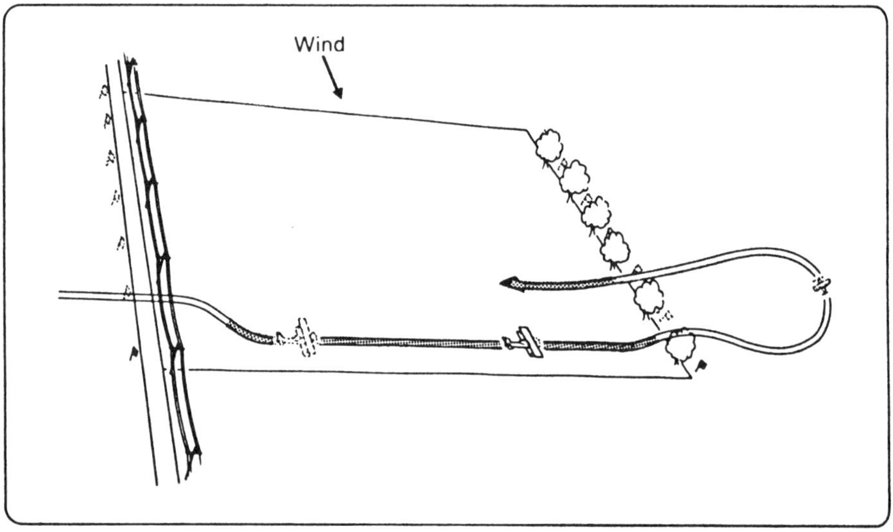

Fig 10.2 Schematic representation of the 'classic' procedure turn (after F.A.O., 1974)

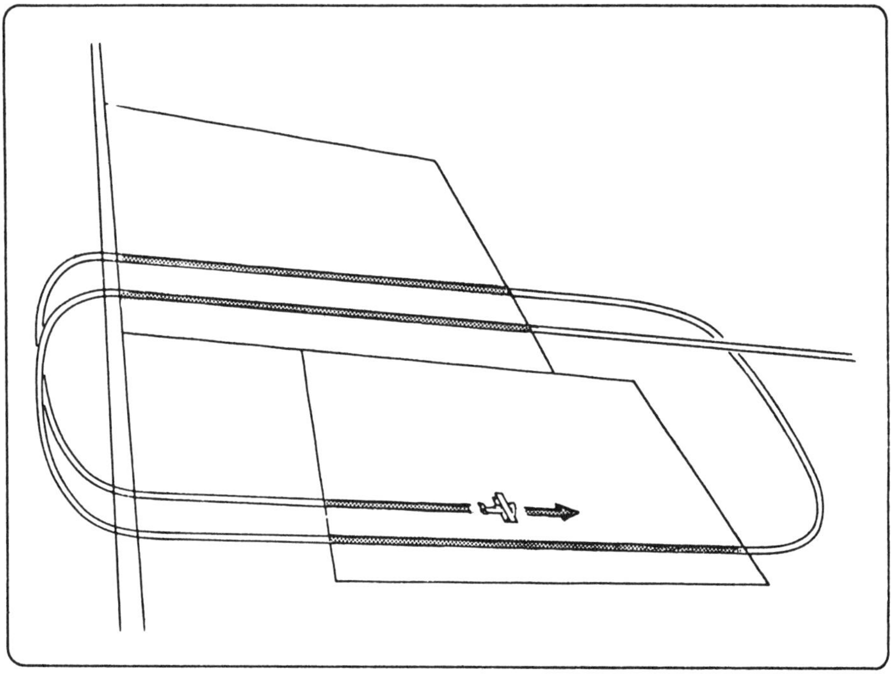

Fig 10.3 Schematic representation of the 'round robin' procedure. Note that two fields or a single large field can be treated by this method, but it requires two additional markers (after F.A.O., 1974)

of hazardous exposure. This of course all leads into the second factor of adequate training, particularly as to why certain procedures are followed, e.g. the reason for the determined swath width, the rudimentary sign system to communicate observations or operational changes between ground/air/ground, crash rescue and first aid actions, etc. (see the section in chapter 4 on hazards to pilots and ground crews).

Some suggestions for markers to follow are:

(1) Wear colour contrast clothing or fluorescent bright waistcoats or jackets (conditions permitting).
(2) Use a mechanical counter to relieve the boredom of counting 1 through 20 (paces) all day. Better, but more expensive, an odometer helps to keep parallel swaths ('the other fellow takes longer paces').

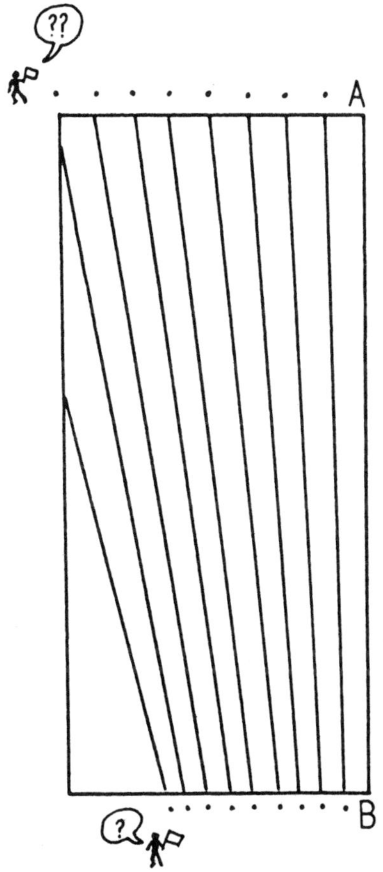

Fig 10.4 A method of measuring the distance between flagging positions is necessary so that each man steps off the same distance (after Haley, 1973)

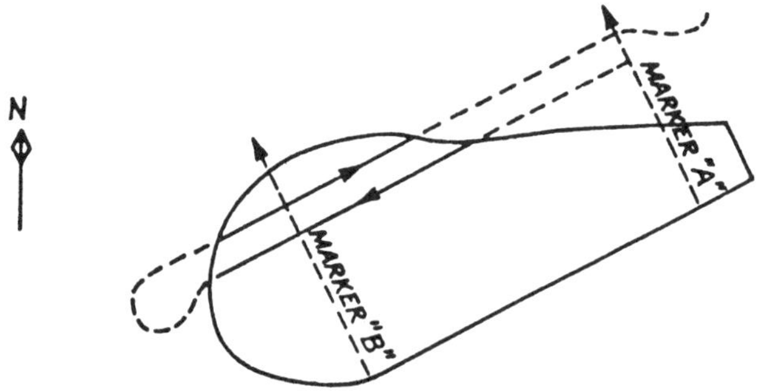

Fig 10.5 Marking in adjacent areas

(3) If possible, use the more expensive, small radios which in CB enlightened countries are relatively cheap communication equipment.

Figure 10.5 shows a field where it may not be important to position the markers in the widest part of the area, since it is possible for marker A to continue measuring the required spacing in the adjacent area, thus continuing to give the pilot the line indication although, of course, the spray is turned on and off at the boundary of the treatment area.

Figure 10.6 shows a similar field but marker A cannot move, and be seen, through the trees. To position him, initially, in the widest part of the area would put him too close to B for an adequate line indication during the long runs on the south-east edge. He should be briefed that when he reaches the north-west fence he should walk directly towards B until he can again turn and measure a swath width towards the north-west, repeating this as often as necessary and taking care always to move either parallel to the aircraft's runs or at right angles to them. Any diagonal movement will, of course, soon result in uneven spacing of the swaths.

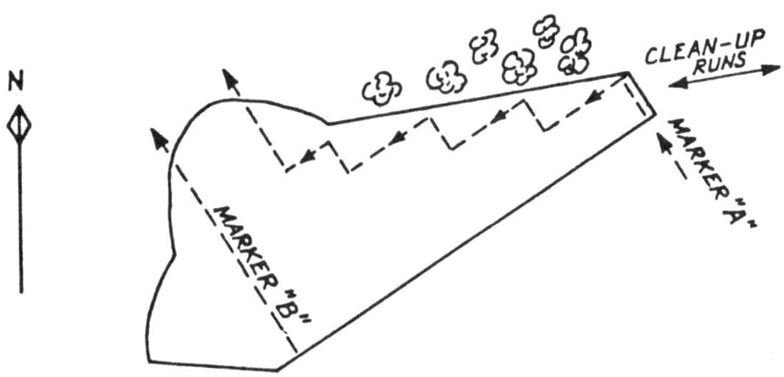

Fig 10.6 Marking within the field but adopting a 'stair' path adjacent to the irregular edge

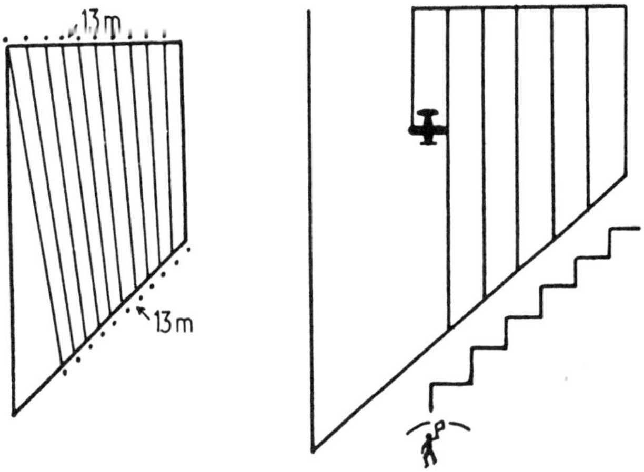

Fig 10.7 'Stair' path of marker when edges of the field are not parallel (after Haley, 1973)

Night flagging

Operating in darkness presents a whole new dimension to this work, as both pilots and flagmen will need to have their own lights in order to see and be seen. The aeroplane is rigged with a set of floodlights which illuminate the flight path across the field. The flagman guides the pilot in the same manner as usual, except that a powerful flashlight is used instead of a flag.

At night, extra precautions must be taken when darkness hides otherwise obvious surface features from the pilot's view. He must determine, from checking the field in daylight, if it is safe to work in relation to obstructions or terrain. *Only the pilot is able to make these judgements.* The preparations by loaders and flagmen are basically the same as for day opeations, with the addition of preparing the lighting equipment. The loader will need runway end lights, and some form of floodlighting for the loading area. The runway lights may be either kerosene goose-neck lights or smudge pots, or electric, preferably battery operated in remote airstrips. The lights must be reliable and, in the case of kerosene lights, long burning. The pilot may require some spares in case a light fails.

The flagman's preparations include the usual equipment – protective clothing, measuring devices for the swath intervals, walkie-talkies (if used), the worksheets, food and water, and any other special requirements, e.g. mosquito repellent. Each flagman should have in addition to his own flashlight, spare bulbs and batteries. What may seem like an excessive redundancy of back-up equipment is actually cheap insurance that the whole job is not brought to a complete halt on account of one little burnt out bulb.

The pilot must brief the flagging team carefully and this should include a tour through the locations where the flagging team are to take up positions. It is more likely that 'flagging the wrong field' is possible at night, even if the personnel consider they are familiar with the area. This is potentially very dangerous, as the pilot may learn too late of an unexpected obstruction. The pilot will be depending on the flagman almost entirely to guide him to the proper field, especially on dark moonless nights, since all he will be able to see is a few stationary farmlights.

The flagman, after locating the field by careful reference to the worksheet, must make a close visual inspection of the crop as a final check that it is the right one. (This would probably be done in the daylight briefing.) The wind velocity should be checked and the second flagman positioned at his end of the field. Another word of caution about operating in darkness concerns where to drive. Since it is more difficult to see the way around at night (and the condition of the road ahead) one should drive only as much as is necessary and drive slowly. There are occasions when it may be necessary to mark (in daylight) the tracks to follow at night by any of the vehicles.

Wearing protective clothing is always important, but especially so for night spraying jobs. As it is more difficult to move around at night, the pilot may not want to change the flight direction because of a change of drift, and he might not even notice one. It may be necessary for the flagman to stand fairly close to the field edge, so use of protective clothing becomes more important.

After getting into position, the flagman should leave the flashlight off until it is possible to see the aeroplane coming, unless the pilot has briefed otherwise. The pilot may require some guidance for his first run at a greater distance, but there are many ways to achieve this, and it comes down to a thorough briefing. The pilot may even wish to do a dummy run on the first approach. In the still, cool and quiet air, it is possible to hear the aircraft from much greater distances than is possible during the daytime, thus ample advance warning is given of its arrival. (Radio communication may well be economically justified with modern high cost equipment and chemicals.)

The flagman should be watching for the aircraft navigation lights, as the pilot will not operate the floodlights until working in the field. It should be remembered that a green light is at the right (starboard) wingtip, and red at the left (port) wingtip (port wine is red!). A white light is displayed at the tail. Remembering these positions will help later in determining the aircraft's direction of flight. As soon as the flagman sees the red and green navigation lights he turns on the flashlight and aims at the aircraft. The signal the pilot will be looking for from the flagman is a 'blinking' light. This is accomplished by pointing the steady beam directly at the aircraft, following its flight path and *slowly* moving it up and down (fig. 10.8). The flashlight must not be held still as there may be other stationary lights around that could confuse the pilot. The reason for signalling while the aircraft is some distance off is to allow the pilot to locate the field, as the light may be the primary reference (subject to the briefing). If the powerful sealed-beam lamps are used instead of flashlights, care is necessary not to blind the pilot by shining it steadily in his eyes.

Once the pilot is lined up, he will operate the aircraft floodlights and make a pass along the field. The flashlight must be continued in use until the aircraft is very close to the end of the field, as the pilot will need a definite point to aim towards in the darkness. The light must be turned away from the aircraft when the next swath is marked or the pilot may follow the light and put a bend in the swath. The flagman must time his moves to the next swath mark at the point where the pilot has about 90° remaining to complete his turn onto the next swath. This allows him to line up and start the application at the correct position. He may also be able to see the other flagman at the far end of the field, and this affords even more precise alignment.

The flagman should monitor the performance of the flashlight, or lamp, in case the batteries are running low. They should be replaced

Fig 10.8 The light should be directed at the aircraft, following its flight path and *slowly* moved up and down; this will be observed by the pilot as a 'blinking' light (Haley, 1973)

as soon as the light appears to get dim, as the pilot will need to see a very bright light. One of the flagmen may have to reposition at the completion of the regular swath application runs, in order that the pilot will be able to line-up for any clean-up runs. Again, the precise order of things would be determined at the briefing.

Electronic systems

General

Electronic track guidance used in the present generation of application aircraft (including helicopters) cannot be taken as the universal answer to all track guidance requirements. There are many spraying jobs that can only be done visually, e.g. spraying in hilly or mountainous country, spraying numerous small irregular plots, spraying in the proximity of wires or other significant obstructions. In other cases, such as application on non-crop areas, e.g. larviciding in rivers, air to air spraying (flying locust swarms), etc., electronic track guidance would not contribute to the efficiency of the operation. However, on the larger areas requiring treatment like large monoculture, or tsetse barrier spraying, accurate track guidance becomes essential. In fact it is probably the only way to exploit the full potential of the aircraft. The ULV rate of application is often limited by the aircraft's safe endurance. For example, tsetse control in East Africa using synergized pyrethrum at 0.18 l/ha (Lee, 1969) means that an aircraft with a 2000 l hopper could treat 110 km^2, if it could stay airborne long enough!

Pest control in crops could show significant savings with accurate track guidance. For example, studies by N.A.S.A. have confirmed that if a pilot could always fly within 5 ft (1.5 m) of the desired ground track when spraying, the amount of chemicals applied could be reduced from 30 to 40% for the same degree of control (Thomson and Mitchell, 1978). It would not take a great effort to justify the investment in electronic track guidance with savings of this order of magnitude.

Electronic track guidance in agricultural aircraft has in the past used systems developed for navigation of ships or transport aircraft. There are now systems developed for the small aircraft and also catering for some of the unique requirements of agricultural operations. The principles of operation of the main systems are now described.

Electronic systems – self-contained

Inertial navigation system (INS)

The INS system, in principle, is derived from very simple laws of mechanics and is one method of accurate navigation or guidance which is completely self-contained requiring no reference to radio, radar, celestial bodies or other external source for its operation. Basically the INS consists of three mutually perpendicular accelerometers mounted on a platform kept level by gyroscopes, with a computer to integrate the sensed accelerations, giving velocity and resolving distances along the axis of the accelerometers. This information can then be presented on indicators as any of the navigational references or data as appropriately required. These accelerometers are mounted on a gyro stabilised platform which isolates them from the effects of gravity and maintains their earth orientated axis regardless of the aircraft attitude (fig. 10.9).

From this basic description of the mechanics of an inertial system it can be appreciated that manufacturing the components is to a very high level of precision, to which the electronics must be matched, and compensated.

Experience in North America with developed systems to include grid guidance capability in addition to the basic line navigation concept has had encouraging results, improving upon the 1 nautical mile per hour error to which INS is limited by specification. The results have shown errors of approximately 600–700 ft cross-track and about 1000 ft along track after one hour but with crew familiarity in operation and thus manual updating over precise map read visual reference co-ordinates have achieved track guidance accuracies of ± 100–200 ft.

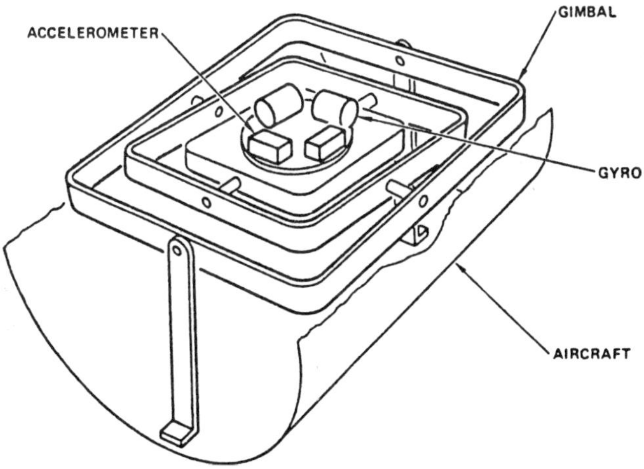

Fig 10.9 Inertia sensing unit functional drawing showing relationships of accelerometers, gyros and gimbals

As gyros are complex mechanical devices the major reservation is that for precise operation any external imposed forces, intentional or otherwise, should be smoothly applied to ensure that they remain accurately controllable without impairing their precession, bearing stiction or inertial characteristics. Thus for agricultural track guidance it would appear preferable that utilisation be limited to more stable aircraft.

This system is not suitable for the smaller aircraft, at least the present generation of INS. At the moment it is a very expensive system and needs high technical support to ensure reliability. The system has been used very successfully by the larger application aircraft, e.g. the Douglas DC-6B used in spruce budworm control in Canadian forests. INS is still being developed, and it could well be that in future a small reliable (and cheaper) system could become available for the agricultural pilot. INS is one of the few systems that is totally independent of external beacons or transmitters, a useful advantage when operating in the more remote and inaccessible areas.

Doppler navigation

Doppler is the alternative completely self-contained system which operates on the principle that the frequency of a wave (microwave, radio, sound, etc.) will change if the receiver is moving relative to the transmitter. The received frequency is increased by V/λ Hz if the closing velocity is V cm/s and the transmitted wavelength is λ cm. Likewise, received frequency is decreased if the receiver is approaching the wave generator. This propagation characteristic is obvious in the pitch change of sound waves emitted by an approaching/receding fast moving vehicle.

Airborne Doppler transmitter/receivers function by emitting three (or four) beams from a special antenna array to be reflected by the ground back to the antenna. Thus a double frequency shift results between the microwave radar (e.g. 13.325 and 13.3143 GHz) continuous wave (CW) transmissions and their reception. Note that one frequency is emitted in the two forward beams and the other is emitted in the third rear left beam whilst the two frequencies are simultaneously emitted from the fourth right rear beam to provide the intermediate (lower) frequency, i.e. the difference between the two, which is used as a reference by the receiver. Another intermediate frequency (i.f.) reference is fed to the receiver by separately mixing the two microwave frequencies internally. The receiver thus extracts the difference between the received and internal source signals from the three radiated beams to provide the i.f. plus Doppler spectrum, which are then processed separately through further receiver and frequency tracking stages.

The narrow conic, radiated beams angles are accurately known in

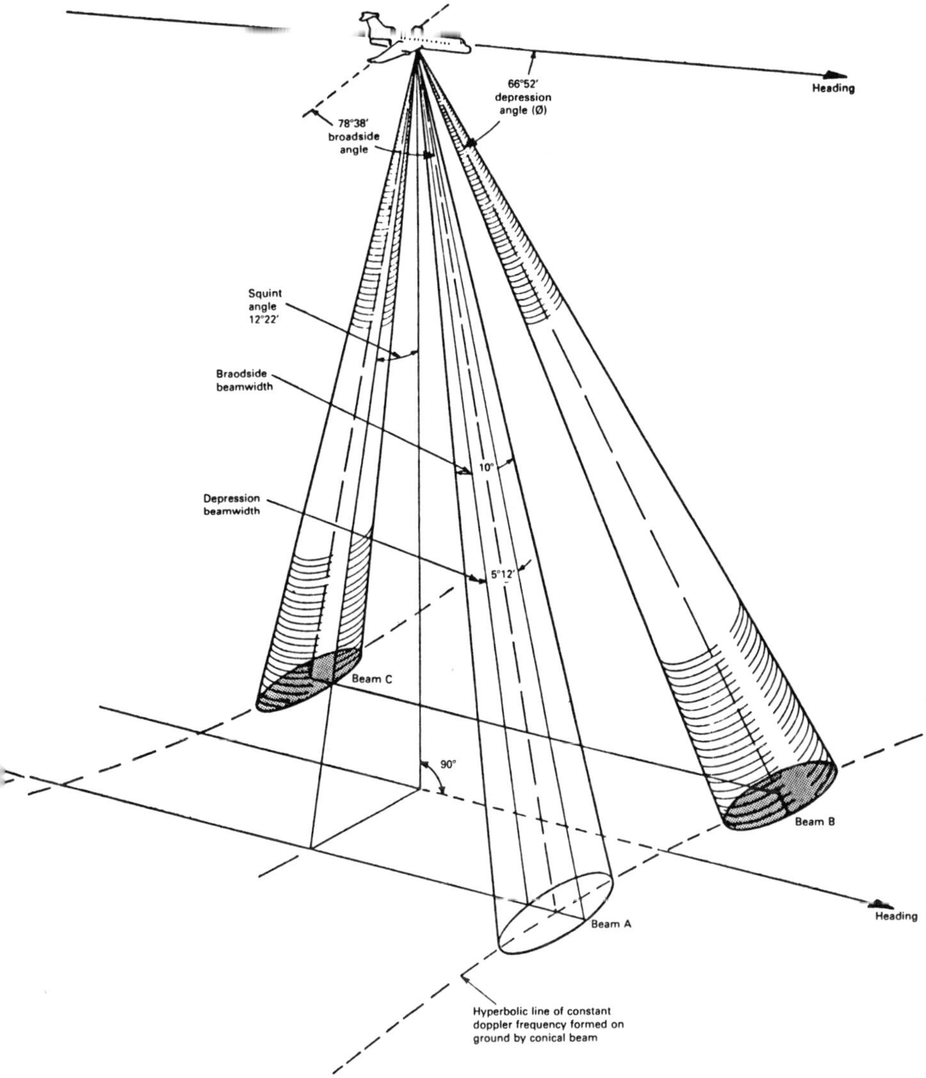

Fig 10.10 Beam pattern of a Doppler navigation system

respect to the antenna (fig. 10.10) and thus by sine or cosine computations are processed into a ground speed and drift indication. Thus we can visualise Doppler as an accurate electronic speedometer providing true ground speed and angle of drift. With an additional computer into which this data is fed, plus a heading or directional input from an accurate gyrocompass, other information can be resolved e.g. left/right indications, a moving map flight log, wind velocity, direction, distance to go, etc.

As an agricultural aircraft track guidance system requiring parallel lane keeping, the gyro compass input to the Doppler computer is necessary as the heading reference for reciprocal turning. This gyro equipment is not accurate to ± 100 ft tolerance unless reasonably short runs, e.g. 5–10 miles, and gentle low rate turns are made. The Doppler groundspeed errors are also cumulative with increasing distance gone and thus the system, if operated by reference to several precisely known positions, can be manually updated by an experienced pilot to achieve ± 100 ft lane guidance.

Further factors complicating its use as an accurate low-level guidance are the fixed antenna and thus radiated beams which suffer from change in angles with varying aircraft flight attitude (a function of airspeed and weight) and effects of pitch and roll also cause errors. In turns, Doppler errors occur with wind, which is invariably present, and the aircraft will be downwind from the indicated or required position. Corrections by pitch and roll altitude data made available to the computer can improve upon these sources of inaccuracies.

During turns a standard gyro magnetic compass is subject to instantaneous errors due to the inherent geometry of the gimbal suspension, and this heading error results in a position error. It is however reduced if the turn is made in dumbbell fashion. Secondly cross track error (CTE) refers to compass accuracy on a straight line course and is a function of the amplitude of the residual one cycle error after calibration, thus very accurate compensation swings of the gyro compass on the aircraft are necessary.

Performance of the latest Doppler/gyrocompass systems have manufacturer claims for navigation accuracies of 0.25–0.35% CEP of distance flown with resolution of readouts of latitude/longitude co-ordinates of 0.1 min of arc, grid position to 10 m and range/bearing of 0.01 km, 0.1 degree arc and velocity computations to 0.15%.

Electronic systems – using external references

Hyperbolic navigation

The following systems all use hyperbolic lines of constant phase difference, and the basic principles are now described.

Radio waves are transmitted omni-directionally from the aerial so that they are standing in space – that is, the phase of a signal received at a fixed point from one transmitter is always the same (fig. 10.11). Thus in fig. 10.11(a) the concentric rings, which are one wavelength apart, represent lines of constant phase, i.e. 10 kHz = 8 *n* miles (14.832 km).

If two transmitters of the same frequency are located so that their signals overlap (fig. 10.11(b)), the circles (representing lines of constant phase) will cross at a point where the received phases are the same. If

(a)

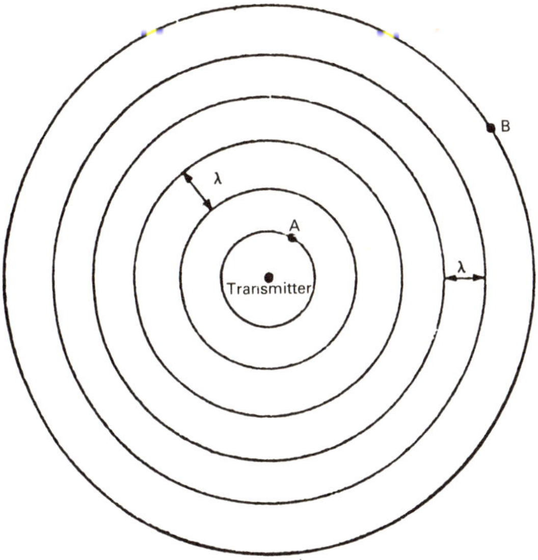

(b)

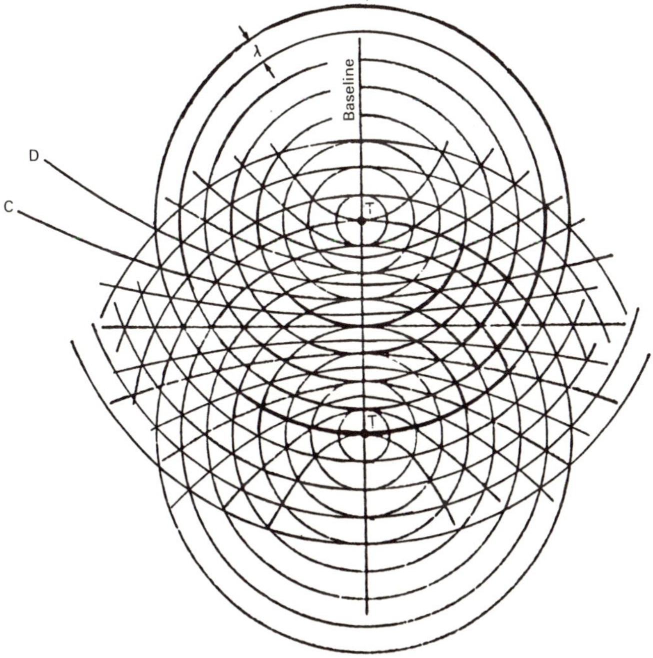

Fig 10.11 Hyperbolic navigation: A and B are points of equal phase; λ is the wavelength; C and D are hyperbolic lines of zero phase difference (occurs every half wavelength)

such points are joined they form a hyperbola with the transmitters at the foci. The line joining the transmitters is known as the base line.

These hyperbolae can be used as lines of constant phase difference (lines of position, or LOP) and, in the case drawn, are lines of zero phase difference. Such a line will recur every half wavelength, a distance known as the hyperbolic lane width.

If a third transmitter is now considered, again using the same frequency, and similar LOPs constructed, a hyperbolic grid is formed. If a navigator knows his starting position on the grid, a lane-counting device will give him a continual position update as his aircraft moves. Charts are available with such hyperbolic grids for established aids like Loran.

Omega is just such a hyperbolic aid, but the advance in computer technology has eliminated – at least in airborne applications – the need for these charts. Lane counting is done by the computer which, given a starting position, converts the counts into latitude and longitude.

Omega long range area navigation systems are intended to replace other older and less accurate although somewhat similar systems such as Loran A and C. In addition another network of ten military transmitters provides a comparable worldwide capability for accurate navigation/guidance and although its future is not certain, it is being used in conjunction with Omega, as its very low frequency (VLF) emission is of simple format and continuous, fixed frequencies between 14 and 25 kHz. The eight current Omega stations transmit three separate frequencies pulsed sequentially from each station during a 10 s complete worldwide synchronised cycle, this precision being controlled by four caesium atomic clocks in each transmitter. The frequencies utilised are in the 10–14 kHz band.

Receivers select the best and strongest signals and determine phase difference. The computer is preprogrammed with diurnal wave shift corrections for every 20 min for several years ahead. Magnetic variation and earth rotation affect radio wave propagation but the navigational computer library compensates for this when processing receiver data into the appropriate guidance information.

Some regions of the world do not have signal reception as yet of adequate strength for optimum accuracy which can be in the order of 100–200 ft (more likely to be about 1000 ft). Again an experienced pilot using observed reference points could achieve much improved accuracy – an advantage of a combined Omega VLF system is that random error occurs continuously about the desired track compared to Doppler and INS in which errors are cumulative.

An experimental improvement to Omega is the differential system, in which an accurately positioned ground receiver relays errors in radio reception in order that the airborne computer can correct for them and so greatly improve system accuracy.

Hyperbolic survey and navigation systems have been produced and developed by the Decca group of companies. Examples are given with frequency and range in brackets. Loran C (100 kHz; 1300 miles, ground wave; 3000 miles, sky wave), Lambda (100 kHz, 400 miles), Decca Main Chain navigator, i.e. Mk 8, Mk 15 with Danac or lightweight Dectrac, Mk 19 (100 kHz; 200–400 miles), Hi-Fix (2 MHz; 100 miles), Sea-Fix and Agri-Fix (2 MHz; 40–100 miles).

Loran C will be phased out of operation on being superseded by the more accurate Omega System and so will not be further mentioned.

Lambda is a range/range two transmitter low-frequency system basically similar to the VLF system and is used for naval survey work.

Main Chain systems are generally semi-permanent sets of three transmitters which are presently located in Europe, the Persian Gulf, eastern Canada, South Africa and Japan, covering limited and mainly coastal regions. This system can provide very accurate navigation and guidance to within tens of metres in optimum areas of coverage, at typical surface vehicle speeds (fig. 10.12). To operate in other areas transportable transmitters are available. Airborne equipment consists of antenna and amplifier, receiver, computer and receiver control box with, depending on the Mk type, either a lane identification meter, three decometers, a flight log, zone identification meter and control box, or the simplified version Dectrac for slower aircraft (below 200 kts) which has two units, position fixing meter and tracking unit which combine the functions of the first version excluding the flight log.

Hi-Fix is modified to update at a faster time interval to permit accurate guidance at aircraft speeds and has been used successfully for agricultural track guidance within limits of the transportable transmitters providing fixed hyperbolic patterns, i.e. fixed direction lanes of equal phase difference which, excepting the base line (connecting the two transmitters) where the bisector is at right angles, curve around the transmitters. This introduces divergence in lane spacing which limits the area for practical purposes where the lanes are sufficiently parallel to avoid over or under application (fig. 10.13 (a)).

Providing lane divergence and directions are planned out using hyperbolic to chart conversion, accuracies of less than 10 m are obtainable. Note that the operational frequency of 1.9 MHz gives a lane width on the base line of 1.5 m (Main Chain at 100 kHz lane width is about 1.5 km). Lane indicators are calibrated to 1/100 of a lane for potential accuracies of 0.8 m and 15 m respectively. Airborne components for Hi-Fix consist of antenna receiver, computer, flight log, left/right indicator and a lane counter.

Sea-Fix was developed from Hi-Fix and miniaturised for compactness and increased portability, with a pulse transmission similar to Hi-Fix.

Agri-Fix, a redesigned Sea-Fix, was produced mainly to increase the

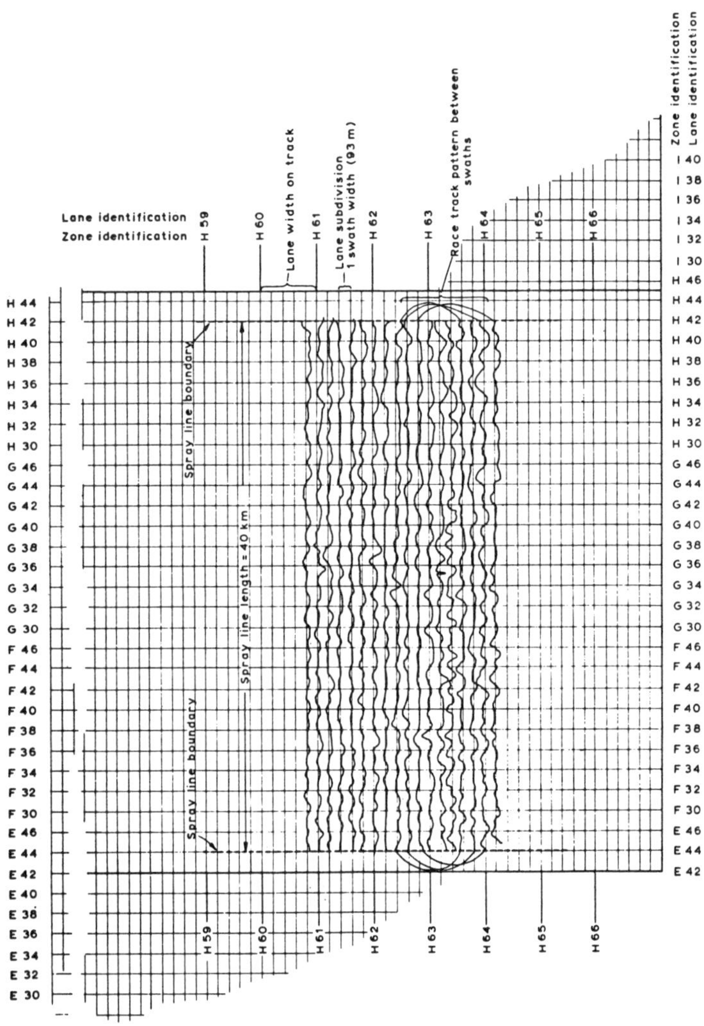

Fig 10.12 Annotated flight log chart record (Decca Main Chain) showing completed spray lines. The trace record exaggerates the actual deviation from the required spray line which in practice is only a few metres. For clarity the trace indications when flying the procedure turn between swaths have been erased and a schematic insert included (Joyce *et al.*, 1968)

(a)

(b)

(c)

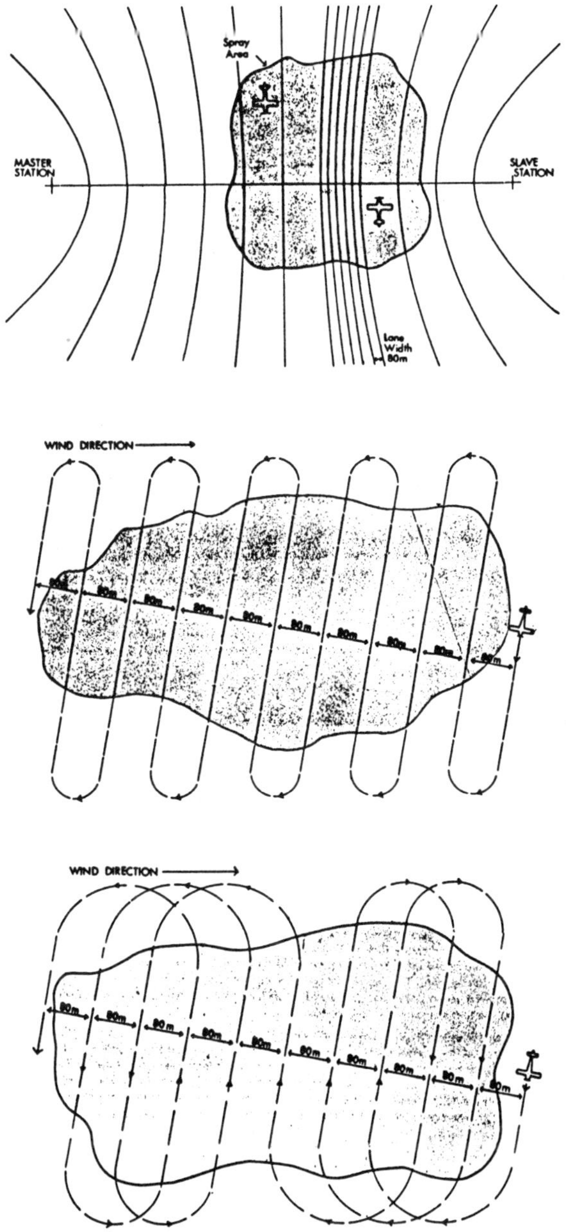

Fig 10.13 Decca Hi-Fix navigation system: (a) shows the pattern transmitted by the TGS system, upon which swath runs as in (b) and (c) may be based; (b) progressive swath application; (c) 'round robin' swath application. (Equipment: modified Hi-Fix units with airborne equipment and display. Frequency: 1890–1905 kcs. Baseline length over rice paddy in excess of 30 miles.) (Joyce *et al.*, 1970)

Plate 10.4 Decca 'flight log' mounted in a Pilatus Turbo Porter; a modified decometer (extreme left of the flight panel) gave 'fly right'/'fly left' indications (photo: I.A.A.C.)

pulse rate to 10 per second to increase resolution at aircraft speeds of the phase locked sequential transmissions from portable master and slave stations (fig. 10.15). This hyperbolic pattern (fig. 10.16) consists of a series of half phase lanes and when processed by the aircraft receiver is indicated on a lane counter graduated in units of 1/100 and a head-up left/right display consisting of multiple horizontal lights. Track spacing or deviation between each light is about 1.7 m on the base line where in the operating band of 1600 to 2000 kHz one whole lane width is 100 to 77.5 m respectively. Figure 10.17 illustrates the Agri-Fix simple first difference utilisation, with a master and one slave station providing only track guidance.

As with Hi-Fix, etc., consistent accuracy is unfortunately not possible due to radio propagation of the ground waves being influenced by

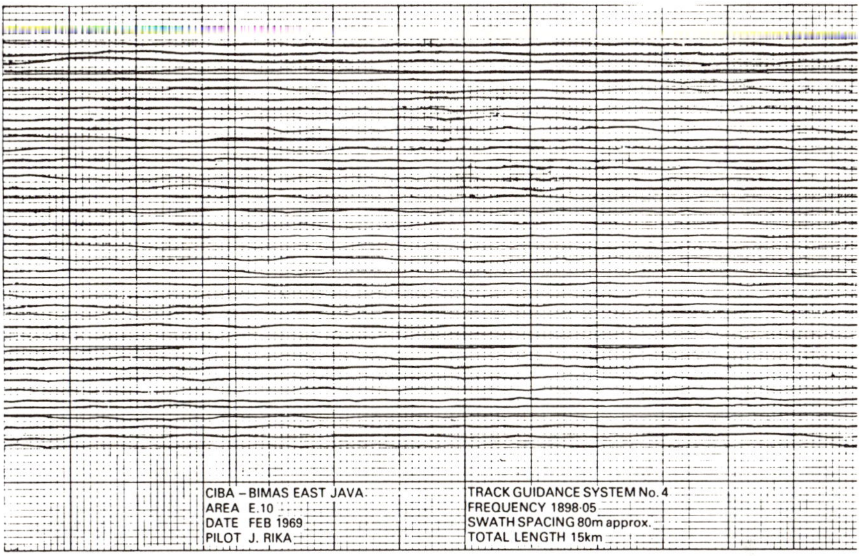

Fig 10.14 Decca Hi-Fix flight log showing tracks flown by the pilot: ULV application on a rice paddy, Indonesia, 1969. From such flight logs it was possible to measure the areas sprayed and provide a check on the insecticide applied (Joyce *et al.*, 1970)

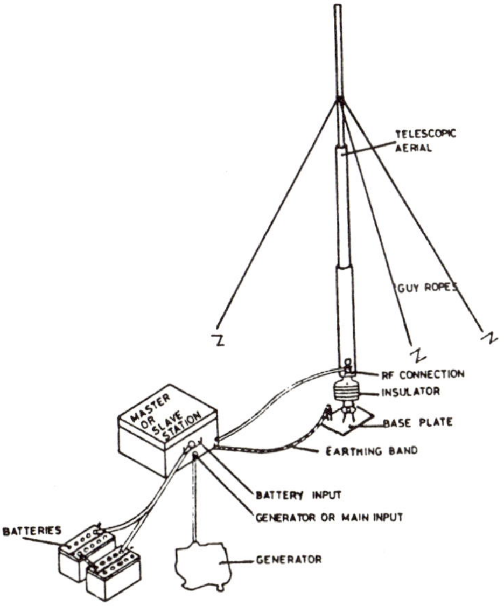

Fig 10.15 Master or slave station: Decca Agri-Fix field layout for master and slave operating stations; in certain conditions a series of ground radial wires are used to assist signal propagation which are laid out radially from the base of the telescopic aerial; operations from a vehicle installation are possible (Walker, 1973)

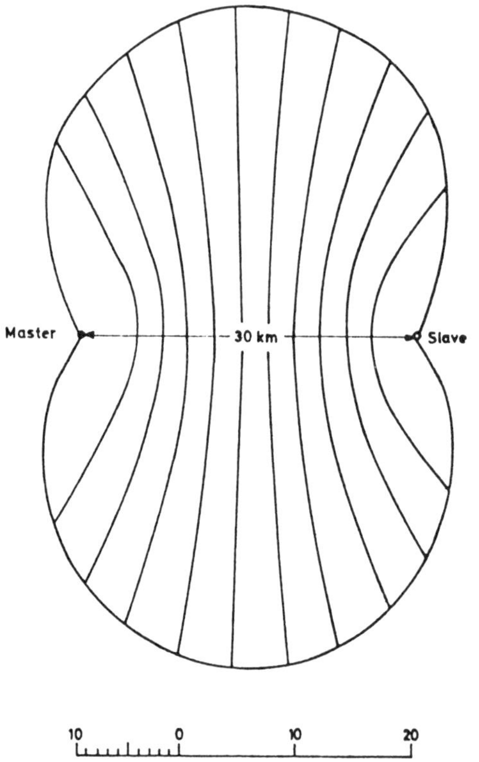

Fig 10.16 Decca Agri-Fix diagram showing phase-locked signal pattern between the two stations on a base line of 30 km illustrating the expansion and directional characteristics of the hyperbolae (Walker, 1973)

magnetic radiation, terrain surface, power lines, electrostatics, spurious radio sources and reflection by buildings which cause swamping, phase unlocking or incorrect guidance. However it is anticipated that these obstacles will be overcome and development of an airborne computer will dispense with the problems of hyperbolic divergence and lane orientation which presently impose constraints on field direction (by way of guided flight line) and location, when these are eliminated, the extensive pre-planning preparation at present required prior to utilisation may be avoided. With development it will then provide an omni-directional track guidance system of sufficient accuracy within a considerable area envelope for any field orientation and/or crosswind component.

Decca Flagman™

This positioning aid for agricultural aviation is the result of a cooperative effort between the Decca Survey Co. of the U.K. (now Racal-Decca Survey Ltd, U.K.) and Del Norte Technology Inc., from the U.S.A. The basis of the system is the Del Norte Trisponder™, which was developed to meet the special requirements for agricultural aviation.

The development of this airborne, high resolution positioning system marketed by the Decca Survey Group under the name 'Decca Flagman'™ was initiated early in 1977 for a number of reasons, some of which were:

- The increasing importance of economical and efficient food production.
- The higher costs for aircraft, fuel, labour, insurance, chemicals and supplies.
- The danger to flagmen from the application of increasingly toxic chemicals.

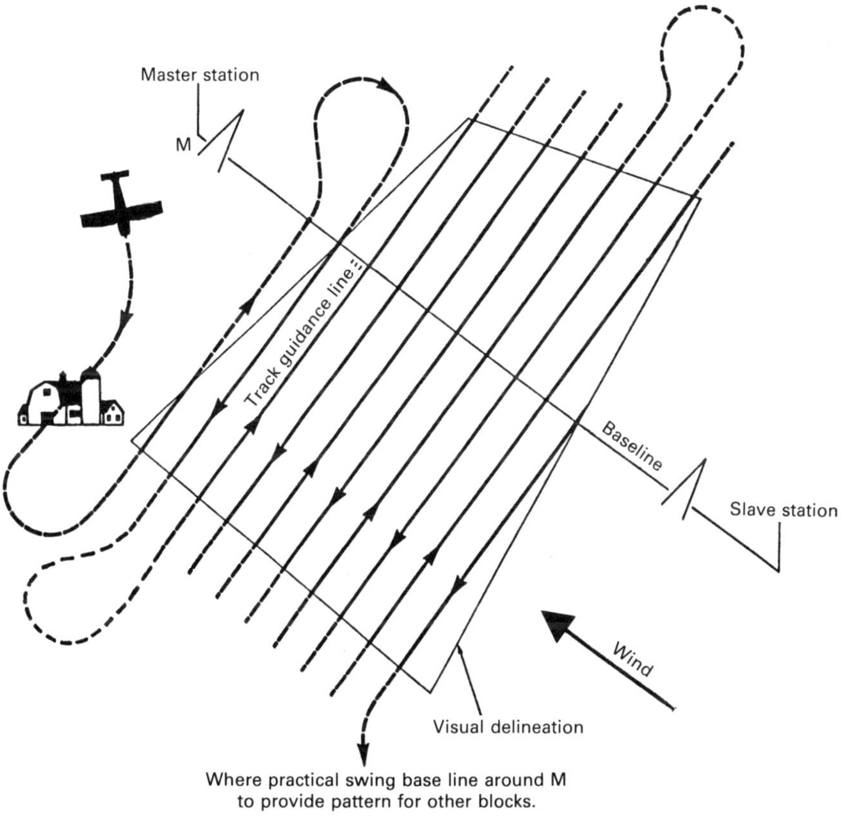

Fig 10.17 Decca Agri-Fix simple first difference utilisation (master and one slave station giving track guidance only)

- The increasing amount of land used for agricultural purposes in remote areas lacking sufficient checkpoints for quick identification.
- The requirement for a method of recording precisely when and where an aircraft applied chemicals.
- The fact that pilots do not fly nearly as accurately as they think they do.

All of these reasons indicated that there was a market for a system that would allow a pilot to apply chemicals very precisely and therefore more efficiently. A reduction in wastage caused by excess application would have benefits for the protection of the environment and cash savings for the aerial operator and the crop farmer.

Before describing the development and operation of the Decca Flagman system, it might be well to review the operational characteristics of the basic Trisponder system. The Trisponder™ is an electronic positioning system that provides accurate line of sight distance information from a master station to one or more remote stations. This is accomplished by measuring the round trip time of RF signals transmitted between the master station and each of the remote stations. Signals to and from each station are coded, and, thus, provide a means of station selection and outside signal rejection. A distance measuring unit, working in conjunction with the master transponder, measures the length of time for this round trip signal and from it computes, averages, and displays the two ranges. Each range displayed is an average of 10 or 100 measurements selected by digital filtering, thereby reducing statistical error and increasing system accuracy and stability. Each measurement requires about one millisecond and the indicated average is updated once per second.

Normally, two or more remote stations are set up at known locations, and the master transponder and distance measuring unit are placed on a boat, land vehicle, or in an aircraft where they will be operated with an unobstructed view to each of the remote transponders. The range/range data observed at the distance measuring unit may be reduced to X/Y position by trilateration.

The basic Del Norte/Decca Trisponder is used worldwide to position boats accurately, and starting in 1974 was used increasingly in both aeroplanes and helicopters for various types of survey flights. As the need for a precise guidance system for agricultural aircraft increased, it appeared that the Trisponder system could be the basis for a new system to satisfy the particularly stringent requirements of the agricultural aviation industry.

Technical research efforts were divided into four primary areas: range acquisition, computation, controls, and displays. It was decided to redesign the well proven Trisponder system to take advantage of the latest microcircuitry techniques and to repackage it suitably for the hostile environment of the agricultural aircraft. The basic Trisponder range/range acquisition method was still employed. The Decca Flagman would use two or more ground based transponders to establish a known base line. Practically speaking, these could be placed anywhere from 2 to 50 km apart without need for a survey. The airborne system would operate within line of sight of these beacons out to 80 km. The round trip time for a transmitted signal from the aircraft to each ground transponder is measured at least twice a second and the range is computed. These Trisponder techniques were well known and well proven and, therefore, presented no problems.

The digital distance measuring unit (DDMU) of the Decca Flagman measures and computes the range to each ground beacon and provides this information to a left/right computer. This second unit monitors all control box inputs, processes all the input data, and provides the outputs for the pilot's display and for tape recording in an ASCII serial format. The controls are placed in two separate control boxes, one for the basic DDMU functions, plus checking and calibration features, and the other, the pilot's control panel, for the selection of swath width, swath offset direction, designation of first swath and stepping button to move to the next swath. The swath identifying number also is displayed on this panel. The DDMU control box need not be placed on the instrument panel, but it should be placed so the pilot can see and reach it to turn the system on and check it out prior to take off. The pilot's control panel usually is mounted on the aircraft instrument panel, highly visible, and within easy reach.

The pilot's display was adapted from a standard cross-pointer indicator, one that most pilots have used. Extensive flight testing of display devices over the past twenty years has revealed several areas of research results applicable to this agricultural equipment. For example, the update rate, the scale, and the needle damping rate must be compatible with the aircraft speed and manoeuvrability so that the total system loop response will provide the required accuracy with an average pilot operating the aircraft. A simplified explanation of this is that if the needle moves too quickly and too far, the pilot will be chasing it and working everything too hard. If the needle moves too slowly, accuracy is impaired and the aircraft flight path will be equally difficult to control.

Extensive flight testing showed that update rates slower than twice per second were unsatisfactory. Also, half scale needle sensitivity should not be less than 13 m for airspeeds of 90 knots. As the airspeed increases, so should the scale. 140 knots is comfortably flyable when the display needle half scale sensitivity is approaching 18 m. The lateral track accuracy in the above examples may be held within 1 m when operating within 15 km of the baseline transponders without working the pilot too hard.

There were many other relationships that were discovered and tested during the research and development flight testing of the Decca Flagman. The horizontal needle of the cross-pointer display is used, for example, to indicate the aircraft's approach to the start of the swath, the end of the swath, or any other specific point a pilot wants to remember. The Decca Flagman display shows a digital display reading in kilometres until 0.5 km from the desired point. During the last 0.5 km, the horizontal needle presents closure rate by moving from the full upward position to the horizontal position. Simultaneously, a light on the cross-pointer indicator is turned on to indicate arrival at a starting point, end point, etc. This allows the pilot to concentrate on flying and gives him peripheral visual indication of time to open or close spray controls. This feature will be very valuable, especially when operating at night. This analogue presentation is a much better way to indicate position to a pilot than a constantly changing digital display. Digital presentations are not suitable when the numbers are changing rapidly since it requires too much of the pilot's attention to extract the information.

The 'round robin' pattern is frequently used by the agricultural pilot (see chapter 7, fig. 7.16, for procedures for reversing the aircraft track) particularly on the larger areas because it is more efficient for the larger Turbo Thrushes and Turbo Ag Cats. This means, for example, they might be flying west on swath number 1, east on swath number 30, west on swath number 2, east on swath number 31, west on swath number 3, etc. The Decca Flagman has an optional feature that allows pilots to do this easily with the pressing of a single button at the end of each swath. They can set up any number without having to fly adjacent swaths consecutively.

There are two methods of establishing the orientation of the Decca Flagman system. The first method enables the positioning of the two ground transponders wherever convenient for visibility, accessibility, and power. Then, if the pilot will fly across the base line between these two positions, the system automatically will measure the length of the base line and orient the system properly. It is not necessary to fly across the base line again as long as the pilot is working in the same area. If he wants to work on the other side of the base line, however, he must fly across it again and let the system reorient itself. An operator conceivably could place the ground transponders so that all of his working area is on one side of the base line, and he would have to cross it only once to orient his system initially. This first orientation method allows a pilot to fly a precise grid or pattern without having to correlate it with maps. The initial swath is located visually and the remaining swaths are oriented with respect to this first one.

There is a second method of orienting the Decca Flagman system with applications in forestry and in survey and mapping projects in particular. Using this method, the ground transponder positions are surveyed and these coordinates in X and Y are inserted into the Decca Flagman computer. Then, it is not necessary for the pilot to fly the aircraft across the base line to measure it since the computer already has that dimension.

If the co-ordinates of the first swath are also known, these also can be inserted into the Decca Flagman computer so the pilot can fly the aircraft out to a specific position and from there to a second position by following the display. He can establish and follow a series of ground tracks parallel to the line connecting these two positions just as he would if he had established the first swath visually. This second orientation method allows the pilot to fly precise tracks over an area

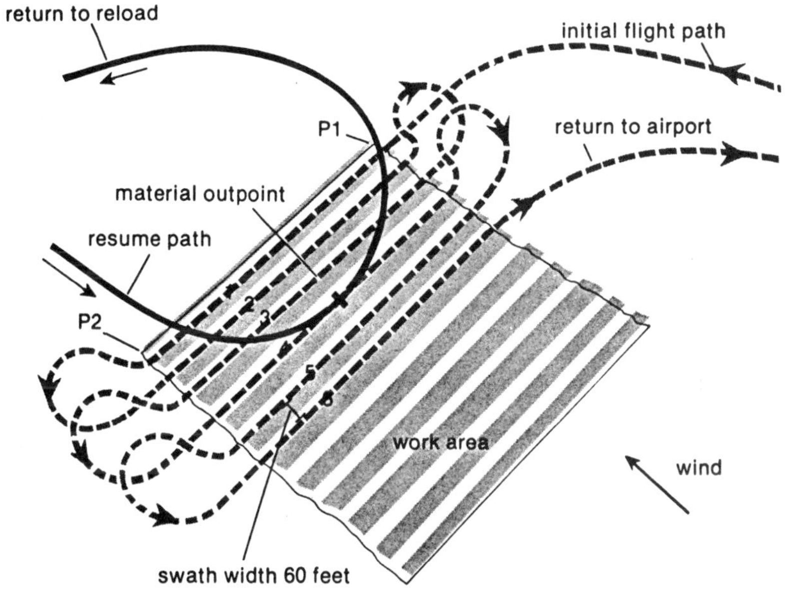

Fig 10.18 When a pilot runs out of chemical while spraying, he presses a 'material out' button located on or near the aircraft throttle quadrant, and returns to reload. When he returns to the field to resume spraying, he presses the 'resume to last stop point' button on the left/right control box. The Flying Flagman will index the proper swath, indicating distance from the point on one-mile increments (1.6 km). The horizontal needle on the cross-pointer indicator begins to centre during the last half mile (800 m), and will centre when the point is reached. At that moment, the 'point reached' light comes on, and the pilot resumes spraying. All functions are activated when switches are released (with acknowledgements to *Ag Pilot International* (1980))

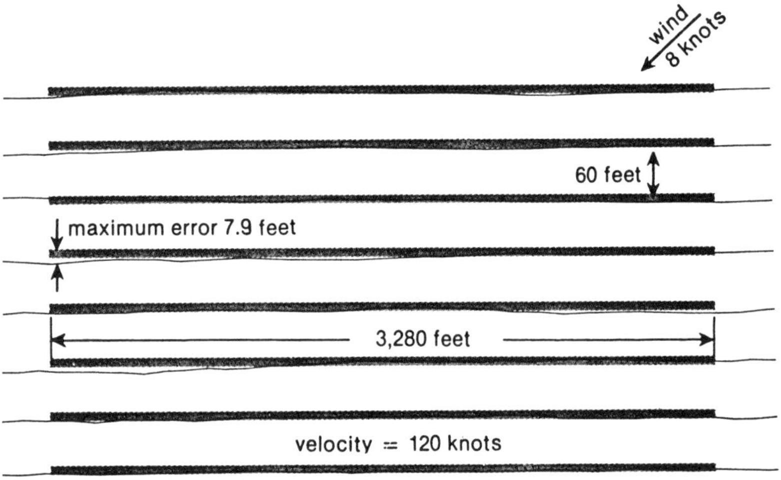

Fig 10.19 Maximum error from the centre line was 7.9 ft (2.4 m) in this test of the Flying Flagman; the flight test was made by a single-turbine powered agricultural aircraft.

Conversions:

8 knots	=	13 km/h
60 ft	=	18.28 m
7.9 ft	=	2.4 m
3280 ft	=	1000 m
120 knots	=	193 km/h

Note that This equipment was marketed under the name of 'Flying Flagman' in the U.S.A. and 'Decca Flagman' in the rest of the world (with acknowledgements to *Ag Pilot International* (1980))

he has not seen before, whether it is for agricultural purposes, survey, or search and rescue.

Racal Micro-Fix

Micro-Fix is a short-range position fixing system employing the proven microwave interrogation technique to achieve a repeatable accuracy of ± 1 m. The system utilises a low power solid state transmitter operating in the 5 GHz band providing a maximum working range of 80 km with line of sight.

Micro-Fix comprises two principal units: a transmitter/receiver unit (T/R) and a control measurement unit (CMU). When deployed, T/R units are sited at known locations around the area and are referred to as remote stations. Remote T/R units are usually mounted on a surveyor's tripod and powered by a +24V battery pack. A master station comprising a T/R unit interconnected to a CMU is located on the user's vehicle within the area and interrogates all remote stations in turn. The reply pulses are received at the master and numerically processed by the CMU to display the corrected ranges. The master station can be powered by the normal range of A.C. supplies (110V/230V 50–400 Hz) or from a +24V battery pack. Both units are designed for minimum power consumption. The master station can interrogate up to eight remote stations from a possible total of thirty-two with each remote T/R unit preset to recognise its own unique station code. By the inclusion of a chain code up to four separate chains can be deployed in the same working area without inter-station interference. Multi-user capability allows a maximum of sixteen users for each deployed chain.

Operator communication is via the keyboard and display of the CMU for all data presentation and control purposes. Operating parameters such as station code, chain code and station heights are stored during power-off thus obviating the need to re-enter on power-up. The CMU design reflects the use of microprocessors to increase the facilities available as standard for the user. These include full self-test, track guidance, plotter drive, *X*/*Y* conversion (full spheroid and multi-range solution) and slant range correction.

T/R units incorpoate automatic calibration to compensate for errors due to the turn around delays associated with microwave ranging systems. This calibration eliminates the need for pre-deployment calibration and T/R units can be inter-changed as required with accuracy maintained over the whole operating temperature range. All the T/R units are identical and operate on the same frequency of 5.48 GHz (5.52 or 5.56 GHz alternative). T/R units can be fitted with either an omni or sector antenna. Normally a master designated T/R unit is fitted with an omni antenna and remote stations with a sector. Both antennae clip onto the T/R unit without the use of waveguide retaining rings or screws. Circular polarisation is employed to ensure null free operation and the rejection of any reflections. Interference suppression is inherent in the operation of the T/R unit.

Units are constructed to meet the expected environmental operating conditions. The T/R unit is fully waterproof and capable of withstanding high impact forces and vibration. The CMU is housed in a lightweight weatherproof case which may be free standing or stack mounted with similar cased units such as Hyper-Fix.

Racal Hyper-Fix

Hyper-Fix is a third generation medium frequency phase comparison positioning system using microprocessor techniques. The range and accuracy show an improvement over earlier equipments. The system radiates frequencies in the base 1600–3400 kHz and depends on the groundwave mode of propagation.

A chain consists of from three to eighteen transmitting stations. One station transmits the trigger signal which controls the timing of the chain. At each station the phase of the transmitted signal can be referenced to the signal from any other station to provide optimum performance and coverage of the chain. Transmitting station equipment includes a sectional monopole antenna available in different heights from 10–30 m to meet operating range requirements.

Two frequencies are operated, between 1600 kHz and 3400 kHz. The recommended separation is in the range of 2–10%. The range is up to 700 km by day and 250 km at night.

The accuracy depends on propagation, geometry and instrumental factors, and corresponds to 0.01 lane under the best conditions. On the base line, 0.01 lane represents 0.44 m at 3400 kHz and 0.94 m at 1600 kHz.

Electronic track guidance at night

The systems so far described would work equally well at night; however, the pilot has less visual cues flying at night to maintain constant height. His vision is restricted to the floodlit area forwards and some beam angle, depending on the lights used. His concentration on the outside world precludes any preoccupation with instruments, except for the briefest glance, and then possibly only using peripheral vision. This is why analogue instruments can be read so quickly, or rather, the meaning interpreted – they are not actually read. It requires that track guidance indication be positioned such that the pilot can monitor it at peripheral vision. This is probably just below eye level and to one side, but pilots may find a favourite direction, or 'area to view' outside while low flying at night, and any obstruction of this particular 'area to view' would not be acceptable. This is a difficult thing to quantify and it would be desirable that the display unit could be repositioned, with certain limits, because pilots would not know where their primary 'area to view' at night is directed, until they actually fly the aircraft at night. Even experienced pilots have noticed that monitoring height requires a different technique than when flying the same aircraft over the same area in daylight.

The pilot also needs advanced warning of the start and end of swath runs. Some of the electronic systems described have provision for this, others only provide track guidance. It is also desirable at night to approach from further out, allowing time to settle onto the correct track, then reducing height to be at the correct height and speed at the start of the swath run. The pilot must also know that when he lets down there are no obstructions, particularly if the approach has been extended. It is also very convenient, and indeed a safety factor, if some visual reference can supplement the electronics for the start and end of swath runs, particularly for long runs. It is not necessary with electronic track guidance to mark each run visually, but lights of some sort in the proximity of the start and end of the treatment area are of considerable help, even a large fire or fires, if conditions permit, but many of the lighting systems described elsewhere could be used. It is a great help, and a safety aspect, to see some form of reference, particularly lights in the distance, not necessarily to aim at, but to indicate to the pilot where to pull up and relax the concentration that is necessary during the swath run.

It is important to remember that no matter how sophisticated the electronics may be, the pilot has practically no time to monitor them while actually on the spray run. This is true of head-up displays (HUD), and audio systems, which are fatiguing after a short period, and moving light bars or other coloured lighting systems are not recommended for night operations. The pilot is looking very hard at *the ground*, or the top of the crop, and is not able, and should not be required to refocus his eyes on any other indicator with different light levels. It is therefore necessary to use at least a minimum of external references for night operations, even with electronic track guidance, at least with the present generation of manned aerial application aircraft.

The future

Almost all the electronic systems described have been used in this industry. With the exception of the Decca Agri-Fix and Decca Flagman, they have been adapted from route or area navigation systems for transport aircraft or ships.

Hyperbolic area navigation seems the most promising, but even the systems developed for agricultural track guidance need further development to meet the specific needs of modern aerial application. Some of the hyperbolic systems 'go out of lock' at low level, often as a result of local screening when flying across undulating country. Pilot displays need attention, specially for night operations. Adequate electrical generation is necessary for all electronics and atomisers (if fitted) and lighting systems, particularly night operations.

Data recording should need greater attention to monitor spray paramaters, system pressures, flow rates, emission and if rotating atomisers are used, the r.p.m. to monitor droplet spectrum. These data should correlate with the electronic track guidance system in order to evaluate the complete treatment over specific areas. There are a number of data recording systems that could be interfaced with the track guidance, and possibly downloaded via a small computer to printout all the parameters in whatever format is required. For the operator, systems monitoring (and indeed pilot monitoring) can be analysed by the engineer or chief pilot after the mission. For the crop protection specialist, pest mortality and application can be related and analysed. For the farmer or crop production authorities, records of treatments performed could be made available. The records could be kept for future reference in relating treatments and pest complexes, which seem to change over the years, particularly over large monocultures.

Application pilots are already finding themselves flying expensive equipment, with turbine power and greater sophistication in the aircraft systems and spray control. The new generation of aircraft are able to improve productivity by flying faster and carrying a heavier load (less number of landings per unit area treated). In many areas of application the potential to improve productivity can only be realised by giving the pilot the electronic equipment to help him. Electronic aids to track guidance are getting more sophisticated and in smaller packages. The technology is already available, and it will be up to the aircraft operators and pilots to press for these systems to become universally accepted in the interests of safety and efficiency and, by definition, to use less chemicals for economic control of insect pests and diseases.

References

Anon. (1980) 'Aerial applicators turn to electronic guidance to meet higher accuracy requirements in applying pesticides.' *Ag Pilot International* **3** (10), 46-50.

Burnett, G. F., Yeo, D., Miller, A. W. D. and White, P. J. (1961) *Bull. ent. Res.* **52** (2), 305-316.

Buyckx, E. J. E. (1962) 'Rapport préliminaire sur la deuxieme campagne de désinsectisation par voie aeriénne contre – *Glossina morsitans* Westw. au Bugesera, Ruwanda.' Inéac R.U. rapport stencilé.

F.A.O. (1972) 'The use of aircraft in agriculture.' Agricultural Services Bulletin 16.

Foster, R., White, P. J. and Yeo, D. (1961) *Bull. ent. Res.* **52** (2), 293-303.

Haley, J. (1973) *Expert Flagging – A Training Manual for Aerial Applicator Ground Crews.* University of North Dakota, Dept. of Aviation, Grand Forks, U.S.A.

Hocking, K. S., Burnett, G. F. and Sell, R. C. (1954) *Bull. ent. Res.* **45** (3), 605-612.

Joyce, R. J. V., Marmol, L. C., Lucken, J., Bals, E. and Quantick, H. R. (1970) 'Large scale aerial spraying of paddy in the Java Ciba-Bimas Project.' *PANS* **16** (2), 309-326.

Joyce, R. J. V. *et al.* (1968) 'Waterless spraying in East Pakistan using Decca navigation system'. *Agricultural Aviation* **10** (4), 118-124.

Lee, C. W. (1969) 'Aerial applications of insecticides for tsetse fly control in East Africa.' *Bull. World Health Organization* **41**, 261-268.

Miller, A. W. D. and Chadwick, P. R. (1963) 'Swathe marking in aerial spraying.' *Agricultural Aviation* **5** (4), 114-120.

Newman, B. (1980) 'Guidance systems.' Lecture to short course, aerial application of pesticides, Cranfield Institute of Technology, U.K.

O'Neal, J. and Markin, G. P. (1979) 'Comparison of three aircraft guidance techniques for use under mountainous conditions.' *Agricultural Aviation* **20** (3), 151-158.

Racal - Decca Survey Ltd, (Racal Positioning Systems), Kingston Road, Leatherhead, Surrey KT22 7ND, U.K.

Thomson, J. M. and Mitchell, H. W. (1978) 'A new positioning aid for agricultural aviation.' E.C.E. Seminar on Techno-Economic Trends in Airborne Equipment for Agriculture and other Selected Areas of the National Economy, Warsaw, Poland, 18-22 September.

Transland Catalogue. Transland, Inc., Harbor City, California, U.S.A.

Walker, D. A. (1973) 'Agri-Fix a track guidance system for aerial application.' *Agricultural Aviation* **15** (4), 99-104.

Whittam, D. (1962), 'Aircraft guidance methods for pest control in the United States.' *Agricultural Aviation* **4** (1), 8-15.

Yule, W. N. (1960) *Bull. ent. Res* **51** (3), 441-460.

11
Night spraying

This chapter is taken mainly from a paper by Norman E. Stanley which was presented at the Agricultural Chemical Application Short Course, Boise, Idaho in November 1968, and is reproduced with his kind permission. (Mr Stanley was former President of the Growers Aerial Service, El Centro, California, U.S.A.)

Adaptive equipment

Most aircraft used in aerial application can be adapted readily to night flying. There are several electrical systems with various arrangements for lights and switching controls, each designed to accomplish the most effective lighting of the target field and obstructions surrounding it. All have similar circuitry, but placement of lights varies according to the needs and purposes of the operator and according to the aircraft and its flight characteristics.

The most common arrangement is a 600-watt retractable worklight under each wing, placed at least ⅔ of the distance from cabin to wingtip, to minimise backlight reflection from the propeller. Retractable lights can be streamlined into the wing for daylight operation, reducing drag. A turnlight of 200 to 300 watts is placed on each wingtip to provide light for turnarounds. These lights should be pointed out at a 45° angle and slightly downwards, and should be adjustable so that by trial and error the best position may be obtained. The attitude of an aircraft in a normal turn will vary on different makes of aircraft and therefore, the position of the lights will also vary. Turnlights should be retractable for efficient daylight operation. Most retractable lights have adjustable stops that can be set to stop the extension of the light at the correct angle so that hunting for the correct position is unnecessary.

Where fields are small and obstructions like trees and power lines border the fields, the addition of obstruction lights is a definite help.

These lights are placed near the turnlights but faced forward and down. When rounding out of a turn and approaching the entry to the field, power lines and trees are better illuminated and depth perception is more accurate than when using only the turnlights. The powerful worklights are ineffective for this purpose because they point forward and above the obstructions and also shed backlight that blinds the pilot in the turns and field entry.

All aircraft are required to have navigation lights when operating after dusk. A rotating beacon is an additional safety precaution, but care must be taken to place it so that it will not reflect on the wings to interfere with the pilot's vision. All lights should be out of the pilot's view and outside the reflecting arc of the propeller. The further out on the wing the less backlight there will be. The control system for lights should be kept simple. The pilot's attention needs to be on the field and obstructions and not confused by a multitude of switches. Keeping the pilot's fatigue level low is essential.

Two popular methods are:

(1) A simple grip control on the stick with a double-contact trigger switch that is pulled to bring on the worklights. Upon release of the trigger the worklights go off and turnlights and obstruction lights come on. The pilot pulls the trigger again when entering the swath run to turn on the worklights as the dual contact switch breaks the connection for the turnlights and obstruction lights. When the pass is completed, the pilot releases the trigger, and the worklights go off and the turnlights and obstruction lights come on. The pilot's only concern is with turning his worklights on or off, and the operation of the other lights is automatic. Solenoids should be used to eliminate the necessity of high amperage wired to the switch in the stick. Each light should be switched on the panel with circuit-breaker switches so any combination can be used. Most operators use a 50-amp generator in a 24-volt system, reducing the risk of overloading the electrical system.

(2) The use of a control grip on the stick that has a trigger switch for the worklights and a multiple selector switch on top of the grip for selecting any other light. Solenoids should be used here too, permitting low amperage and small wiring in the control stick. The control on top of the stick selects the left turnlight when the button is pushed to the left, the right turnlight when pushed to the right, and the obstruction lights when pushed forward. The system can also be wired for selecting both turn and obstruction lights on either left or right. More demanding of the pilot's attention than the first system, this system requires fewer lights in the turn.

Checks and techniques

When aircraft are operated at night, routine inspections should be increased. A visual inspection should be made at least every ten to twenty hours, with special attention to oil leaks, cylinder hold-down nuts, propeller nicks, throttle and mixture-control linkage, pilot control cables and pulleys, electrical system, lamps, selector switches and adjustments. In addition to an enhanced inspection programme for night flying, the pilot should make a daily habit to spend a few minutes checking for obvious defects. Preventive maintenance programmes are vital for all aspects of flying.

Some pilots have a tendency to overlook such things as excessive magneto drops or rough running during daylight hours. Such reliance on chance is dangerous at any time, and particularly at night. Any slight detail of engine performance that is 'not quite right' demands immediate attention, and operations should be halted until the problem is identified and corrected.

Most agricultural aircraft in use today are adaptable for night work. Important to look for are good visibility, safe stall characteristics, and plenty of power to gain and keep emergency altitude. Complete electrical failure can occur at any time, and if a pilot should happen to be working under wires, he is very likely to either catch them or hit the ground beneath. If a pilot always works over power lines or other wires, a failure in the electrical system will only require him to pull up. A good working altimeter is a necessity. A flashlight is also a necessity. If a complete electrical failure should occur, the altimeter and the flashlight will be invaluable. The flashlight should be kept in a secure place, so that it won't fall into the fuselage and jam the controls.

The 'loudest silence in the world' to a pilot is the one when an engine fails. There may be only time to roll the wings straight and set the aircraft down level and straight. If every pilot has this procedure preplanned, he will be more apt to do the proper thing in an emergency. If he does not, he may in the resulting confusion try to stretch a glide, producing a stall that may result in a serious accident. Of most importance is landing the aircraft on the ground in a partially controlled attitude so that it will not hit anything solid. Sudden stops are the major cause of serious injuries. The cockpit area of most agricultural aircraft is strong enough to protect the pilot, even through violent cartwheels, if the forward motion of the plane can be stopped somewhat gradually.

Planning night flights

Efficient night operation requires thorough planning and preparation.

Minor problems of daylight flying become major ones at night. The flagging crew may set up in the wrong field and the pilot may be unable to identify the error in the dark, resulting in treating the wrong area. Sometimes the pilot cannot find his flagmen, and hours are wasted searching for them, or before they can find their way back to the strip. The heavily loaded aircraft is not a safe search aircraft. The pilot, too, has special difficulties, like mistaking headlights for field worklights. While lanterns have been tried, they are unsatisfactory since they produce a steady light that may be confused with other ground lights. A flashlight held at eye level, pointed at the aircraft and wiggled sideways, produces a blinking effect that the pilot does not confuse with other lights. Once a crew is located, getting them to the right field becomes a problem and sometimes a pilot must land his plane with the full load still on board, increasing the risks to a safe landing. Problems like these are largely preventable. A good two-way radio will assure the pilot, before take off, that his flagging crew is in the correct place. The recognition that night flying requires extra time, even for experienced pilots, especially in turnarounds and on the strip, will result in unrushed operations.

The pilot should never avoid visiting the field during the day to plan how he will fly it that night. He should note obstructions in the area, and he should never rely on the visit of a week ago. New power lines and guy wires can be erected very quickly. Careful consideration of the problems in advance will produce greater safety and more efficient operation.

Pilot selection

The selection of pilots for night flying requires good judgement on the part of the operator or the chief pilot. Qualifications to look for are:

Agricultural aviation experience The mechanics of aerial application should be perfected to the point of second nature. A night pilot should not have to think about opening or closing the gate handle, or the timing of pull-ups and turnarounds. He will know the airspeed by feel and will not need to look at the airspeed indicator to know. He will not have to think about wheel height, drift correction, or power settings for the swath run. In general, a new night spraying pilot should have had two or three seasons' experience and 1500 to 2000 hours in day flights. These stiff requirements may be somewhat modified according to the individual and the circumstances under which he will work. For example, an area of large fields and few obstructions will not demand quite as much experience as one of small fields and many obstructions.

Personal Habits A good pilot is serious, purposeful, conscientious and responsible. He is able to plan and organise a period of work efficiently and methodically. He is patient, and can be counted on to sort out problems in time of pressure, and stress. His personal habits will help his efficiency and skill. Night flying pilots with personal problems, those who need the stimulant of alcohol, and those who may be called temperamental are poor risks.

Night pilot training

The introduction of night flying needs special consideration and procedure. A thorough briefing with experienced pilots can reveal many valuable 'tips' and forewarn of special problems. For the first night flight choose a moonlit night and a field with no obstructions. Have the pilot inspect the field and its immediate area during the day, and plan the exact procedure. One or two fields are sufficient for a first night flight. Tension will be high, so proceed in a leisurely way. Allow enough time to complete each job and to follow it at the strip with a discussion of results. Operations may be discontinued after the first load if necessary in order to iron out problems. Be sure to use a trained crew until the new pilot has mastered night flying. He will be too busy to coordinate the rest of the operation.

For the pilot there are many problems that occur at night that do not exist in the daytime. Disorientation is a common occurrence during night spraying. A car driving down a nearby road sometimes appears to take off at a ridiculous speed, or the flagman and his flashlight will start moving sideways at high speed. This is caused by the turning motion in the aircraft and the motion is transferred by the pilot's eyes to the other light, making the plane seem stationary instead of the groundlight. The quickest way to stop this illusion is to turn the worklights on the moving light thus fixing it with the earth so that the sense of motion returns to the plane. Good turn and obstruction lights minimise this problem. Even with turnlights, there are conditions that may produce disorientation as when turning over an open field that has just been flooded, and the field is black and without texture; a sense of true relationship to the ground is difficult to maintain. Most such problems occur on dark nights when there is no moon, stars, or faint horizon; although power lines and trees are more visible at night than in daylight, as worklights silhouette them against the black night. Finding the strip or field to be treated is often difficult. This may be solved by having the pilot signal with his worklights as he approaches and the tankerman or field crew flag him in with a flashlight.

Safety keynotes

Almost everything related to night flying concerns safety: placement of lights, an accelerated preventive maintenance programme, selection and training of pilots, planning and procedure of work, coordination of air and ground personnel. There are many additional practices that will keep accidents at a minimum:

- All pilots and personnel must have time to get enough sleep – at least eight hours out of every twenty-four. A twenty-four hour work schedule with ten hours of sleep is not an efficient system.
- Tranquillizers, cold medicines such as antihistamines, and any narcotics are dangerous because of their mental and physical inhibiting characteristics.
- Excessive worry and mental strain distract attention. Daytime habits can result in problems at night.
- Daytime requirements are also not the same as those for night-time operations. Some pilots count a certain number of loads or a certain length of time between refuellings. Night operations require more fuel due to higher turns and advanced power settings to allow a greater margin of safety.
- Long periods without food lower efficiency. If the night crew will work all night, a good meal and drink (non-alcoholic) will help to reduce fatigue.
- A ground crew that is working with one pilot soon learns his style of flying. An alert crew can detect a change in this style and warn the pilot. If this should occur, the night's work should stop until the reason is found. The same watchfulness should hold true for ground personnel. Listlessness, forgetfulness, and any change from normal behavior suggest a cholinesterase depressed condition.
- When there is unusual pressure and time is short, safety and efficiency will be better served by a conscious effort to relax and slow down.
- If two aircraft are working together, the pilots should agree upon a procedure. When working small fields, a circular pattern with each aircraft on opposite swaths and turning at opposite ends of the field will greatly reduce the chance of one aircraft getting in the other's propeller wash. Clean-up runs can also be planned so each aircraft has a set routine, so that, for example, one pilot treats the north and east ends, and other other south and west ends.

Advantages and disadvantages

Night application will be profitable to an operator if a surcharge is imposed. Night application does not generally produce the gross hectares per hour of application that is produced in the daytime. The incentive for experienced pilots to do this work is a higher rate of pay. Additional rates of pay, substantial increase in fuel consumption per engine hour, accelerated engine wear and subsequent reductions in engine life, additional man-hours for gross hectares treated, are all adequate reasons for imposing additional charges for night application.

For the farmer, there are situations which make night application distinctly advantageous even with the increased costs, particularly for seed growers. Before the advent of night application of pesticides, many bees died when daytime controls of the pest were carried out. The reduction in the bee population resulted in substantial seed loss. Farmers were faced with a dilemma: whether to treat and kill the harmful insects and many of the bees, or not to treat the pests and lose seed to them. But with night application this 'lesser of two evils' situation was changed. After dark, when the bees have returned to the hive, the field can be treated safely. Toxic organophosphate pesticides can be used during the evening hours after dark, allowing several hours for the chemical to dissipate before the bees return in the morning. This method results in only minor kills of the bees and excellent control of the damaging insects.

Other advantages of night applications are:

- Less evaporation – higher deposits of material on insects result in a higher percentage of kill and require smaller amounts of insecticide.
- Better exposure – at night many damaging insects are active in the upper portions of the plant, a distinct advantage where thick foliage presents a penetration problem.
- Certain selective insecticides that fail during the daytime produce results on specific insects at night. Again, some insects are more frequently on the tops of the plants and better coverage is possible.
- Most moths are active at night and hide during the day.

Many of the disadvantages of night flying have been covered already, but a few more should be mentioned. One is the possibility of an aircraft going down during ferrying. Quick location at night is nearly impossible unless two aircraft are operating together. Many times it is not economical or feasible to send two aircraft to every job. If it is a one aircraft operation, then everyone must be doubly alert. The tankerman should keep track of the aircraft if it is within his range of vision, until it reaches the field and starts to work. The flagging crew should also watch the aircraft until it lands at the strip for another load. Flagmen should never leave a field until the pilot has treated the ends and left the field for the next strip or to return to the base. If long ferries are involved, the only sure way is for two aircraft to be on the job, each pilot checking on the other.

Another problem is the onset of sudden storms at night. The pilot who is aware of this can usually avoid sudden engulfment by wind, dust, and low visibility. Warning comes when distant lights become dim or suddenly disappear. Any pilot so warned should return to the strip where there will be help to secure the aircraft until the dust clears. To be caught in the almost zero visibility created by the thick dust that comes with the first part of a wind is a harrowing experience when flying close to the ground and trying to find home base or a strip on which to land. In areas where fog forms or rolls in, getting caught while spraying could end in disaster.

Chemicals drifting onto adjoining crops are always cause for concern. During night operations additional precautions should be taken against this. At night when the air is cool and more stable, drift will deposit more residue and travel farther than during the day when wind and turbulence are favourable elements. To avoid contaminating a bordering crop some jobs may have to be postponed until the direction of drift changes.

Summary

Aerial application at night is successful in many areas. For those who are contemplating the addition of this phase to their present operations, there are opportunities, advantages, and the addition of another important service for customers. There are special hazards and problems, but these can be successfully overcome or lessened by thorough planning, anticipation, common sense and the constant concern for safety. Practise preventive maintenance, highly train personnel, perform preflight field inspection, demand preflight aircraft inspection by mechanics and pilots, initiate ground crew briefing, secure weather reports and forecasts and allow ample time to complete work without the pressure of being rushed.

Appendix 1

Tabulation of agricultural aircraft

Reproduced with the kind permission of the Editor of Flight International.

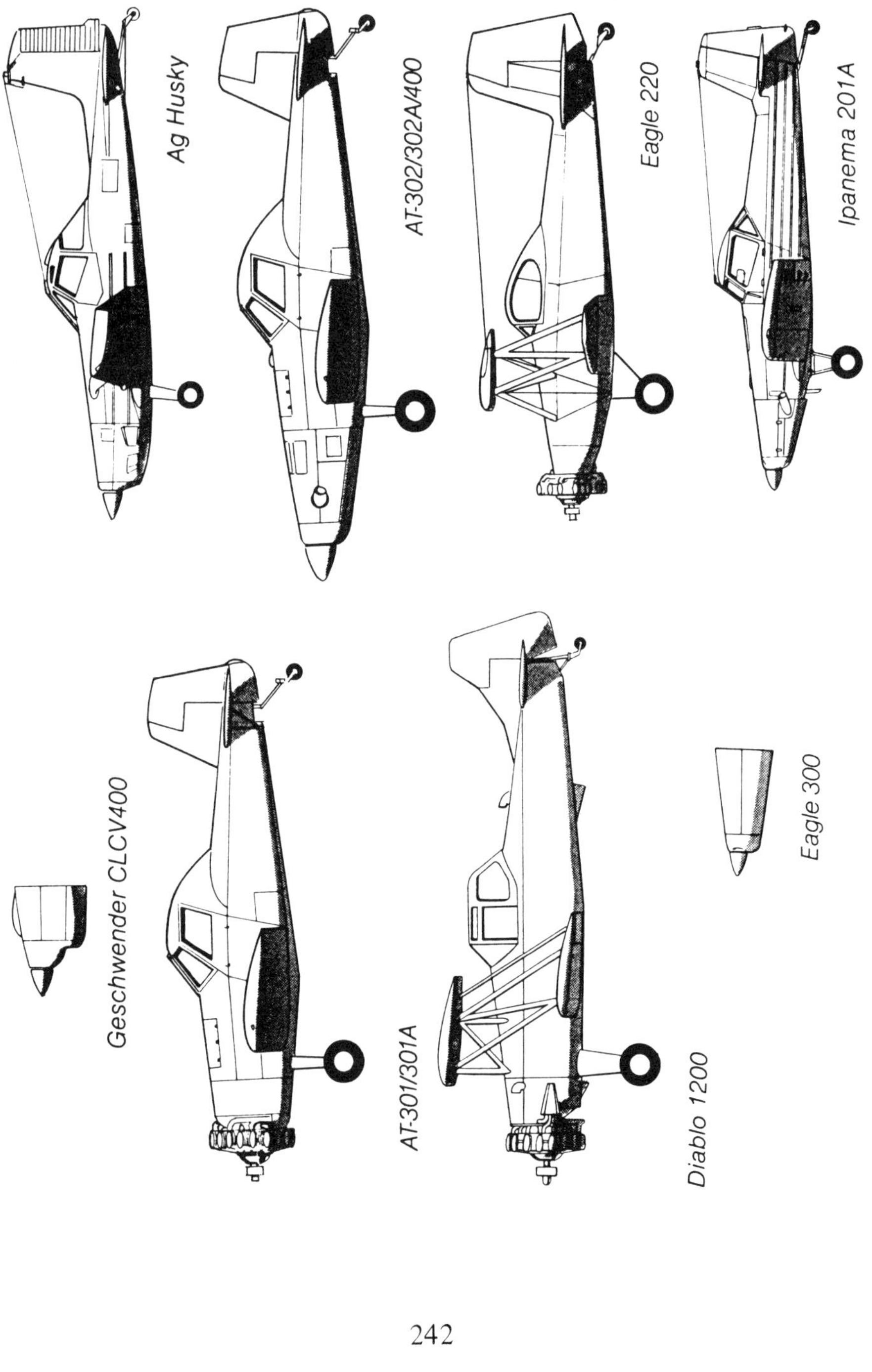
Ag Husky
AT-302/302A/400
Eagle 220
Ipanema 201A
Geschwender CLCV400
AT-301/301A
Diablo 1200
Eagle 300

Type	Manufacturer	Engine	Span	Gross weight	Disposable weight	Hopper capacity	Price
Ag Husky	Cessna Aircraft Wichita, Kansas 67201, U.S.A.	Continental TSIO-520T 310 b.h.p. at 2700 r.p.m.	41 ft 8 in 12.7 m	4400 lb 1966 kg	2078 lb 943 kg	280 U.S. gal. 1060 *l*	$79 900
Ag Truck	Cessna	Continental IO-520-D 300 b.h.p. at 2850 r.p.m. (take off) 285 b.h.p. at 2700 r.p.m. (max. continuous)	41 ft 8 in 12.7 m	4200 lb 1905 kg	1970 lb 894 kg	280 U.S. gal. 1060 *l*	$71 200
AT-301	Air Tractor, P.O. Box 485 Olney, Texas 76374, U.S.A.	Pratt & Whitney R1340, 600 h.p.	45 ft 13.7 m	6900 lb 3130 kg	3250 lb 1473 kg	320 U.S. gal. 1211 *l*	$81 500
AT-301A	Air Tractor	Pratt & Whitney R1340, 600 h.p.	45 ft 13.7 m	7300 lb 3311 kg	3450 lb 1565 kg	350 U.S. gal. 1325 *l*	$83 500
AT-302	Air Tractor	Avco Lycoming LTP101 600 s.h.p.	45 ft 13.7 m	6600 lb 2994 kg	3350 lb 1522 kg	320 U.S. gal. 1211 *l*	on request
AT-400	Air Tractor	Pratt & Whitney PT6A-15AG 680 s.h.p.	45 ft 13.7 m	7800 lb 3538 kg	4250 lb 1928 kg	400 U.S. gal. 1514 *l*	$187 500
Diablo 1200	Emair, Hangar 38, Industrial Airpark, Harlingen, Texas 78550, U.S.A.	Wright Cyclone R1820 1200 h.p.	41 ft 8 in 12.7 m	8400 lb 3810 kg	4000 lb 1814 kg	475 U.S. gal. 1798 *l*	on request
Eagle 220	Eagle Aircraft, Box 4127, Boise, Idaho 83704, U.S.A.	Continental W-670-6N 200 h.p.	55 ft 16.8 m	5400 lb 2450 kg	2750 lb 1247 kg	250 U.S. gal. 945 *l*	$81 495
Eagle 300	Eagle	Lycoming IO-540-M1B5D 300 h.p.	55 ft 16.8 m	5400 lb 2450 kg	2750 lb 1247 kg	250 U.S. gal. 945 *l*	$96 450
Ipanema 201A	Embraer, P.O. Box 343 12,200 Sao José dos Campos, Sao Paulo, Brazil	Avco Lycoming IO-540-K1FSD	38 ft 4 in 11.7 m	3968 lb 1800 kg	1841 lb 835 kg	180 U.S. gal. 680 *l*	$91 080

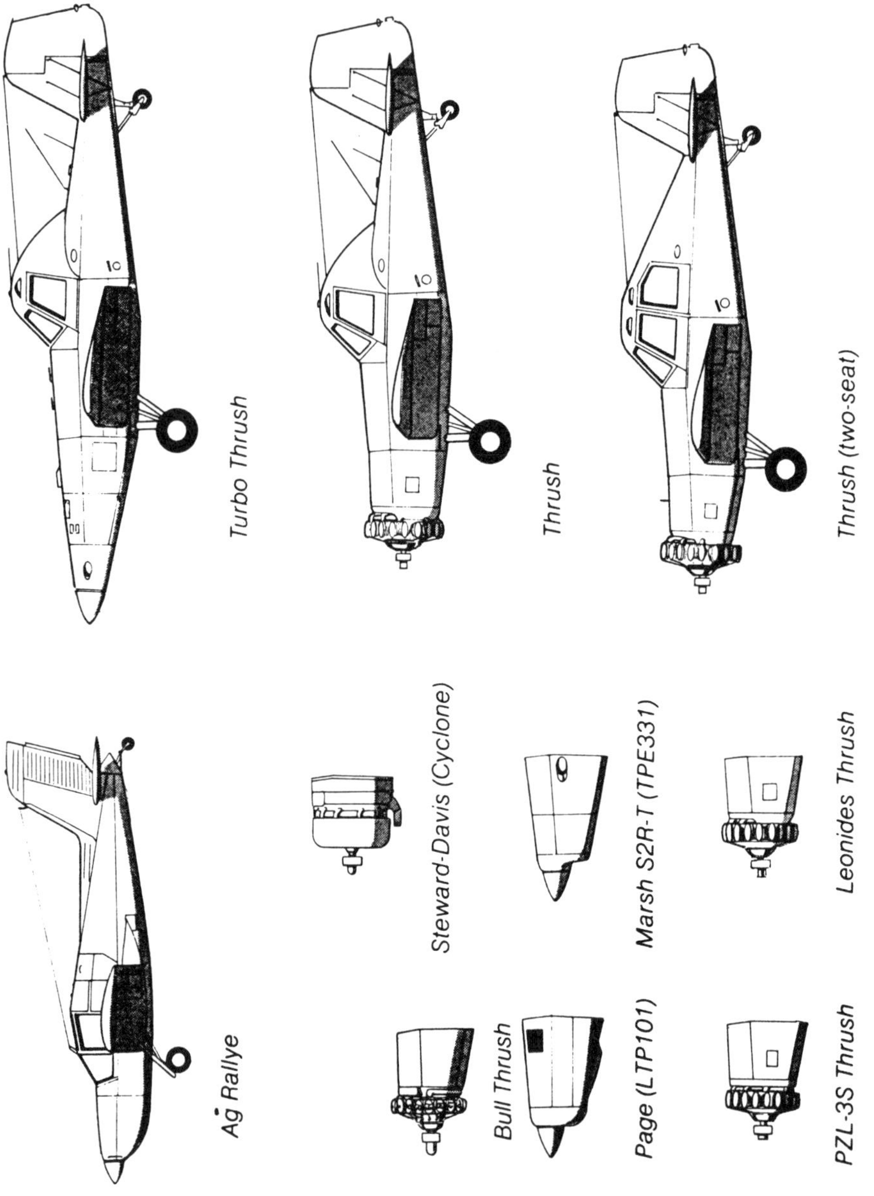
Turbo Thrush
Thrush
Thrush (two-seat)
Ag Rallye
Steward-Davis (Cyclone)
Marsh S2R-T (TPE331)
Leonides Thrush
Bull Thrush
Page (LTP101)
PZL-3S Thrush

Type	Manufacturer	Engine	Span	Gross weight	Disposable weight	Hopper capacity	Price
Thrush	Ayres Corporation, P.O. Box 3090, Albany, Georgia 31706, U.S.A.	Pratt & Whitney R1340, 600 h.p.	44 ft 4 in 13.5 m	6900 lb 3130 kg	3200 lb 1450 kg	400 U.S. gal. 1514 *l*	$116 500
Turbo Thrush (500 gal)	Ayres	PT6A-34AG 750 h.p. or PT6A-15AG 680 h.p.	44 ft 5 in 13.5 m	8500 lb 3855 kg	4600 lb 2086 kg	500 U.S. gal. 1893 *l*	$259 000 $228 500
Turbo Thrush (400 gal)	Ayres	PT6A-34AG 750 h.p. PT6A-15AG 680 h.p. PT6A-11AG 500 h.p.	44 ft 5 in 13.5 m	8200 lb 3719 kg	– –	400 U.S. gal. 1514 *l*	$251 500 $221 000 $209 500
PZL Thrush	Ayres	PZL-3S 600 h.p.	44 ft 4 in 13.5 m	6900 lb 3132 kg	–	400 U.S. gal. 1514 *l*	$122 500
Bull Thrush	Ayres	Wright R-1820 1200 h.p.	44 ft 5 in 13.5 m	10000 lb 4536 kg	–	510 U.S. gal. 1930 *l*	$149 500
Leo-Thrush	R. W. Harker, 40 Pont St, London S.W.1, U.K.	Alvis Leonides 550 h.p.	44 ft 4 in 13.5 m	6900 lb 3130 kg	3200 lb 1450 kg	400 U.S. gal. 1514 *l*	$18 000 (engine)
S2R-T	Marsh Aviation, 5060 East Faldon Drive, Mesa, Arizona 85205, U.S.A.	TPE 331-1-101	44 ft 4 in 13.5 m	9200 lb 4173 kg	– –	400/500 U.S. gal. 1515/1893 *l*	on request
Cyclone	Stewart-Davis, 3200 Cherry Ave., Long Beach, California 90807, U.S.A.	Wright R-1820 1200 h.p.	44 ft 4 in 13.5 m	6903 lb 3130 kg	3200 lb 1450 kg	600 U.S. gal. 2273 *l*	on request
Page	Page Industries, Box 191, Yukon, Oklahoma 73099, U.S.A.	Avco Lycoming LTP 101, 600 s.h.p.	44 ft 4 in 13.5 m	6900 lb 3130 kg	3200 lb 1450 kg	400 U.S. gal. 1514 *l*	on request
Ag Rallye	Aérospatiale (Socata) BP38, 65001, Tarbes, France	Avco Lycoming O-540 235 h.p.	31 ft 11 in 9.7 m	2980 lb 1350 kg	1450 lb 655 kg	153 U.S. gal. 579 *l*	on request

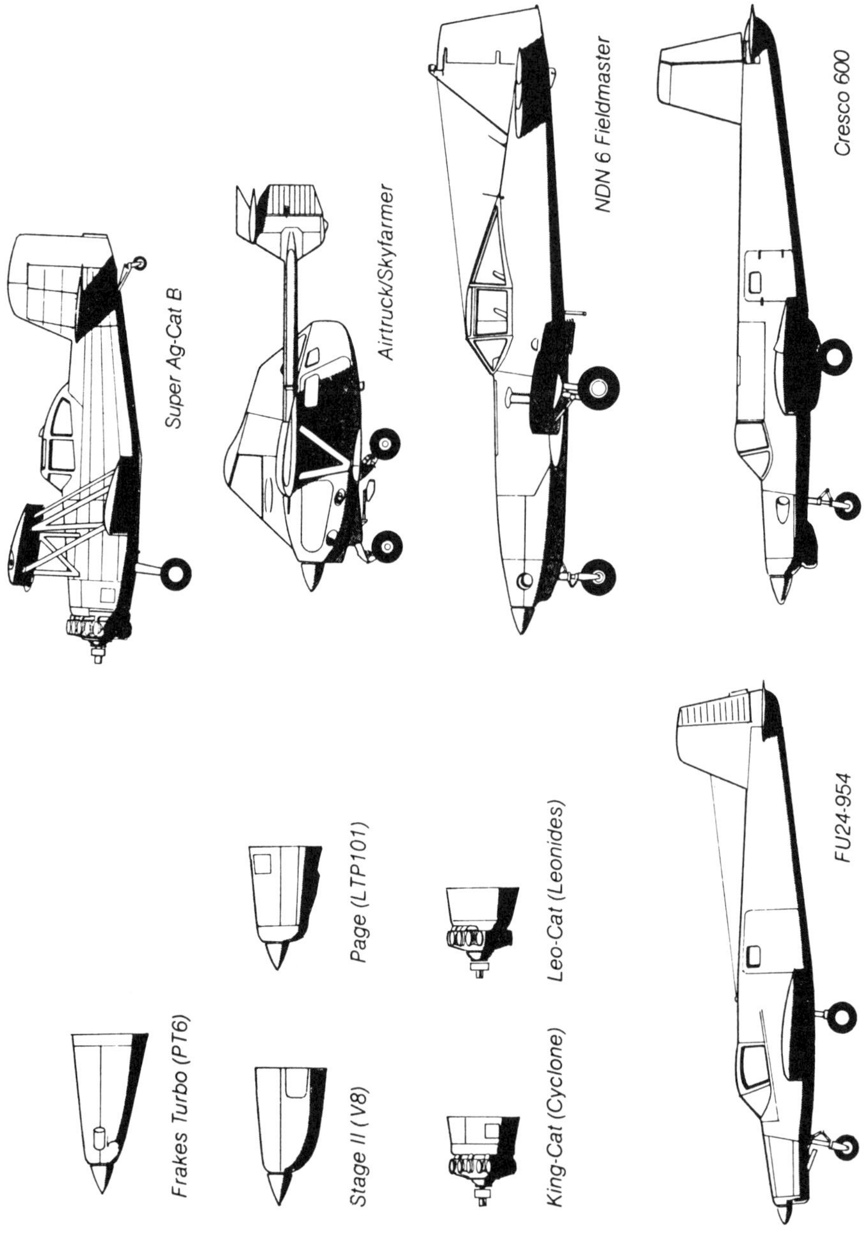
Super Ag-Cat B
Airtruck/Skyfarmer
NDN 6 Fieldmaster
Cresco 600
Frakes Turbo (PT6)
Stage II (V8)
Page (LTP101)
King-Cat (Cyclone)
Leo-Cat (Leonides)
FU24-954

Type	Manufacturer	Engine	Span	Gross weight	Disposable weight	Hopper capacity	Price
Super Ag-Cat B	Schweiger Aircraft, Box 147, Elmira, NY 14902, U.S.A.	Pratt & Whitney R985 450 s.h.p. or R1340 600 s.h.p.	42 ft 12.9 m	6075 lb 2758 kg	– –	400 U.S. gal. 1514 *l*	$121 995
Leo Cat	R.W. Harker, 40 Pont St, London S.W.1, U.K.	Alvis Leonides 550 h.p.	42 ft 3 in 12.9 m	6075 lb 2756 kg	3000 lb 1360 kg	300 U.S. gal. 1136 *l*	$18 000 (engine)
Marsh/Gulfstream C164-C-T	Marsh Aviation, 5060 East Faldon Drive, Mesa, Arizona 85205, U.S.A.	Garrett TPE 331-1-101	42 ft 2 in 12.9 m	9000 lb 4082 kg		500 U.S. gal. 1892 *l*	on request
Frakes Turbo	Frakes Aviation, Route 3, Box 229B, Cleburne, Texas 76031, U.S.A.	Pratt & Whitney PT6A-34AG 750 s.h.p. (derated 540 s.h.p.)	42 ft 3 in 12.9 m	8500 lb 3856 kg	5150 lb 2336 kg	500 U.S. gal. 1893 *l*	on request
Stage II	Stage II, 3013 Airport Avenue, Santa Monica, California 90405, U.S.A.	Liquid cooled V8 450 h.p.	42 ft 3 in 12.9 m	6075 lb 2758 kg	3075 lb 1393 kg	300 U.S. gal. 1136 *l*	on request
Page	Page Industries, Box 191, Yukon, Oklahoma 73099, U.S.A.	Avco Lycoming LTP 101, 620 s.h.p.	42 ft 3 in 12.9 m	6075 lb 2756 kg	3475 lb 1568 kg	300 U.S. gal. 1136 *l*	on request
King-Cat	Mid-Continent Aircraft, Hayti, Missouri 63851, U.S.A.	Wright Cyclone R1820, 1200 h.p.	42 ft 3 in 12.9 m	8500 lb 3856 kg	– –	500 U.S. gal. 1893 *l*	$152 000
NDN 6 Fieldmaster	NDN Aircraft, Isle of Wight Airport, Sandown, Isle of Wight, U.K.	Pratt & Whitney PT6A-34AG 750 s.h.p.	50 ft 3 in 15.3 m	8500 lb 3856 kg	3500 lb 1588 kg	698 U.S. gal. 2642 *l*	$400 000
PL-12 Airtruk	Transavia, 73 Station Road, Seven Hills, NSW 2147, Australia	R-R Continental IO-520-D flat 6	39 ft 4 in 12 m	4090 lb 1855 kg	1850 lb 839 kg	83 Imp gal. 379 *l*	on request
T-300 Skyfarmer	Transavia	Avco-Lycoming IO-540-K145	39 ft 4 in 12 m	4090 lb 1855 kg	3800 lb 1723 kg	83 Imp gal. 379 *l*	on request
FU24-954	New Zealand Aerospace, Hamilton Airport, N.Z.	Avco Lycoming IO-720, 400 h.p.	42 ft 12.8 m	5430 lb 2463 kg	2420 lb 1100 kg	276 U.S. gal. 1045 *l*	on request
Cresco 600	New Zealand Aerospace	Avco Lycoming LTP101, 600 s.h.p.	42 ft 12.8 m	7000 lb 3175 kg	4005 lb 1817 kg	450 U.S. gal. 1705 *l*	on request

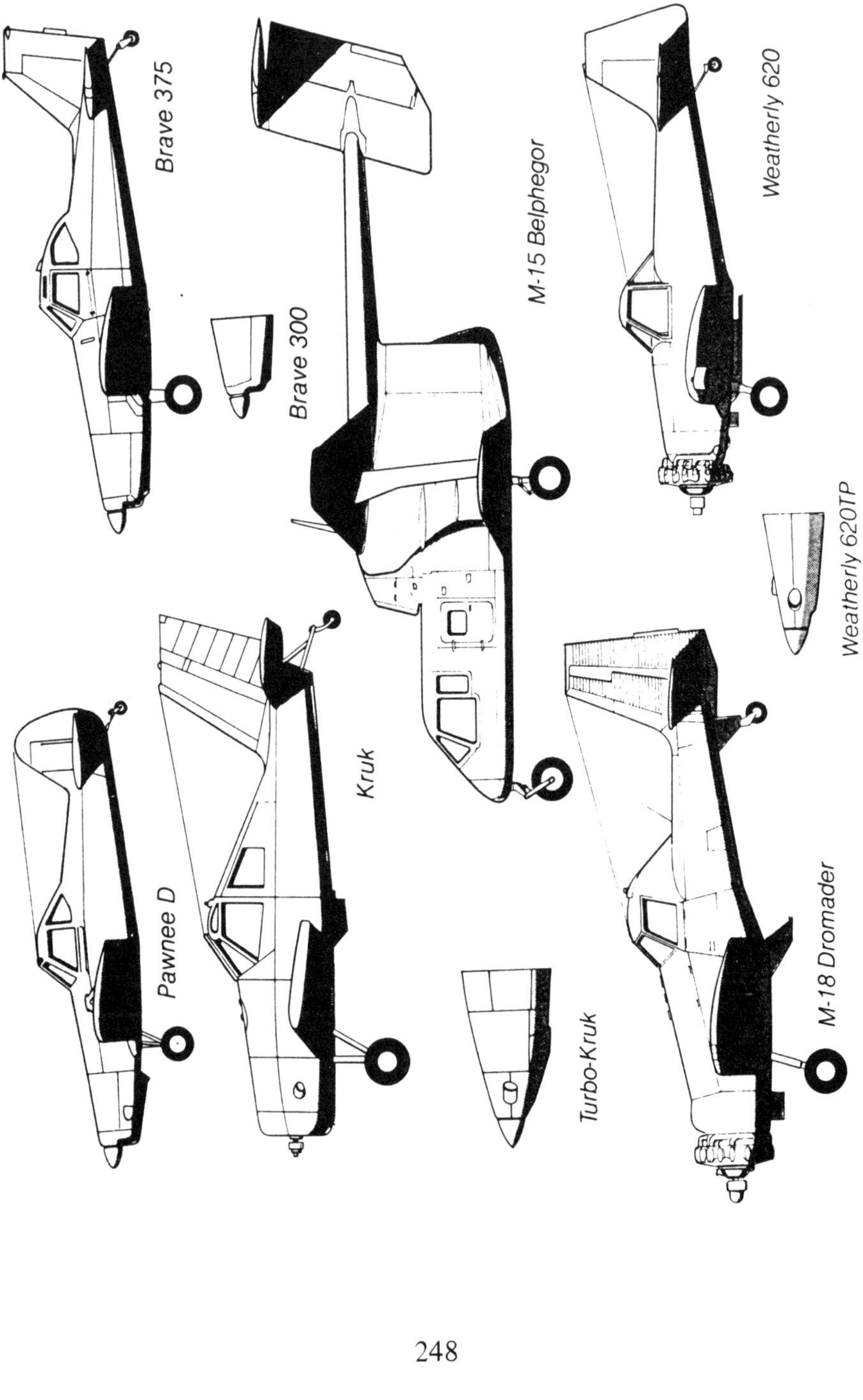
Brave 375
Brave 300
M-15 Belphegor
Weatherly 620
Weatherly 620TP
Pawnee D
Kruk
Turbo-Kruk
M-18 Dromader

Type	Manufacturer	Engine	Span	Gross weight	Disposable weight	Hopper capacity	Price
Pawnee D	Piper Aircraft, Lockhaven, Pa 17745, U.S.A.	Avco Lycoming IO-540, 235 h.p.	36 ft 2 in 11 m	2900 lb 1316 kg	1301 lb 544 kg	150 U.S. gal. 572 *l*	$53 130
Brave 300	Piper Aircraft	Avco Lycoming IO-540, 300 h.p.	38 ft 10 in 11.8 m	4400 lb 1996 kg	2202 lb 999 kg	225 U.S. gal. 852 *l*	$74 740
Brave 375	Piper Aircraft	Avco Lycoming IO-720, 375 h.p.	38 ft 10 in 11.8 m	4800 lb 2177 kg	2335 lb 1059 kg	275 U.S. gal. 1041 *l*	$99 850
Kruk	PZL-Warszawa, 02-256 Warsaw-Okecle, Al Krakowska, 100/114, Poland	Pezetel PZL-35 600 h.p.	48 ft 6 in 14.8 m	6614 lb 3000 kg	2205 lb 1000 kg	370 U.S. gal. 1400 *l*	on request
Turbo Kruk	PZL-Warszawa	PT6A-34AG	48 ft 6 in 14.8 m	6614 lb 3000 kg	2645 lb 1200 kg	370 U.S. gal. 1400 *l*	on request
M-15	PZL-Mielec ul. Ludowego Polskie- A1-25, go 3, 39-301 Mielec, Poland	Ivchenko	73 ft 6 in 22.4 m	12676 lb 5750 kg	4850 lb 2200 kg	766 U.S. gal. 2900 *l*	on request
M-18 Dromader	PZL-Mielec	Pezetel ASZ-621R 1000 h.p.	58 ft 1 in 17.7 m	9259 lb 4200 kg	3307 lb 1500 kg	660 U.S. gal. 2500 *l*	$145 000
620	Weatherley Aviation, 2304 San Felipe Road, Hollister, Calif. 95023 U.S.A.	Pratt & Whitney R985, 450 h.p.	41 ft 12.5 m	5800 lb 2640 kg	3000 lb 1360 kg	335 U.S. gal. 1270 *l*	$74 000
620TP	Weatherley Aviation	PT6A-11AG	41 ft 12.5 m	5800 lb 2640 kg	3000 lb 1360 kg	335 U.S. gal. 1270 *l*	$156 000

Appendix 2

Guide to droplet size for particular applications and definitions

Table A.1 Guide to droplet size for particular applications (after E.P.P.O., 1982)

Approximate volume median diameter in μm	Use	Remarks
$\leqslant$ 20	Space spraying in enclosed structures	Little, if any, lasting effect
20– 60	Contact sprays against flying insects	Low deposition on large obstacles (drift-prone)
60–150	Contact and residual sprays against most pests and diseases	Check volatility; good canopy penetration
150–250	Not normally used in ULV application, but used in VLV	Good deposition but possible loss of cover density at low application rates
$\geqslant$250	For larvicide application, bait-spraying against mobile insects and herbicide application from ground spraying equipment	Good deposit, but with loss of cover density
>600	Oil-slick control	Dispersal in sea water

Table A.2 Definitions. The term 'reduced volume application' covers ULV (ultra low volume) and VLV (very low volume) pesticide applications. Generally, HV (high volume) is a term which usually indicates that the crop is wetted over most of its surface. MV (medium volume) is a term which usually indicates that a proportion of the crop surface is totally wetted. The term LV (low volume) is also widely used for aerial spraying in the range 5–50 *l*/ha. These terms have been defined as follows (E.P.P.O., 1982)

Category	Bushes and trees	Ground crops
ULV	<5	<5
VLV	$>$ 5–200 *l*/ha	$>$ 5–50 *l*/ha
LV	$>$ 200–500 *l*/ha	$>$ 50–200 *l*/ha
MV	$>$ 500–1000 *l*/ha	$>$ 200–700 *l*/ha
HV	$>$ 1000 *l*/ha	$>$ 700 *l*/ha

Reference

E.P.P.O. (1982) *Guidelines for Reduced Volume Pesticide Application.* 2nd edn. 1, rue Le Nôtre, Paris: European and Mediterranean Plant Protection Organization.

Appendix 3

Corrosion effects of some agricultural chemicals

Chemical	Effect on airframe (aluminimum base materials)	Remarks
Fertilisers		
Superphosphate fertilisers	+ +	pitting
Copperised super	+ +	
Cobaltised super	+	
Agric. lime	o	
Basic slag	o	
Nitro lime	o	corrodes Mg-alloys
Nitrates	o	
Ammonium sulphate	+	
Chlorides	+ +	
Insecticides		
Insecticides in oil solutions	o	
BHC	+	
DDT	+	
Aldrin	–	
Dieldrin	–	
Parathion	–	
Chlordane	–	
Heptachlor	–	
Sulphur	o	
Toxaphene-sulphur	+	
Lime-sulphur	–	
Fungicides		
Copper base fungicides	+	
Carbamates	o	
Organic mercurial compounds		suspected, but data lacking

Chemical	Effect on airframe (aluminimum base materials	Remarks
Herbicides		
2,4-D salt or ester	°	
MCPA salt or ester	°	
2,4,5-T salt or ester	°	
Potassium cyanate	°	
Sodium cyanamide	++	
Trichloracetates	++	
Sodium trichloracetate	+	
0.7% sodium dichromate	–	
Dalapon	–	

Explanation:

°no corrosion, – slight and acceptable corrosion
+ corrosion, ++ severe corrosion.

Note: Some organic phosphates are harmful to many plastics (except to fibre glass reinforced polyester plastic) and also soften doped fabrics.

Appendix 4

Conversion and miscellaneous tables

Conversion table

Dosage: solids		
1 cwt (short) per acre	=	112 kg per ha
1 cwt (long) per acre	=	125 kg per ha
1 kg per ha	=	0.892 2 lb per acre
1 g per ha	=	0.014 28 oz per acre
Dosage: liquids		
1 gal. (U.K.) per acre	=	11.23 *l* per ha
1 gal. (U.S.) per acre	=	9.35 *l* per ha
1 pt (U.K.) per acre	=	1.40 *l* per ha
1 pt (U.S.) per acre	=	1.17 *l* per ha
1 *l* per ha	=	0.712 1 pt (U.K.) per acre
1 *l* per ha	=	0.855 2 pt (U.S.) per acre
1 *l* per ha	=	0.089 02 gal. (U.K.) per acre
1 *l* per ha	=	0.106 9 gal. (U.S.) per acre
1 *l* per ha	=	114 fl oz (U.K.) per acre
1 *l* per ha	=	0.7125 pt (U.K.) per acre
1 *l* per ha	=	136.9 fl oz (U.S.) per acre
1 *l* per ha	=	8.557 pt (U.S.) per acre
1 *l* per ha	=	0.089 gal. (U.K.) per acre
1 ml per ha	=	0.014 24 fl oz (U.K.) per acre
1 ml per ha	=	0.013 68 fl oz (U.S.) per acre
1 fl oz (U.K.) per acre	=	0.070 20 *l* per ha
1 fl oz (U.S.) per acre	=	0.073 08 *l* per ha
Pressure		
1 kg per cm^2	=	14.22 lb per in^2
1 lb per in^2	=	0.07 kg per cm^2
1 lb per ft^2	=	4.9 kg per m^2
1 kg per m^2	=	0.205 lb per ft^2

Conversion table – *continued*

Density		
1 kg per m^3	=	0.0624 lb per ft^3
1 lb per ft^3	=	16.10 kg per m^3
Speeds		
1 (stat.) mile per h	=	1.466 ft per s
1 (naut.) mile per h	=	1.689 ft per s = 1 knot
1 (stat.) mile per h	=	0.445 m per s
1 (stat.) mile per h	=	1.609 km per h
1 knot	=	1.152 mile (stat.) per h
1 knot	=	1.853 km per h
1 knot	=	0.515 m per s
1 km per h	=	0.621 4 mile (stat.) per h
1 km per h	=	0.277 8 m per s
1 m per s	=	2.237 mile (stat.) per h
Liquid measure		
1 gal. (Imp.)	=	1.2 gal. (U.S.)
1 gal. (U.S.)	=	0.832 gal. (U.K.)
1 *l*	=	1 kg
1 gal. (Imp.)	=	4.546 *l*
1 gal. (U.S.)	=	3.785 *l*
1 *l*	=	0.220 gal. (U.K.)
1 *l*	=	0.264 gal. (U.S.)
1 *l*	=	1.76 pt (U.K.)
1 *l*	=	2.114 pt (U.S.)
1 cl	=	1/100 *l* (0.01 *l*)
1 pt (Imp.)	=	0.568 *l*
1 pt (U.S.)	=	0.473 *l*
1 ml	=	0.035 20 fl oz (U.K.)
1 ml	=	0.033 81 fl oz (U.S.)
1 cc	=	1 ml=1/1000 *l*
Square measure		
1 acre	=	4047 m^2
1 acre	=	0.404684 ha
1 acre	=	4840 yd^2
1 $mile^2$ (stat.)	=	640 acre
1 ha	=	2.471 acre
1 km^2	=	100 ha
1 ft^2	=	929 cm^2
1 cm^2	=	0.0011 ft^2
1 cm^2	=	0.155 in^2
1 in^2	=	6.452 cm^2

Conversion table – *continued*

1 ha		=	10 000 m^2
1 km^2		=	0.3861 mile $(stat.)^2$
1 m^2		=	10.76 ft^2
1 mm^2		=	0.001550 in^2
1 ha		=	2.380 Feddan
1 Feddan		=	0.420 ha
1 acre		=	0.963 Feddan
1 Feddan		=	1.038 acre
Latin America			
Argentina	1 manzana	=	1.000 ha
El Salvador, Handuras, Costa Rica, Guatemala	1 manzana	=	0.699 ha
Nicaragua	1 manzana	=	0.750 ha
Central America	1 fanegada	=	0.640 ha
Peru	1 fanegada	=	2.890 ha
Volume			
1 m^3		=	35.31 ft^3
1 m^3		=	1.308 yd^3
1 m^3		=	1000 *l*
1 ft^3		=	6.229 gal. (U.K.)
1 ft^3		=	7.480 gal. (U.S.)
Linear measure			
1 mile (stat.)		=	5280 ft
1 mile (naut.)		=	6080 ft
1 mile (stat.)		=	1.6093 km
1 mile (naut.)		=	1.854 km
1 mile (stat.)		=	0.8684 mile (naut.)
1 mile (naut.)		=	1.16 mile (stat.)
1 km		=	0.5395 mile (naut.)
1 km		=	0.621 mile (stat.)
1 m		=	3.28 ft
1 m		=	1.0936 yd
1 yd		=	0.9144 m
1 ft		=	0.3048 m
1 in		=	2.54 cm
1 cm		=	0.3937 in
1 mm		=	0.03937 in
1 μm		=	0.00003937 in

Conversion table – *continued*

Weights		
1 cwt (short)	=	45.36 kg
1 cwt (long)	=	50.80 kg
1 kg	=	0.0220 cwt (short)
1 kg	=	0.0196 cwt (long)
1 kg	=	2.205 lb
1 cwt (long) (U.K.)	=	112 lb
1 cwt (short) (U.S.)	=	100 lb
1 tonne	=	1000 kg
1 tonne	=	0.984 2 ton (U.K.)
1 tonne	=	1.102 ton (U.S.)
1 oz	=	28.35 g
1 g	=	0.035 27 oz
1 lb	=	0.454 kg

Miscellaneous tables

Bar	=	14.50 lb f/in^2
KW	=	1.341 hp
KW	=	1.360 metric hp
mN/m	=	1000 dyne/cm
°C	=	$\frac{°F - 32}{1.8}$
°F	=	(°C x 1.8) + 32

The payload of some aircraft is limited when carrying solid materials by the capacity of the hopper; the densities of three representative materials, two of them fertilisers, are as follows

	Density		Particle length (approx.)	
	lb/ft^3	kg/m^3	in	mm
Ammonium sulphate	64	1030	3/32	2.4
Urea (prilled)	45.5	732.5	1/16	1.6
Rice	38.7	623	3/16	4.8

Theoretical plant coverage from 10 l applied volume per hectare

	Drops per cm^2		
Drop dia. (μm)	Flat surface	Field and row crops (divide by 5)	Orchards (divide by 10)
25	12 174	2 435	1 217
50	1 522	360	152
100	191	46	19
200	23	6	2.3
300	7	1.6	0.7
500	1.5	0.4	0.15
600	0.83	0.2	0.08

Index

Index